THE LEGENDS OF
ABERDEEN

THE LEGENDS OF
ABERDEEN

by Paul Smith

The Press and Journal

breedon **books**
PUBLISHING

First published in Great Britain in 2007 by
The Breedon Books Publishing Company Limited
Breedon House, 3 The Parker Centre,
Derby, DE21 4SZ.

ISBN 978-1-85983-575-3

Printed and bound by Cromwell Press,
Trowbridge, Wiltshire.

Contents

To Finlay and Mia,

The two true inspirations in everything I do.

Acknowledgements

In the opening pages of my first book in 2006 I thanked those nearest and dearest for their love, support and encouragement, and those same people are the first to be thanked again. Heartfelt appreciation goes to Mum and Dad, for a love of writing and a love of football, and to my wife Coral, for another six months of patience and support, laughter and fun. To my son Finlay, special thanks for his winning smile and help with the statistics, despite his tender years, and to my baby daughter Mia, for her company on so many of the late shifts during the process of putting this book together. Professionally my appreciation goes to Steve Caron and Michelle Grainger along with the rest of their team at Breedon Books, at *Aberdeen Journals* the support and enthusiasm of Susan McKay was vital in getting the project over the finish line, while Duncan Smith and Tom Cooper deserve enormous credit for their tireless work in sourcing and perfecting the images which bring the words to life. Without those images, and the photographers behind them, it simply would not have been possible. Without the 15 players past and present who gave up their time so willingly to share their own thoughts in the pages where possible, it simply would not have been half as interesting and my final thanks are reserved for them.

Introduction

If music is the food of love then debate is surely the oxygen of football. The 100 players listed in the pages that follow are not a definitive collection of the greatest ever to wear the red shirt, simply some of the greatest.

Nor does the list even attempt to scratch the surface of the iconic men who achieved legendary status for their contributions off the hallowed turf. Men such as the late chairman Richard Donald, visionary director Chris Anderson, talent scout extraordinaire Bobby Calder, revered mentor to a succession of stars Teddy Scott, or managerial masters Dave Halliday, Eddie Turnbull and Sir Alex Ferguson. And that is only to name a few of those who did not achieve greatness as Dons players but had such a telling input in other capacities.

So how do you categorise a playing legend? It was supposed to be an exact science. You simply go back through the team sheets and pick out every man who has ever starred in one of the 13 domestic and two European Cup-winning sides for Aberdeen and then add in the stars who started more than half of the games in each of the four title-winning squads. For good measure blend in the men who have represented Aberdeen with distinction in the dark blue of Scotland and you have your completed set of legends.

Only it is not quite as simple as that. Using that equation the 100 barrier is smashed through in some style.

Then there's no accounting for emotion. Charlie Cooke and Zoltan Varga do not tick any of the boxes above, failing to win silverware during their Pittodrie stays and Cooke having to wait until after his departure for pastures new to win a cap. Yet, according to anyone who has seen them play, it would be sacrilege to omit either.

Instead of a neat package of 100 legends who fit nicely into defined lines, the collection has turned into a selection of those who won on the big stage, those who starred for Scotland and one or two who did neither but did win the hearts and minds of the Pittodrie faithful. The list of those who are not included but could quite easily have been is long and varied. That collection of talented footballers and dedicated athletes more than anything demonstrates just how spoilt the Dons fans have been in more than a century of Aberdeen Football Club.

Willie Waddell from the 1947 Scottish Cup Final, a man who will forever be a Rangers legend, played fewer than 100 games for the Dons and misses this selection. For the same reason 1956 League Cup-winner Bobby Wilson misses the cut, although others who also failed to break the 100 mark are included. Doug Considine, a Premier Division medal winner in 1980, just failed to creep over the 50 percent total for games played in the League that season, just as courageous 1950s star Joe O'Neil did in the club's maiden League win 25 years earlier.

Billy McCall and Joe McLaughlin were victims as much as anything of limited information in the otherwise fruitful archives of the *Press and Journal* and *Evening Express*, while Scotland star Alex Jackson, the epitome of a one-season wonder following his arrival in 1924, is another deserving case absent from these pages.

There is no room, either, for the men who played cameo roles in many of the other trophy successes, with Cup Final substitutes Andy Watson, Steve Gray, Willem Van der Ark, Graham Watson, Hugh Robertson and Peter Hetherston edged out in the final draft. Had it not been for Watson's converted penalty in the 1990 Scottish Cup Final shoot-out against Celtic, the trophy may never have been taken north. John Inglis, a veteran of the 1995 League Cup success, is also relegated to the reserve list.

There are many non-Scottish internationals that have graced Pittodrie who are also absent, from giant Danish goalkeeper Peter Kjaer and enigmatic Norwegian striker Arild Stavrum, to the late Moroccan talisman Hicham Zerouali, in recent times right-back to Northern Ireland cap Eddie Falloon and Irish international Charlie O'Hagan in the club's earlier years. It was O'Hagan who became the first Aberdeen player to represent his country when he turned out for Ireland against England in 1907.

Of course, there are also many, many long-serving players from every era who also fail to fall into the categories used to determine entrants to this particular chart of Dons' past and present. Popular goalkeeper John Tubby Ogston is one and the devoted Ally Shewan, who played a staggering 314 consecutive games in the second half of the 1960s, is another in that group.

All of those players and more unmentioned may be exiled from the following pages but they are true legends in their own right and plentiful enough to ensure a second volume would be as feasible as it would be fascinating.

In the meantime, enjoy the stories behind the 100 men in the pages that follow and the thoughts of the select band of 15 who have shared their memories to provide an intriguing insight into life at Aberdeen Football Club through the generations. Then let the debate begin.

Jack Allister

Date of birth: 30 June 1927, Edinburgh
Died: 1999

Aberdeen record:
Appearances: League 117, Scottish Cup 21, League Cup 25
Goals: League 18, Scottish Cup 4, League Cup 2
Debut: League, 11 October 1952 v Third Lanark (h) won 4–3

Also played for: Chelsea, Chesterfield, Elgin City, Deveronvale

In 1955 Aberdeen lived the dream that the club's supporters had been harbouring for more than half a century when the Scottish League crown was claimed. Now, more than half a century on, the majority of the Championship-winning heroes live on only in memory.

Jack Allister, the first player in this collection of greats, died in 1999, but his part in the club's first-ever title success will survive for as long as football records are preserved. He and his teammates earned legendary status as part of Dave Halliday's dominant Dons team and demonstrated their manager's talent for piecing together a winning side.

Allister was recruited by Halliday in 1952 for the not inconsequential fee of £6,000, having taken his first steps in football with Chelsea. He had made just four appearances for the Stamford Bridge club, having moved south from Tranent Juniors in 1949, but Halliday was convinced he was the man to make the number-six shirt his own and thrust the new half-back straight into his side following his arrival six games into the 1952–53 campaign.

His relationship with the Pittodrie fans was not always smooth, with his strong tackling and competitive spirit failing to win over some sections of the crowd. That all changed within two seasons of his arrival when he formed part of the formidable half-back line of Allister, Young and Glen as Aberdeen marched triumphantly to the 1955 Championship.

Allister played in 21 of the 30 League games that term, weighing in with four goals in the top division as the Dons beat Celtic by three points to lift the prize.

Not surprisingly, it proved to be the highlight of Allister's career, although he came close to adding to his collection of honours in two major Finals prior to that.

The first was the Scottish Cup Final of 1953, when Rangers were taken to a replay before the Ibrox men ran out 1–0 winners. The second came the following year in the same competition when the Dons were beaten 2–1 by Celtic in the Hampden showdown. Allister had been among the goalscorers when Rangers were dumped 6–0 in the semi-final.

In 1955 he came within an ace of earning full Scotland recognition, turning out for the B team but just failing to win promotion to the senior side. Having requested a transfer the same year, Allister changed his mind and opted to stay. Two years later, at the end of the 1957–58 season in which he made just 11 appearances, he again looked for an escape route and found it in the form of a £500 switch to Chesterfield.

Allister tried Canadian football briefly in 1958 after failing to settle back in England but returned to the north-east of Scotland just months later to join Elgin City. He went on to add Deveronvale to his Highland League credits as he combined his playing commitments with a career as a plumber in Aberdeen.

In 1961 he moved into coaching, was appointed trainer at Stirling Albion for a short spell, but it was after emigrating to Australia that he found the opportunity to truly get his teeth into that role.

He returned to the plumbing trade in Edinburgh in the 1970s before a heart attack forced his retirement.

Russell Anderson

Date of birth: 25 October 1978, Aberdeen

Aberdeen record:
Appearances: League 263+17, Scottish Cup 23+1, League Cup 20, Europe 4
Goals: League 18, Scottish Cup 1
Debut: League, 4 January 1997 v Dunfermline (h) lost 2-0

Also played for: Scotland (9 caps up to June 2007), Sunderland

Through one of the most turbulent periods in Aberdeen's history, Russell Anderson was the one constant. At the age of 27, in 2006, he was honored with a testimonial match against Everton in recognition of the influential Dons defender's contribution to the club. Well before his 30th birthday the Aberdonian had amassed enough experience to be classed as a veteran.

After making his debut as an 18-year-old under Roy Aitken in January 1997, he became a first-choice selection for a further five managers. Alex Miller, Paul Hegarty, Ebbe Skovdahl and Steve Paterson all came and went during Anderson's decade in the top team.

More than 10,000 fans turned out to voice their approval of Anderson's contribution to the cause, a humbling experience for a local boy turned Dons star. He said 'I felt honoured to be given a testimonial by the club. Some really great players received them before me – I don't think I'm at the same level, but it was a delight to be honoured. The supporters have always been good to me. I've realised they appreciate those who put in the effort. The least you can give the fans is full effort.'

Under Paterson he was installed as captain and retained the armband when Jimmy Calderwood took over as manager in 2004, holding the coveted position until his £1 million move to Sunderland in the summer of 2007.

The transfer was the chance of a lifetime for Anderson, but the decision to move to the Premiership was not taken lightly. He said 'I've a lot of happy memories from my time with Aberdeen. I've had some good seasons and some not so good seasons, but, all in all, the time I had with the club was really enjoyable. The opportunity to join Sunderland was a massive challenge for me and one I couldn't turn down.'

A player who started life as a right-back has become established as one of Scotland's leading central defenders, and he was nominated as the SPFA's Players' Player of the Year in 2007 before losing out to Shunsuke Nakamura. The Aberdonian made his international debut as a late substitute in a 2–0 win over Iceland in Reykjavik in 2002, earning the bizarre distinction of having to wait for his second cap, three days later against Canada on home soil, to win his first touch of the ball.

Scotland manager Alex McLeish, following his appointment in 2007, was quick to sing the praises of Aberdeen's captain, giving hope that elevation to international regular appearances could be on the horizon.

However, domestic honours eluded Anderson. Appearances in two national Finals were the closest he came to success, but on both occasions the showpiece game ended in defeat. In March 2000 the Dons fell 2–0 to Celtic in the Final of the League Cup. Just two months later Rangers were the conquerors in the Scottish Cup Final, winning 4–0 against an Aberdeen side featuring striker Robbie Winters as a makeshift goalkeeper after an early injury to Jim Leighton.

Anderson's determination saw him overcome two potentially career-threatening injuries along the way. During pre-season for the 2000–01 season, he suffered a cruciate ligament injury which kept him out for the entire campaign. He did not return to first-team action until November 2001, after a 16-month absence. In 2004 the same knee was damaged in a Scottish Cup tie against Livingston, leading to another five months of recovery work.

Each time Anderson came back stronger and in his final season in a red shirt he led his club back into Europe, earning a UEFA Cup spot courtesy of a third-place finish in the SPL behind Celtic and Rangers.

In his time as Aberdeen captain he became firmly established as mentor to Aberdeen's next generation of emerging stars. As he begins a new life in English football, his one piece of advice to those around him is to make the best of the chance they have with the Dons back in his home town.

Anderson said 'The past 10 years have gone really quickly and I think that intensifies more as you get older. People talk about the benefits of experience in the game and I'm not sure you fully understand that when you are younger. Over the years you realise how important it is to savour every good experience as well as trying to learn from every circumstance and experience you face. Trying to take it all in and appreciate the opportunities you have is important.'

Ian Angus

Date of birth: 19 November 1961, Glasgow

Aberdeen record:

Appearances: League 84+21, Scottish Cup 15+3, League Cup 10+4, Europe
11+6

Goals: League 9, Scottish Cup 2, Europe 1

Debut: League, 6 December 1980 v Morton (a) lost 1–0

Also played for: Dundee, Motherwell, Clyde, Albion Rovers, Stirling Albion

Ian Angus did not play the amount of games as many Aberdeen stars, he did not earn the same plaudits as many Aberdeen stars and he did not earn international recognition. What he did walk out of the Pittodrie main entrance with when he moved to Dundee in 1986 was a Premier Division winners' medal and that is something many, many players past and present would walk over hot coals to emulate.

The Glaswegian, a product of Eastercraigs Boys Club, enjoyed his most productive season in a red jersey in the 1984–85 campaign. He was still only 24 when he helped the Dons to sweep to the League title by a margin of seven points but already had four seasons under his belt before that Championship-winning term even began.

Up to that point he had been a valuable squad man for Alex Ferguson but far from a first-team regular. After breaking into the team just a fortnight after his 19th birthday, Angus quickly forced his way into Ferguson's starting XI and spent the remainder of his rookie season vying for the number-10 jersey with Drew Jarvie and Andy Harrow.

Injury stalled his progress and after a frustrating second term, in which he made just a single appearance, he had to be patient in his quest for regular football at Pittodrie. In the famous 1982–83 season he was again restricted to a bit-part role, his starts in the final three League games the only time he made it into the starting XI in the Premier Division and bringing a haul of three goals. Angus made a cameo appearance in the run to the European Cup-winners' Cup trophy, coming on as a substitute in the semi-final second leg against Waterschei and on the bench for the Final.

He enjoyed his first taste of success as a professional when he helped the Dons to the Championship in 1984, with nine starts and three substitute appearances. In 1985 he stepped up to take a central role in the successful defence of the Premier Division prize, in the first team a total of 21 times and used from the bench in seven other games. The same year brought European Cup heartache for Angus and his Dons teammates, as his goal in the 2–1 defeat against Dinamo Berlin in the second leg of the first round was enough to take the tie to a penalty shoot-out, which was lost on German soil.

There was more agony in the same competition the following season when Angus was part of the team held to a 0–0 draw by IFK Gothenburg in Sweden in the second leg of the quarter-final. The Scandinavian side progressed courtesy of their away goal in the 2–2 draw at Pittodrie in the first game.

In the summer of 1986 he moved down the A90 to join Dundee as part of the deal that took Robert Connor in the opposite direction and helped the Dens Park side maintain mid-table security in the top flight for three seasons until their relegation in 1990.

Motherwell stepped in with a £40,000 bid to offer Angus a Premier Division lifeline and he grabbed it with both hands, going on to score the third goal for the Steelmen in the pulsating 4–3 Scottish Cup Final victory against Dundee United in 1991 to cap his first season in Lanarkshire in style.

Angus made more than 100 appearances for Well over four years before winding down his senior career with Clyde and Albion Rovers.

Steve Archibald

Date of birth: 27 September 1956, Glasgow

Aberdeen record:
Appearances: League 76+2, Scottish Cup 10, League Cup 18, Europe 6
Goals: League 29, Scottish Cup 11, League Cup 6
Debut: League, 7 January 1978 v Ayr United (a) drew 0–0

Also played for: Clyde, Tottenham Hotspur, Barcelona, Espanyol, Hibs, St Mirren
Managed: East Fife, Airdrie

Enigmatic, charismatic...infuriating, frustrating. Everyone has their own opinion of Steve Archibald and his colourful career in football.

The Glaswegian was recruited by Billy McNeill in January 1978 as a raw 21-year-old midfielder from Clyde. It proved to be the first leg of an altogether more exotic football journey, which ultimately led him to his current home in Spain.

From First Division midfielder he was converted to Premier League striker with the Dons. He made his debut for McNeill's side in the red number-eight jersey in a 1-1 draw with Ayr United at Somerset Park on 7 January 1978. Archibald's first goals came in the shape of a double in a 3-0 win over Rangers at Ibrox. Joe Harper, who became his strike partner in a formidable pairing, was the other scorer.

The Pittodrie side were runners-up to the Gers in the Premier League in Archibald's first season. Alex Ferguson was the new man at the helm by the time the 1978–79 campaign kicked-off and Archibald had a taste of things to come when he and his teammates marched to the Final of the League Cup.

His first taste of the big occasion ended in bitter disappointment, though, with Rangers winning 2-1, but the following term provided sweet success. Archibald was the key man as the Dons swept aside all challengers to win the Premier League title by a single point from Celtic. It was the first Championship triumph in 25 years and he had missed just two of the 36 games along the way, scoring 12 League goals in the process. It was the Pittodrie swansong for Archibald, who made his final appearance for the Reds in the 1-1 draw with Partick on the final day of the 1979–80 season to complete a 15-game unbeaten run.

His relationship with Ferguson was stormy. Legend has it that the manager named a chair in his office after his bolshy striker, such was the frequency of his visits to see the top man. In May 1980 the divorce was completed when Spurs weighed in with an offer Aberdeen could not refuse. A fee of £800,000 took Archibald to White Hart Lane.

He was England's leading scorer in his first season with Tottenham and won the FA Cup in 1981 when he played in the 3-2 win over Manchester City at Wembley. By that time he was also a fully-fledged international, making his debut in dark blue on 19 May 1980 against Northern Ireland. His confidence extended to the international arena, scoring within 20 minutes of his introduction as a substitute for Kenny Dalglish as Scotland won 2-0.

In all, Archibald made 27 appearances for his country, including at the 1986 World Cup Finals in Mexico, although he scored just four goals. It was a disappointing return for a striker who netted 77 times in just 189 appearances for Spurs, winning another FA Cup-winners' medal in 1982, the UEFA Cup in 1984 and scoring in the 4-3 penalty shoot-out victory over Anderlecht. That propelled him to a global audience and a £1.15 million switch to Barcelona, coached by Terry Venables, followed in August 1984.

Archibald was quickly accepted by the Catalan fans, in no small part because of his willingness to learn the language and adapt to the culture, and he helped the club to the Spanish title in 1985.

Spells as a player with Espanyol, Hibs and St Mirren followed, before Archibald's first venture into management. He steered East Fife to promotion to the First Division before quitting the club, questioning their ambition.

Archibald then added club chairman to his portfolio in 2000 when he took control of struggling Airdrie while the club were in the hands of administrators. He had the grand plan of importing foreign talent, winning promotion to the Premier League and making profit in the process by selling on the gems his network of contacts in Spain unearthed.

The blueprint was not without its merits but never got off the ground – Archibald left in 2001 and the club folded. He returned to Spain to concentrate on business commitments.

Gone from Scotland but his reputation lives on.

Matt Armstrong

Date of birth: 12 November 1911, Newton Stewart
Died: 1995, Aberdeen

Aberdeen record:
Appearances: League 191, Scottish Cup 24
Goals: League 136, Scottish Cup 19
Debut: League, 21 November 1931 v Falkirk (a) lost 3–0

Also played for: Scotland (3 caps), Port Glasgow Juniors, Elgin City

The statistics say it all when it comes to Matt Armstrong's career with Aberdeen: 215 games, 155 goals. It puts him second in the club's all-time scoring chart, behind Joe Harper with 200 goals in 308 games, and guarantees him legendary status.

A succession of managers throughout the 1990s and beyond have searched for a striker who could consistently pass the magical 20-goals-a-season mark. Armstrong, who died in Aberdeen in 1995, beat 30 in four consecutive seasons in the 1930s.

Which makes it all the more surprising that he was almost shipped out of Pittodrie in his early days as a Dons player. He had been signed on a provisional form with Celtic, having starred with Port Glasgow in the junior ranks, but Aberdeen manager Pat Travers took advantage of a lapse in the paperwork to nip in and recruit the 19-year-old.

Opportunities were limited in the Pittodrie first team and after making his debut in a 3–0 defeat at Falkirk on 21 November 1931, Armstrong endured a frustrating two seasons in which he made just 17 appearances and scored six goals. The first of those goals came just a fortnight after his first game in a 2–1 win against Leith in Edinburgh.

It was in the 1933–34 season that Armstrong began to make his mark – scoring five in the first game of the season as the home crowd were treated to an 8–0 win against Ayr United. That helped take his tally to 14 goals in just 13 games and convinced Travers that his rising striker could be depended on to wear the number-nine shirt week in and week out.

The following season was the most prolific in his Aberdeen career, with the staggering return of 39 goals in 43 games. Hat-tricks against Queen's Park and Ayr were joined by doubles in eight League and Cup encounters. Armstrong was in unstoppable form, but even his heroics could not lift the Dons higher than sixth in the final First Division standings.

That 1934–35 tally made him the leading scorer and he retained that billing for the next three years, thanks to hauls of 31, 30 and 22 goals. Armstrong's ability to hit the target at club level brought three caps for Scotland to add to the junior international cap he had won as a teenager. He was never on the losing side for the national team, playing in a 1–1 draw against Wales on his debut in 1935 as well as a 2–1 win over Northern Ireland later that year and a 2–0 win over Germany in 1936.

Honours proved agonisingly elusive for one of the finest attacking talents Aberdeen has ever had. In 1936–37 he came the closest he would get, scoring in the Scottish Cup Final against Celtic in front of 146,433 as his side fell to a 2–1 defeat. In the League it was Rangers who stood between the Dons and the League title, winning by seven points.

To put the season's achievements in context, the club had only ever reached the heady heights of second place once in its history up to that point and had never before reached the Final of the Cup. It was the only time the original black and gold striped kit was worn in the Final, with red adopted as the club colours two years later.

The war interrupted Armstrong's career when he was in full flight, but, at the age of 34, he returned in 1945–46 to ease the club back into competitive action and still knew the way to goal, netting eight goals in just 13 appearances.

Armstrong, born in Newton Stewart, remained in the north and continued playing well into his 40s with Elgin City, where he remained a potent striker. He later acted as a scout for Falkirk, among other clubs.

Post-football Armstrong worked in the motor trade in Aberdeen, combining work with his love of golf – a member of Murcar Golf Club who played off a handicap of two at his prime – before returning to Aberdeen FC as manager of the Pittodrie Development Association. He retired in 1976 after a 45-year association with the Dons.

Archie Baird

Date of birth: June 1919, Rutherglen

Aberdeen record:

Appearances: League 104, Scottish Cup 17, League Cup 23
Goals: League 26, Scottish Cup 2, League Cup 9
Debut: League, 11 August 1945 v Third Lanark (h) won 3–0

Also played for: Scotland (1 cap), St Johnstone

Aberdeen supporters waited 43 years to savour the taste of success. For Archie Baird, the 1946 Southern League Cup victory was even sweeter. Baird wore the number-10 shirt with pride as the Dons defeated Rangers 3–2 in front of 135,000 fans at Hampden to lift their first major piece of silverware, the precursor to the League Cup, since the formation of the side in 1903. Baird had scored the opener after just 90 seconds and was joined on the scoresheet by George Taylor and Stan Williams.

The Glaswegian signed for the Pittodrie side in 1938 on a £4-per-week contract. The outbreak of war meant it was not until 1945 that he made his debut for the club.

Not that he spent the years in between living the quiet life. In fact, his military service took him to the deserts of North Africa and after being captured by a squadron of German tanks, a prisoner of war camp in Italy. In 1943 Baird made a break from the camp in Rimini, through a gap in a wire fence, and found refuge with an Italian family for nine months. When the Germans eventually pulled out of Italy, he was free to return to Scotland and live out his football dream.

Baird's first competitive action came on 11 August 1945, against the famous old name of Third Lanark at Pittodrie. His side won 3–0, competing in the Scottish Southern A League. He waited just another month to open his goalscoring account, on the scoresheet in a 4–1 win over Motherwell early that season. The club went on to finish third in the League, behind champions Rangers and runners-up Hibs.

His first season would prove to be his most prolific as an Aberdeen player, bringing 17 goals in total. Nine came in the League, two in the Scottish Cup and, most crucially, six were bagged in the League Cup campaign. In addition to his vital strike in the Final, Baird scored in the semi-final against Airdrie to earn a 2–2 draw and was on target again in the replay of that tie, which the Dons won 5–3 after extra-time, to help his side to the Final.

The Southern League Cup success in 1946 was followed the next season by a 3–2 victory over Hibs in the Scottish Cup Final, with Baird again resplendent in the red number-10 shirt.

The Scottish Cup win was a momentous occasion for the club, a fact demonstrated by the 15,000-strong welcome committee that greeted the team when it pulled in at Aberdeen's Joint Station to parade the famous trophy on home soil.

It was a glorious period for Baird, who made his debut for Scotland in 1946 against Belgium. The solitary appearance in dark blue was in a 2–2 draw at Hampden.

Baird underwent three cartilage operations and also recovered from a fractured leg during his time in the game. After an association stretching back 15 years, he waved farewell to his Pittodrie terracing backers in January 1953, his final appearance coming in a 2–2 League draw against Dundee.

Each of his 144 appearances came under the stewardship of manager Dave Halliday, who himself departed three years later. Baird's spirit and skill led St Johnstone to tempt him to Muirton Park when his Dons career ended after 37 goals for the Pittodrie side.

He served as a sports journalist and teacher before his retirement, and the war hero, who lives in Cove Bay on the outskirts of Aberdeen, added author to his list of credits in 1989 when his biography, *Family of Four*, was published.

Dougie Bell

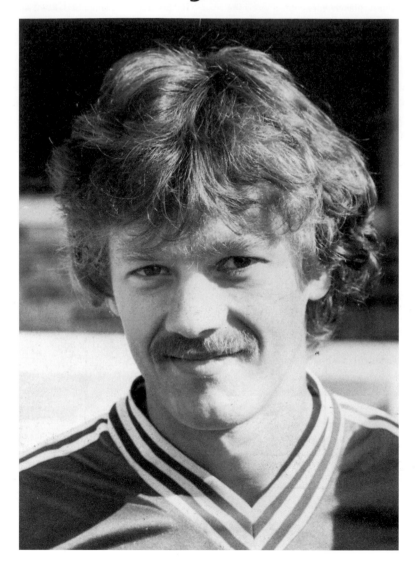

Date of birth: 5 September 1959, Paisley

Aberdeen record:

Appearances: League 109+22, Scottish Cup 22+11, League Cup 28+5, Europe 25+5

Goals: League 6, League Cup 7, Europe 1

Debut: League, 11 August 1979 v Partick Thistle (a) lost 1–0

Also played for: St Mirren, Rangers, Hibs, Shrewsbury, Hull, Birmingham, Partick, Portadown, Clyde, Elgin City, Alloa, Albion Rovers

Dougie Bell could not have picked a better season to walk through the front door at Pittodrie for the first time. The Paisley-born player was signed by Alex Ferguson from St Mirren on a free transfer and made his debut in the opening game of the 1979–80 season.

Few who played a part in the 1–0 defeat at the hands of Partick Thistle at Firhill could have predicted what the campaign would yield, except perhaps the manager with the midas touch. Bell was a substitute in that game and proved a reliable squad man as the Dons pipped Celtic to the Premier Division title by a single point.

The classy midfielder made 10 appearances in that League-winning run, his first start in a 4–0 win at Dundee on 29 September 1979. Bell scored his first goal for Aberdeen on 27 August in an 8–1 League Cup victory against Berwick Rangers at Pittodrie.

After contributing to League success in 1980, Bell's second experience of that winning feeling came in the 1982 Scottish Cup Final when he came on from the bench to help the Dons to a 4–1 extra-time win over Rangers. He missed the rematch with the Ibrox side in the Final the following year, which the Dons won 1–0, but had established himself as a regular by then. He wore the number-eight jersey in each of the four rounds leading to that Final but was sidelined by injury for the Hampden showdown with the Gers.

The same injury forced him to miss out on the club's finest hour in Gothenburg, having started eight of the 11 European Cup-winners' Cup ties in that legendary tournament and scoring the only goal of the game in the second-round second-leg tie against Lech Poznan to give the Dons a 3–0 aggregate win.

Bell did add a European-winners' medal to his collection when he played a key role in the 1983 Super Cup win over SV Hamburg – a main man as Aberdeen won 2–0 over two legs to confirm their place among Europe's elite. The 1983–84 season also brought further Premier Division success and Bell was a mainstay, making 23 appearances in the League as the Dons beat Celtic by seven points to take the crown.

He came on from the bench in the tense 2–1 extra-time win over Celtic in the Scottish Cup Final and also played in every tie as the Dons came agonisingly close to earning a shot at a third European title, beaten 2–0 on aggregate by Porto in the semi-final of that season's European Cup-winners' Cup.

Bell's final winners' medal in the red shirt of Aberdeen came in 1985 as he helped the club claim a second consecutive Premier Division title, this time clocking up 22 appearances in the dominant Dons side of the day to take his total to 227 games and 14 goals.

He was snapped up by Rangers for £160,000 that summer and stayed at Ibrox for two seasons before heading across the country to Hibs in 1986. He went on to play in England with Shrewsbury, Hull and Birmingham, and he added Northern Ireland to his playing CV when he joined Portadown in 1992 after a stint with Partick Thistle.

Bell played out his career with Clyde, Elgin in the Highland League, Alloa and Albion Rovers. More recently he has been on the coaching staff of Clyde in the First Division, drafted in by former Pittodrie teammate Joe Miller.

Paul Bernard

Date of birth: 30 December 1972, Edinburgh

Aberdeen record:
Appearances: League 93+8, Scottish Cup 11, League Cup 10+1, Europe 2
Goals: League 6, Scottish Cup 2
Debut: League, 30 September 1995 v Raith Rovers (h) won 3–0

Also played for: Scotland (2 caps), Oldham Athletic, Barnsley, Plymouth, St Johnstone

As football clubs count the cost of past extravagance and budgets creak and groan under the strain of historic debts, it is difficult to envisage a day when Paul Bernard will be dislodged from his unique place in the history of Aberdeen.

Bernard became the club's record signing in September 1995 when Oldham Athletic pocketed a fee in the region of £1 million, in the form of £850,000 up front and additional payments as the contract progressed. The deal eclipsed the £800,000 it took to take Billy Dodds to Pittodrie, the £750,000 paid to Hull for Dean Windass or the £500,000 paid to recruit Robbie Winters from Dundee United, although the Winters deal does not factor in the worth of Dodds when he moved in the opposite direction as part of the package.

In cash terms at least, Bernard is the costliest player ever to cross the threshold at Pittodrie after chairman Ian Donald backed manager Roy Aitken's judgement to the hilt. The big question is whether he provided value for money, and the majority of Dons fans would argue that he did not.

The hefty price tag saddled Bernard with a weight of expectation. While he sparkled at times, looking every ounce a £1 million player, he struggled to produce his best form consistently as a series of injuries restricted him to 114 starts in six years, bringing just eight goals.

Bernard's time at the club started on a high, as within two months of his arrival he got his hands on a League Cup-winners' medal following the 2–0 win over Dundee. With one prize in the bag and two Scottish caps already nestling at home, courtesy of appearances in the Kirin Cup in May 1995, the stock of the young midfielder was at an all-time high. However, those Scotland games, as a substitute in a 0–0 draw with Japan and 90 minutes in a 2–1 win against Ecuador, proved to be his last.

He was still only 22 when he achieved those milestones, having burst onto the English scene as a teenager with Oldham as they battled for Premiership survival in 1992. He played two seasons in the top flight before the Latics dropped down to the First Division for the 1994–95 season. The following term,

after the club's failure to regain their seat at the top table, the Dons made their move.

Bernard, complete with Ferrari, rolled into the Pittodrie car park for the first time a month after the start of the season in 1995, making his debut from the bench in a 3–0 win at home to Raith Rovers on 30 September. The League Cup Final followed on 26 November, by which time he had been eased into Aitken's starting XI. He appeared in all but five of the Premier Division fixtures as the Dons finished third behind Rangers and Celtic, having arrived after the first four, and he was on his way to 36 appearances in all competitions. It proved to be a rare full campaign for the midfielder.

An ankle injury first feared to be a broken leg sidelined the record buy for a month in the first half of the 1996–97 season and a groin injury struck at the turn of the year. All in all he made just 15 appearances. This stop-start introduction meant Bernard never truly won over the Aberdeen supporters, even though he was more consistently available for selection in 1997–98 as the club switched manager from Aitken to Alex Miller. He did enough to persuade the new manager to extend his contract but it proved to be a false dawn for the former Oldham star, who made just eight appearances the following season due to injury.

Bernard returned to full fitness in Ebbe Skovdahl's debut campaign, sitting out just eight League games and every one of the seven Scottish Cup ties which culminated in the 4–0 defeat in the 2000 Final against Rangers following an early injury to goalkeeper Jim Leighton. He had also played in the 2–0 defeat in the Final of the League Cup against Celtic earlier that season.

Just as he had established himself as a mainstay the old injury problems returned, with just three appearances in the Millennium season as his contract was allowed to run down by the club. Short spells with Barnsley and Plymouth Argyle followed before Bernard returned to Scotland with St Johnstone in 2003 and later wound down his career in Ireland with Drogheda. He is now back in England and carving out a new niche in the house building industry.

Jim Bett

Date of birth: 25 November 1959, Hamilton

Aberdeen record:
Appearances: League 256+2, Scottish Cup 27, League Cup 31+1, Europe 21
Goals: League 33, Scottish Cup 2, League Cup 10, Europe 2
Debut: League, 10 August 1985 v Hibs (h) won 3–0

Also played for: Scotland (26 caps), Airdrie, Rangers, Lockeren, Hearts, Dundee United

Dougie Bell's departure coincided with the arrival of Jim Bett, recruited by Alex Ferguson in a £300,000 deal in the summer of 1985. That fee, paid to Belgian side Lokeren, represented a record for the Dons at the time but proved to be money very well spent.

At the time, Sir Alex Ferguson said 'Jim will give us quality. He'll give us stature. He will give us stability and his European experience will be invaluable. He's a player of the same class as Gordon Strachan. In short, Jim is an outstanding player.'

High praise indeed from the highest source of all at Pittodrie for a man who had starred in Belgian football and had also made an impression in the Icelandic League.

The cultured midfielder started on the long and winding road to stardom with Airdrie before heading for the continent. He went on to make more than 100 appearances for Rangers between 1980 and 1983, a rare bright spot in a miserable period for the Ibrox time. Bett then switched to Lockeren for a second spell with the club in 1983 and when it was time to return to Scotland two years later there was no shortage of offers, including from Ibrox.

Instead, he chose Aberdeen and made the perfect start to his Dons career, scoring in a 3–0 debut win over Hibs on 10 August 1985. He was the creative force as the team stormed to a Cup double that season.

Bett did not play in the League Cup Final due to an ankle injury but wore his familiar number-10 jersey for the Scottish Cup win against Hearts, helping his side to a 3–0 win over the Edinburgh side who, just a week earlier, had blown their Premier Division title hopes in the final League game of the season. The Dons and Bett, not surprisingly, were in no mood to be sympathetic.

The Lanarkshire-born player was a loyal servant in a transitional period for the club: at the heart of the team under first Ferguson, then his successor Ian Porterfield and, more successfully, Alex Smith and his co-manager Jocky Scott. Smith and Scott's spell at the helm brought the Dons fans and players the silverware they had taken for granted under Ferguson, and Bett was there to enjoy it as his side claimed a dramatic and nerve-shredding 9–8 penalty shoot-out win over Celtic in the 1990 Scottish Cup Final after the match had ended without a goal.

To cap a memorable campaign Bett was voted Scotland's Player of the Year by his fellow professionals. Teammate Alex McLeish won the Scottish Football Writers' Association and Tartan Special Player of the Year awards to make it a Dons hat-trick that year.

Bett was an ever present in the Premier Division campaign in 1990–91 when Aberdeen came within 90 minutes of winning another League title. However, his prompting from midfield could not unlock a resolute Rangers defence as the Light Blues ran out 2–0 winners in the infamous final-day decider at Ibrox to win the Championship by just two points...the value of a single win in those days.

He was part of the Scotland set-up throughout his time at Pittodrie, amassing 26 caps in a senior career spanning from 1982 to his final appearance as an Aberdeen player in 1990. Bett's international career took in the World Cup Finals in Italy in 1990, where he made his final appearance in dark blue in the 1–0 defeat against Costa Rica. He was also a squad member at the 1986 World Cup Finals in Mexico, having featured in every qualifying game. His single international goal came against Iceland, the homeland of his wife, in a 1–0 win in 1985.

Bett eventually left Pittodrie in the summer of 1994, by which time former teammate Willie Miller was the man steering the ship. His final appearance came in a 4–0 League win over Raith Rovers at Pittodrie on 12 February that year, taking his tally to 338 games and 47 goals. He went on to turn out for Hearts and Dundee United over the following two seasons, making more than 20 appearances for each before retiring to the north east.

Bett's association with Aberdeen did not end when he called time on his own playing career, with sons Baldur and Calum both turning out for the club under Ebbe Skovdahl. Baldur made his first appearance in 1998 and Calum followed in his bootsteps in 2001.

Bett, who still lives in the Aberdeen area, served as a youth coach with both Dundee United and Celtic in the Aberdeen area following his retirement from playing.

Eric Black

Date of birth: 1 October 1963, Bellshill

Aberdeen record:
Appearances: League 115+19, Scottish Cup 25+3, League Cup 18+4, Europe
                22+4
Goals: League 45, Scottish Cup 5, League Cup 12, Europe 7
Debut: League, 31 October 1981 v Dundee United (h) draw 1–1

Also played for: Scotland (2 caps), Metz
Managed: Motherwell, Coventry City

The Gothenburg triumph in 1983 not only produced a team of legends, it created a legacy. Whether it was the inspiration of savouring European success or the indelible mark left by Sir Alex Ferguson, a disproportionate number from that European Cup-winners' Cup side have gone on to make their mark in coaching.

Black is no exception, most recently serving as assistant to Birmingham City boss Steve Bruce in the Premiership and Championship. He led Motherwell and Coventry City in his own right, having cut his teeth on the coaching staff at Celtic. He also came very close to taking over the Pittodrie manager's office following the departure of Alex Miller in the 1990s and tantalisingly to this day refuses to rule out the possibility of a Dons homecoming in the future.

His playing career with the club began in 1980, when he was taken south as a teenager straight from Alness Academy in the Highlands by Alex Ferguson and his far-reaching scouting network. He introduced himself to the fans with a goal on his debut in a 1–1 home draw against Dundee United in the Premier Division on 31 October 1981.

Black was eased into life with the club, starting 10 top-flight games that term, and came on from the bench in the 4–1 extra-time triumph over Rangers in the Final of the Scottish Cup to cap his introductory campaign with a medal. By the time the memorable 1982–83 season started he was still short of his 20th birthday but was one of the first names on Ferguson's team sheet. He was integral to the double success the year brought.

Against Real Madrid in that Final he scored the opener in the 2–1 European Cup-winners' Cup Final win to earn himself a permanent place in the hearts of the Dons faithful. Black was a thorn in Madrid's side throughout the game, hitting the crossbar in the opening minutes before tucking home his goal after just six minutes when he met an Alex McLeish knock-down inside the box. He continued to force saves from the Real 'keeper before limping out injured to make way for the other goalscoring hero, John Hewitt, in the second half. Ten days later, on the home soil of Hampden Park, he again showed his aptitude for the big occasion when his solitary goal gave the Dons victory over Rangers in the Scottish Cup Final. Black had arrived, in style.

Rangers were not alone in suffering at his hands, with Black's first Dons hat-trick destroying Celtic in the League earlier that season as they were beaten 3–1. He went one better in the following season's League Cup, bagging four in a 9–0 romp against Raith Rovers.

The League medal was added in the 1983–84 campaign and a third consecutive Scottish Cup-winners' prize joined it on the mantelpiece, Black again on target as the Dons claimed a 2–1 win over Celtic in a tense Final that went to extra-time. By that time, he had already helped the side to success in the European Super Cup against SV Hamburg.

In the summer of 1984 Aberdeen lost the services of Mark McGhee, leading scorer for the previous two terms. Would it prove terminal to Ferguson's hopes of dominating domestically? The answer was a resounding no.

Frank McDougall took over the mantle as the ultimate danger man but Black stepped up his contribution and in what proved to be his penultimate campaign in red, he made the most prolific contribution of his Dons career with 20 goals in all competitions in 1984–85.

The team retained the Premier Division trophy and Black's 17 goals in the League, including the mandatory hat-trick (this time in a 5–0 success over Hibs), were vital to that success.

It proved to be the final medal for Black, who missed the 1986 Scottish Cup Final after scoring in the 3–0 semi-final win over Hibs. He was dropped for announcing, before the campaign had ended, that he would be leaving for new pastures. Not common in those pre-Bosman ruling days.

In the summer of that year he moved on, broadening his horizons with a switch to Metz in France when his Dons contract expired. While on the continent he became a Scotland international, capped twice in 1987 in a 2–0 win over Hungary and a 0–0 draw against Luxembourg during Andy Roxburgh's tenure as national coach. In France, at the age of 28, a back injury cut short his playing career and hastened his entry to the coaching ranks.

Black's decision to turn his back on the Dons after 210 appearances and 69 goals in 1986 angered Alex Ferguson, who made no secret of his displeasure at the time.

But, more than a decade later, the Manchester United coach was the first to send a congratulatory card to his former player on his appointment at Motherwell. The message simply read 'Welcome to the rat's world.'

And so the Ferguson legacy continued.

Henning Boel

Date of birth: 15 August 1945

Aberdeen record:

Appearances: League 105+1, Scottish Cup 16, League Cup 22, Europe 6
Goals: League 2, Scottish Cup 1, League Cup 1
Debut: League, 4 January 1969 v Dundee United (a) won 4-1

Also played for: Denmark (15 caps), Ikast, Boston Beacons, Washington Whips, New England Revolution

Aberdeen has welcomed its share of continental imports, but very few have left the shores of the north east with a precious souvenir from their time at Pittodrie. Henning Boel earned his memento in the 1970 Scottish Cup Final, when Celtic were humbled by the Dons as they ran out 3–1 winners to lift the old trophy for the first time since 1947. Boel played an important role, thwarting the attacking threats of John Hughes and Jimmy Johnstone during that pulsating Final.

It was the undoubted high spot for Boel, who had been taken to the club by Eddie Turnbull mid-way through the 1968–69 season having first been spotted playing for the Washington Whips while the Dons toured America. The Dons finished the campaign 15th, just two places clear of relegation, and Boel's addition to the squad was an attempt by Turnbull to close the door on the dreaded possibility of dropping out of the elite.

The defender proved a popular addition among both players and supporters, and he stayed longer than many imports. After his debut in a 4–1 win over Dundee United at Tannadice on 4 January 1969, Boel established himself as a regular in Turnbull's rearguard and played every game in the run-in to the end of the season.

By the time his first full season began he had been shifted from the centre of the defence to the right side, although he continued to deputise at centre-half when called upon, and the Dons enjoyed a more fruitful period. They shrugged off the relegation fears of the previous season to finish in the comfort of eighth and clinched the Cup.

In the 1970–71 season Boel played a major part in a British club-record run of 12 consecutive games without conceding a goal. He also chipped in with four goals, breaking his Dons duck when he netted in a 4–0 win at Kilmarnock early in the season. Aberdeen went on to miss out on the Premier Division title by just two points, with Celtic taking the honours. Boel, an ever present in the League, could take a share in the small consolation that his side's defensive record could not be bettered, with a miserly 18 goals conceded by a steely unit over 34 games. Not even the champions could match that.

The foundations began to crumble the following season, with manager Turnbull departing for Hibernian and captain Martin Buchan, another vital cog in the defensive machine, moving south in a dream move to Manchester United. Boel, who had vied with George Murray for the number-two jersey under new boss Jimmy Bonthrone, played out the season for the club as they again finished runners-up to the Hoops, this time by a margin of 10 points.

The Dane, who made 17 appearances for his country, was still on the books as the 1972–73 campaign burst into life, but made only 13 further appearances. A broken ankle suffered in the 1972 UEFA Cup tie against Borussia Monchengladbach pushed him out of the frame at Pittodrie.

The Danish international did make a comeback after that, returning to football in America with New England Revolution in the NASL's era of Pele and George Best, but never hit the same heights.

Boel, who appeared 150 times for the Dons with a single goal to his credit, worked as a sales representative for sports firms Nike and Hummel in his homeland before moving into the oil industry.

In 2006 he was voted by fans as one of the top five foreign imports ever brought to Scotland by the Dons.

Scott Booth

Date of birth: 16 December 1971, Aberdeen

Aberdeen record:
Appearances: League 170+15, Scottish Cup 6+1, League Cup 6, Europe 4+3
Goals: League 51, Scottish Cup 3, League Cup 1
Debut: League, 28 April 1990 v St Mirren (h) won 2–0

Also played for: Scotland (22 caps), Borussia Dortmund, Utrecht, Twente Enschede

Scottish football may not have seen the last of one of Aberdeen's best home-grown players. Alongside a certain Alan Shearer on the list of budding young coaches to have passed the SFA's A-licence in the summer of 2006 was a Mr S. Booth. Like Shearer, Booth starred for his home-town club. And like Shearer, he hung up his boots when it appeared to most he could have played on.

In 2004 Booth, then aged 32 and in his second spell at Pittodrie, was told by new manager Jimmy Calderwood that he would not be retained. There were other options on the table in Scotland but he instead signed for Setanta, not an exotic far-flung club but the Irish satellite broadcaster.

Booth has taken to his new role as a television presenter, reporting on Scottish Premier League football week in and week out before stepping up to become the station's co-commentator, with the same type of ease as he played the game.

The fact he has passed his coaching qualifications hints that he may yet be returning to the other side of the lens. Putting Booth through his coaching paces on behalf of the SFA was Alex Smith, the manager who 16 years earlier, in 1990, had given a teenage striker his big break for Aberdeen.

Booth took his bow on 28 April in a 2–0 win at home to St Mirren as a substitute. He waited just a week for his first start, entrusted with the number-nine jersey for a 3–1 win over Celtic at Parkhead. The first goals came on 2 February 1991, with a double in a 5–0 win at home to Hearts. His return in the League, as the Dons missed out on the title on the final day of the season at the hands of Rangers, was six goals in just eight starts.

Booth, along with sidekick Eoin Jess, went from strength to strength under Smith's considered tutelage. His successor Willie Miller also put his faith in the confident and cultured youngster. Miller's side, sent on their way by a Booth hat-trick in the 4–1 first-round win over Hamilton, his first senior treble, ran to the Final of the 1993 Scottish Cup but tasted defeat when Rangers won 2–1 and also finished second to the Ibrox side in the League.

The Light Blues again stood in the way of Booth and the Premier Division winners' medal he craved in 1993–94. His solitary reward for his endeavours at Pittodrie should have come in the League Cup of 1995, by which time Roy Aitken was in charge. Booth was joint top scorer in that 1995–96 campaign, tied with Billy

Dodds on 12, and he scored three in the League Cup before agonisingly missing out on the Final triumph over Dundee due to injury.

The pain of that club disappointment was eased by international recognition, Booth making his Scotland debut against Germany in a 1–0 defeat when he was selected by Andy Roxburgh. He went on to appear in the dark blue 22 times, including at Euro '96 and the World Cup Finals in France in 1998 – scoring six goals in the process.

Having come through the ranks alongside Jess and Stephen Wright, both sold in seven-figure deals in 1996, it was perhaps no surprise that Booth himself opted to test the water away from his boyhood team.

His path was not a well-trodden one, stunning the Dons fans in 1997 when he clinched a move to German giants Borussia Dortmund having fallen out of contract at Pittodrie. He stayed on the continent, with spells at FC Utrecht and Twente Enschede in Holland, for six years before returning to Scotland and Aberdeen in 2003 to play for Steve Paterson.

The coaching staff raved about the new-look Booth, following his studies in the Leagues of Europe, but his return did not bring an upturn in fortunes for the club as they struggled in the top flight.

Booth, brought up on a diet of European football and Championship challenges in his early days with the Dons, was in a very different era but at least ended his career with the merit of only ever playing for one Scottish side. In two spells he turned out 228 times and hit the back of the net on 70 occasions.

Martin Buchan

Date of birth: 6 March 1949, Aberdeen

Aberdeen record:
Appearances: League 133+3, Scottish Cup 20, League Cup 23, Europe 12+1
Goals: League 9, Scottish Cup 0, League Cup 1, Europe 1
Debut: League, 8 October 1966 v Dunfermline (a) drew 1–1

Also played for: Scotland (34 caps), Manchester United, Oldham Athletic
Managed: Burnley

In November 2006 Martin Buchan was named as one of only three football players among 21 stars from all genres to earn a place in the newly-created Aberdeen sporting hall of fame. The trio was completed by Denis Law and a former Dons player featured later in the pages of this book, inducted alongside Olympic medal-winning heroes and champions from the upper echelons of golf and rugby.

The Dons have been blessed with a string of home-grown talents throughout the decades but Buchan is regarded by fans of his home-town club as one of the finest Pittodrie products. Unlike Law, he launched his career at home, signing for Aberdeen straight from school having grown up playing school and boys' brigade football.

It was Eddie Turnbull who recruited the 16-year-old, a pupil at the Robert Gordon's College in the city, in 1965. The following year, on 8 October 1966, he made his debut wearing the number-six shirt in a 1–1 draw against Dunfermline at East End Park.

It was a transitional period for the club under Turnbull, who made sweeping changes to the playing squad as he built a side around his new-found defensive rock. Buchan went on to become Turnbull's captain and his crowning glory in the red of Aberdeen came at Hampden in May 1970, when, at the age of just 21, he held aloft the Scottish Cup in front of 108,324 supporters at the national stadium. The Dons defeated Celtic 3–1 with a double from Derek McKay and a Joe Harper goal, ending a 23-year famine in the national Cup competition for the Dons. Buchan's place as a hero for the Pittodrie faithful was assured.

His standing in the Scottish game was also being elevated to new levels and in 1971 he was named as the Scottish Football Writers' Player of the Year, becoming the first Aberdonian ever to win the honour. He would be followed by another north-east player the following year, another man featured in the pages which follow.

Buchan was growing accustomed to getting his hands on prized football mementoes but admits the moment he collected the League Cup passed in a blur. He recalled, 'I remember a picture of myself and Billy McNeill shaking hands before the Cup Final in 1970. It looked like a big man with a wee laddie. We rose to the occasion as a team - Aberdeen were seen as underdogs but didn't feel that way. We had beaten Celtic at Parkhead in the League in the weeks leading up to the

Final. They only needed a point to win the title - there were crates of champagne stacked up outside the home dressing room and that made Eddie Turnbull's team talk easy. Eddie simply said to us "Do you think they are going to celebrate tonight at our expense?"'

Buchan also won the first of 34 Scotland caps while with the Pittodrie side. He was selected by Tommy Docherty and made his debut in a 1–0 win against Belgium in Aberdeen courtesy of a John O'Hare strike.

The promise of the budding international defender was reaching a wider audience and early in 1972 a clutch of English clubs moved in on Scottish football's hot property. Leeds United and Liverpool were keen but it was Manchester United who won the chase, shelling out £125,000 to take Buchan to Old Trafford. Buchan, who scored 11 times, played 192 games for Aberdeen over the course of five years and four months. Many have served the club for longer but nobody on the Pittodrie terraces grudged their local hero the chance to test himself in the English League.

Frank O'Farrell was the manager who did the deal for Manchester United but within months he was replaced by Docherty and Buchan was given another big break, appointed captain of the Red Devils to follow Bobby Charlton. As he had done with the Dons he led United to Cup glory, lifting the FA Cup at Wembley after a 2–1 win over Liverpool at Wembley in 1977.

While with the English giants he featured in both the 1974 and 1978 World Cup Finals with Scotland and had contrasting fortunes. He played twice in the German tournament in 1974 and helped the national side earn draws against Yugoslavia and Brazil, as the men in dark blue were knocked out despite an unbeaten record. In Argentina in 1978 he played in the ill-fated opening games against Peru and Iran before helping save face with a 3–2 win over Holland. His career with the national team spanned seven years, including a 13-month break when he and a group of players were used as scapegoats in the wake of a 5–0 defeat at the hands of England in what was designed to be a celebration of the SFA's centenary in 1973. That did not deter him and he was back in 1974 to fight for the cause once more.

Buchan, who captained Scotland twice, remained at Old Trafford for 11 years before joining Oldham Athletic in 1983. He also had a brief spell as a manager with Burnley before moving into the sportswear industry with Puma. He remains based in Manchester and now works with the Professional Footballers' Association.

Paddy Buckley

Date of birth: 31 January 1925, Leith

Aberdeen record:
Appearances: League 106, Scottish Cup 20, League Cup 26
Goals: League 58, Scottish Cup 16, League Cup 18
Debut: League Cup, 9 August 1952 v Motherwell (a) lost 5–2

Also played for: Scotland (3 caps), Bo'ness United, St Johnstone

In 1955 Aberdeen were crowned champions of Scotland for the first time since the club's formation in 1903 and it is safe to say that success would not have been possible without the goals of one man.

His name was Paddy Buckley and his prolific form as the feared number nine of the Championship-winning Dons team was a key factor in the title success savoured by the Pittodrie faithful. Buckley smashed home 17 goals in that Division A campaign as his side pipped Celtic by just three points to lift the trophy.

The speedy Leith-born forward missed just two of the 30 League games that term and consistently provided a match-winning contribution. As the title race went to the wire, he crashed home a hat-trick in a 4–0 win over Rangers as the season entered its final month and a double in a 3–2 win over Raith Rovers on the final day of the season.

The 1954–55 season was Buckley's most profitable as a Dons player. He netted six goals in six games in the League Cup and five in six games in the Scottish Cup for a return of 28 in just 40 appearances, securing his place as leading scorer at the club. It was a strike ratio worth millions in the modern game.

Buckley was no stranger to celebrating before that glorious season, on target 27 times the previous campaign. That form propelled him onto the international stage and he made his debut for Scotland in a 1–0 win over Norway in May 1954. Two further caps followed all in the same year, the highlight coming when he scored the winner in a 1–0 win over Wales in Cardiff.

Buckley faced fierce competition from Hibs legend Lawrie Reilly in the fight for Scotland places, but at club level he could not be budged from the Aberdeen team.

He cut his teeth with Bo'ness United before switching to the senior game at the age of 23 in 1948 with St Johnstone, although Celtic had also been on the trail of one of the stars of the junior game. After four years in Perth it cost Aberdeen manager Dave Halliday the considerable sum of £7,500 to tempt Saints to part with their striker, now in his prime.

In fact, in the week leading up to his switch to the north east he scored an incredible eight goals in seven days. He hit four against East Fife for St Johnstone at the start of the week, added a midweek hat-trick against Breadalbane in the Dewar Shield and then signed off with his final goal for the Muirton men against Clyde in the Supplementary Cup. Not bad form.

Buckley's first appearance in red came in a 5–2 League Cup defeat at the hands of Motherwell on 9 August 1952. It was a miserable game but his goal on his debut at least gave a glimmer of hope for the Dons fans in the crowd at Fir Park. He remained at Pittodrie until 1957, when a serious knee injury brought the curtain down on a glittering career.

Buckley remains one of the top-50 strikers at the top level in the post-war Scottish game, with his record of 198 goals at club and international level putting him on a par with Andy Penman of Dundee and Rangers. For the Dons he grabbed 92 goals in the space of 152 games.

A giant in the Scottish game and a giant for the club he served so well.

Dave Caldwell

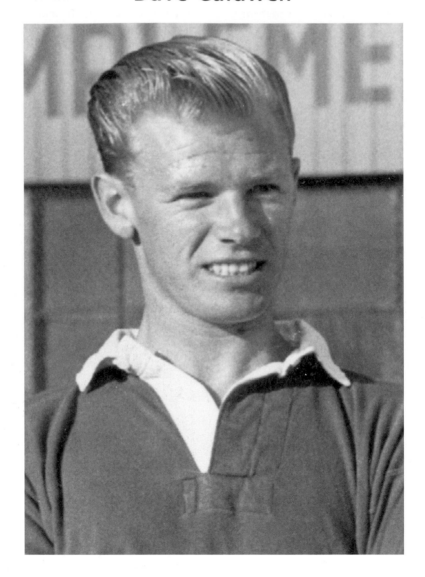

Date of birth: 7 May 1932, Clydebank

Aberdeen record:
Appearances: League 132, Scottish Cup 16, League Cup 30
Debut: League Cup, 22 August 1953 v Celtic (h) won 5–2

Also played for: Duntochter Hibs, Rotherham, Morton, Toronto City, Wick
Academy, Forres Mechanics, Fraserburgh, Keith
Managed: Sunnybank

The Aberdeen team of the 1950s has gone down in history as one of the greatest in the history of the club. Attacking flair was mixed with defensive resilience and one of the key components for the bulk of that decade was defender Dave Caldwell.

Caldwell moved to Pittodrie from Duntocher Hibs, in Clydebank, in 1953 and was a mainstay for the Dons until his departure in 1960. He made his debut in a 5–2 League Cup win over Celtic on 22 August 1953, and the tenacious full-back made the number-three jersey his own that term with 35 appearances, including the 2–1 Scottish Cup Final defeat at the hands of Celtic.

In the following season, the Championship-winning campaign, Caldwell was sidelined for most of the term. He returned for the final five League games to help the Dons clinch the title with four wins.

If he had been a bit-part player in the club's momentous triumph he was firmly in the limelight for the 1955–56 season's trophy success. This time it was the League Cup, which was taken back to the Granite City and Caldwell played in nine of the 10 games on that victorious run. St Mirren provided the opposition in the Hampden Final, which attracted a crowd of 44,000 people, and Caldwell played through the pain barrier to make sure he had a place on centre stage.

The defender had suffered an ankle knock the previous week. He knew he wasn't fully fit and manager Dave Shaw knew he wasn't fit, but the pair agreed to take a gamble and it paid off. It was Shaw's first season in charge and it was capped with Cup success thanks to a Jimmy Mallan own-goal and Graham Leggat's deft chip.

Before departing for a brief stint at Rotherham in 1960 Caldwell wracked up 178 appearances for Aberdeen but could not add a Scottish Cup-winners' medal to his League and League Cup success, in the side that lost 3–1 to St Mirren in the 1959 Final as 108,591 supporters crammed into Hampden. After just 10 minutes he suffered a calf strain and up against the pace of winger Gerry Baker, he toiled. He was eventually pushed up field and out of the danger zone by Shaw as he limped to the final whistle. It was not the dream end to what proved to be his swansong with Aberdeen.

Caldwell, who never scored for the Dons, went from Rotherham to Toronto City the following season, making a short return to home soil with Morton in

1961, and stayed with the Canadian outfit for four years. He earned rave reviews in north America and played into his 30s with Toronto.

In 1965 he returned to Scotland and the Highland League, first with Wick Academy and in the following two years making appearances for Fraserburgh, Forres Mechanics and Keith.

Caldwell's experience as a League and Cup winner with the Dons was tapped into by the city's junior giants Sunnybank when he was appointed coach in 1973, spending four years in charge of the Heathryfold side before resigning in 1977 in protest at the club committee's attempt to influence his team selection for an important League match.

Alex Cheyne

Date of birth: 28 April 1907, Glasgow
Died: 1983

Aberdeen record:
Appearances: League 127, Scottish Cup 11
Goals: League 48, Scottish Cup 7
Debut: League, 2 January 1926 v Hibs (a) drew 0–0

Also played for: Scotland (5 caps), Shettleston, Chelsea, Nimes
Managed: Chelmsford, Arbroath

Aberdeen Football Club has had its share of dark blue heroes and Alex Cheyne falls distinctly into that category. Cheyne was a star of the 1920s for his club and was one of the first Aberdeen players to be capped at international level, with the team still in its infancy.

He helped put the Dons on the British map in 1929 when he defeated England, stunning the 110,512 crowd at Hampden with a goal directly from a corner-kick in the final minute of the match. His vicious swerving set piece gave Scotland the British International Championship bragging rights over the Auld Enemy and made Cheyne the pride of Pittodrie, coming on his first appearance for Scotland.

The Glaswegian inside-forward arrived as a raw 18-year-old in 1925 from Shettleston Juniors, recruited by Pat Travers after Alex Jackson had been lost to Huddersfield. Cheyne made his debut at Easter Road in a 0–0 draw against Hibs on 2 January 1926, but had to wait until the following season to bag the first of 55 career goals for the club in just 138 appearances. That strike came in a 6–1 win over Morton in Aberdeen. Pittodrie's new star number eight had arrived.

Pittodrie was also the scene of arguably Cheyne's best performance for the club, netting a hat-trick in the space of just 10 minutes in a 4–2 win over Hibs in September 1927.

However, his goalscoring heroics were not reserved for Aberdeen and he joined Scotland's own treble club in May 1929 when he claimed a hat-trick in a 7–3 win over Norway in Bergen.

Despite his blistering start in international football, with those four goals coming inside his first three appearances, chances at the top level were few and far between. Cheyne's Scotland career ended in 1930 but he could console himself with an unbeaten record in five appearances for his country, with wins against France and Holland and a draw against Germany adding to his experiences against England and Norway.

When Cheyne left Pittodrie for Chelsea in 1930 the Londoners had to pay £6,000 for his services, equalling the club's record sale at that time.

The talented Scot went on to star for French side Nimes before landing back on British soil for a second stint at Stamford Bridge. After retiring he turned to management with Chelmsford in 1937, coming back to his roots in Scotland when he took charge of Arbroath in the 1950s.

Cheyne wore the red of Aberdeen 138 times, scoring 55 goals, at a time when the club was not in a position to challenge the dominant Old Firm teams of the era but his goals helped propel the team from a mid-table outfit to genuine challengers, finishing third behind Rangers and Motherwell in his final season in the north east.

Even without a medal to show for his Dons career, Cheyne left with five caps as his reward at a time when Aberdeen players barely registered on the radar of the national selectors. His contribution to the Scotland cause, as an ambassador for his club, assured him legendary status among the Pittodrie faithful.

Bobby Clark

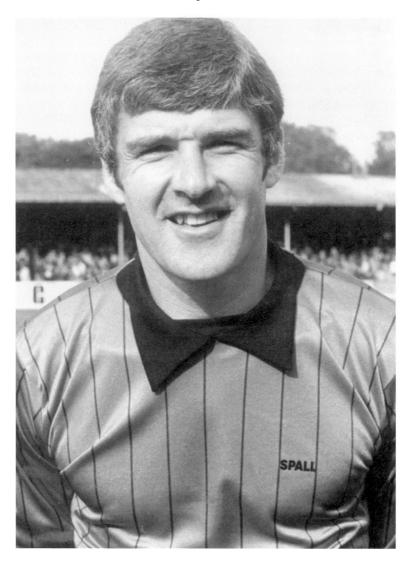

Date of birth: 26 September 1945, Glasgow

Aberdeen record:
Appearances: League 425+1, Scottish Cup 49, League Cup 95, Europe 23
Debut: League Cup, 28 August 1965 v Clyde (h) won 2–0

Also played for: Scotland (17 caps), Queen's Park Rangers
Managed: Highlanders (Zimbabwe), Dartmouth, Stanford, Notre Dame
     (all US)

In the list of great Aberdeen goalkeepers of all time, the name of Bobby Clark looms as large as the man himself. Throughout the 1960s, 1970s and 1980s managers came and went, but Clark remained a rock-solid constant at the spine of the team.

Significantly he was Eddie Turnbull's first signing, the boss determined to send out a message about the changing of the guard. Clark, at just 19, was young and determined to make a name for himself. He fitted the bill perfectly for Turnbull.

He arrived from amateurs Queen's Park Rangers in 1965, the club Turnbull had coached before he had taken up the challenge at Pittodrie. Clark was thrust into the first team in a 2-0 win against Clyde on 28 August at the expense of Tubby Ogston and never looked back. That debut win came against the club at which his father served as a director.

He was already well known to the Dons fans, having starred in two Scottish Cup ties for Queen's against Aberdeen the season prior to his transfer. It took extra-time in the replay to knock the plucky Glasgow side out. In only his second season at the club he was an ever present and voted Player of the Year for the Dons. His performances earned him a Scotland debut against Wales in 1967.

There was an incredible twist in Clark's career when he found himself out of the team in the 1968–69 season and instead playing centre-half for the reserves. He even appeared as an outfield substitute in the second game of the following campaign in a 2-0 defeat against Rangers, replacing striker Jim Forrest. He would soon return to the first team as first-choice goalkeeper, though, and did so in time for the last four games in the famous Scottish Cup run of 1970, culminating in the celebrated 3-1 win over Celtic which brought the 'keeper his first medal. He was again voted Player of the Year at Pittodrie.

His Dons comeback also put Clark back in the national reckoning and he established himself as Scotland's number one for a three-year period from 1970, singled out by Portuguese star Eusebio after one tie in Lisbon. Clark won 17 caps, an Aberdeen record

at the time. He also set a record of 12 consecutive clean sheets in 1971.

Clark came close to leaving on several occasions, notably in 1970 when a switch to Rangers broke down after Bobby Watson refused to head in the opposite direction and two years later when a £100,000 move to Stoke fell through, but Clark's heart was at Pittodrie. By 1974 he had 400 first-team appearances to his credit and a year later he was appointed captain by Jimmy Bonthrone, who had succeeded Turnbull in 1971.

Bonthrone was soon replaced by Ally MacLeod but Clark still had an important part to play and battled through a hand injury to turn out in the League Cup Final of 1976, when he was part of the Dons team which defeated Celtic 2-1 thanks to goals from Drew Jarvie and Davie Robb. Clark had chipped a bone in his thumb during a League match the previous week but that was not enough to prevent him picking up another winners' medal.

He retained his place as number one under Billy McNeill, who took Aberdeen to within two points of the League title in the 1977–78 campaign before Alex Ferguson's arrival the following term. By that stage Clark was vying with up and coming youngster Jim Leighton for the Pittodrie gloves, holding off the challenge long enough to complete his set of domestic honours when he played in 34 of the Premier Division games on the way to Aberdeen's first Championship success since 1955. The Dons beat Celtic to the prize by a single point and the miserly record of 18 goals against was a major factor.

A back injury kept Clark sidelined for two years. By the time he returned to full fitness he was 36 and Leighton was firmly established as Ferguson's main man. After 570 games for Aberdeen he embarked on the first stop of a global coaching career when he left the north east in 1983 to coach Highlanders in Zimbabwe. He moved on to the college scene in America and has become established as one of the leading coaches in the US after a succession of trophy wins with Dartmouth, Stanford and current institution Notre Dame.

Jim Clunie

Date of birth: 4 September 1933, Kirkcaldy
Died: 2003

Aberdeen record:
Appearances: League 104, Scottish Cup 16, League Cup 21
Goals: League 9
Debut: League, 19 April 1954 v Hibs (a) lost 3–0

Also played for: Raith Rovers, St Mirren, Ballymena, Forfar, Irvine Meadow
Managed: St Mirren, Kilmarnock

The imposing Fifer earns a place among Aberdeen's list of all-time greats thanks to his role in securing the club's first League Cup triumph in 1955, anchoring the defence in the 3–1 win over St Mirren at Hampden. The club had won the Southern League Cup previously but the 1955 victory was the first time the League Cup had been taken back to the Pittodrie trophy cabinet since the competition's inception in 1946. It coincided with Clunie establishing himself in the Aberdeen team, having made only four first-team appearances before that 1955–56 campaign.

The six-foot tall centre-half was signed by David Halliday in 1953 for £7,000 and combined his playing commitments with his day job as an electrician in the mines. He was a schoolboy international who had attracted interest from Newcastle United but it was Halliday and the Dons who won the day.

Clunie made his debut in the final game of the 1953–54 season on 19 April 1954. It was not a happy occasion, the Dons losing 3–0 against Hibs at Easter Road, but the new boy did enough to keep his place in the side for the next game – the Scottish Cup Final against Celtic five days later.

Before even playing a game at Pittodrie he turned out in front of 130,000 fervent supporters at Hampden in the biggest game on the domestic calendar. The Final ended 2–1 in favour of the Hoops but Clunie would enjoy his moment of Cup glory just 18 months later in the League Cup. It proved impossible for the young pretender to shift the defensive rock of Alec Young in the Championship-winning season and the following year a broken leg, the first of three he would suffer throughout a long playing career, stalled his attempts to establish himself.

There was no doubting his promise. After just 12 games for the Dons he was named in the Scottish League select to face England in 1955, his reputation as the country's most-improved player cemented by his composed display in the League Cup Final.

Clunie was a rarity of his generation, a ball-playing centre-half who preferred to turn defence into attack with incisive passing rather than looking for a simple clearance. He had attacking flair and was even used as a striker towards the end of his Dons career, scoring seven goals in the 1959–60 season including two doubles against Dunfermline and Third Lanark.

Clunie was another veteran of the 1959 Scottish Cup Final, when Celtic won 3–1, and left the club the following year when his association with St Mirren began. He had played 141 games for Aberdeen and scored nine goals.

Joining the Buddies as a player and staying for five years, he then moved south of the border with Bury in 1965. A year later he was back on the playing staff at Love Street before winding down his career with Ballymena in Ireland, Forfar and junior side Irvine Meadow.

In 1971 Clunie launched his coaching career when he joined Lawrie McMenemy on the Grimsby coaching staff and followed the Englishman to Southampton before being appointed manager in his own right at St Mirren in 1978, helping to foster the talents of a certain young striker by the name of Billy Stark. He was surprisingly sacked by the Paisley outfit just two years later but went on to have a stint in charge of Kilmarnock in 1981. Clunie, who died in 2003, spent four years at the Rugby Park helm.

Donald Colman

Date of birth: 14 August 1878, Dumbartonshire

Aberdeen record:
Appearances: League 324, Scottish Cup 23
Goals: League 1
Debut: League, 21 September 1907 v Dundee (a) lost 1–0

Also played for: Scotland (4 caps), Maryhill, Motherwell, Dumbarton

Player, captain and trainer. Donald Colman was a loyal servant to Aberdeen in the club's formative years and an innovator who ensured the Dons were at the forefront of the rapidly-developing game. Colman's influence extended beyond the field of play and to the infrastructure of the Pittodrie stadium he graced. As trainer, in the 1930s, the Dumbartonshire-born fans' favourite invented the dugout to replace the traditional bench on the sidelines. He wanted shelter and a low point of view to observe the footwork of his players – the dugout was the solution. Colman's love of football led him to explore the worlds of boxing and dancing for pointers on how his players could improve their groundwork. Everton visited the north east on friendly duty soon after his blueprint became reality and took the idea south of the border to Liverpool. The rest, as they say, is history.

That well-worn piece of trivia only scratches the surface of Colman's far more meaningful contribution to the club he grew to love. He grew up playing junior football on the west coast with leading Glasgow club Maryhill and became an international at that level before turning senior with Motherwell in 1905. Two years later, at the age of 27, he was released by the Steelmen but Aberdeen came to the rescue and took him north.

The relationship would be long and fruitful, replacing Alex Halkett as captain two years after his arrival as the Dons strived to establish themselves in the game. He made his debut on 21 September 1907, in a 1–0 away defeat at Dundee. It was an exciting time under the stewardship of Jimmy Philip, with a new attendance record of 18,000 set at Pittodrie that season.

Over the course of the 1908–09 and 1909–10 seasons the defender did not miss a single League or Cup match as he led by example on and off the pitch. His club performances earned international recognition late in life, called up at the age of 33 in 1911. He played in all three internationals that season as Scotland drew against Wales and England either side of a 2–0 win against Northern Ireland. Colman won his fourth and final cap in 1913 when he captained the side to a 2–1 win over the Ulstermen at Dalymount Park.

At the end of World War One, at the age of 42, Colman made a surprise comeback for an injury-ravaged Aberdeen side in 1920 before leaving to play for Dumbarton in-between summer stints coaching the game in Norway. The fact he continued playing for the Dons until after his 47th birthday was testimony to his fitness and devotion to the game.

Coleman arrived back at Pittodrie in 1931 as trainer under manager Pat Travers at the age of 53. He was in his element, implementing a philosophy ahead of its time and earning a reputation as one of the game's great thinkers before tuberculosis claimed his life in 1942.

Always immaculately presented, Colman's intelligence was coupled with a personality that charmed those who crossed paths with him. His international achievements, at a time when Aberdeen were not among the leading lights of the domestic game, coupled with his loyalty and appearance record of 349 games, with a solitary goal, ensured him a permanent place in the Dons hall of fame.

Robert Connor

Date of birth: 4 August 1960, Kilmarnock

Aberdeen record:

Appearances: League 197+9, Scottish Cup 17, League Cup 21+1, Europe
                  16+1
Goals: League 17, Scottish Cup 2, League Cup 3
Debut: League, 16 August 1986 v Hamilton (h) won 2–0

Also played for: Scotland (4 caps), Ayr United, Dundee, Kilmarnock, Partick
                  Thistle, Queen of the South
Managed: Ayr United

Robert Connor's stay in Aberdeen provided him with the best of times and the worst of times. The dark day, without question, came on 11 May 1990. The Dons, under Alex Smith, travelled to Ibrox needing a point against Rangers to win the Premier Division title. The home side won 2–0, the trophy stayed in Glasgow and Connor and his teammates returned north with only thoughts of what could have been. That low was countered by a succession of highs for Connor, who played for the Dons at a time when they ran Graeme Souness and his Rangers side to the wire in every competition.

A native of Kilmarnock, Connor launched his career with Ayr United in 1977 before moving on to Dundee seven years later in a £50,000 deal. By that time he had collected eight caps for Scotland's Under-21 team. Dens Park was a temporary staging post, as Pittodrie boss Alex Ferguson parted with £275,000 in cash and £75,000-rated Ian Angus in exchange for the versatile left-sided star. It was Ferguson's penultimate signing before his departure for Old Trafford and Connor went on to play under Ian Porterfield, Alex Smith and Willie Miller at his new club.

It was Smith and co-manager Jocky Scott that got the best out of Connor, who was an ever present in the duo's first campaign as part of a midfield quartet completed by Jim Bett, Brian Grant and English winger Paul Mason. It was a group any Scottish club would have been happy to have had access to.

With the likes of Charlie Nicholas and Hans Gillhaus in attack, there was no doubt Aberdeen could mount a serious challenge in the League. The difficulty was turning that challenge into success.

Between 1988 and 1994 Conner and his team finished runners-up in the top flight five times. His first taste of the winning feeling came in the League Cup in the 1989–90 season when Smith's men beat Rangers 2–1 to lift the trophy. It was a sweet occasion after losing to the Light Blues in the two previous Finals. Connor played in that showpiece match and helped the Dons complete the double with a penalty shoot-out victory over Celtic in the Scottish Cup to round off the season.

He also shone on the international stage and was an exemplary representative for both Dundee and Aberdeen, making his debut while still a Dens Park employee in a 0–0 draw against Holland in Eindhoven in 1986.

Three further caps followed for the cultured midfielder with a sweet left foot, with a record of one win and two draws against one defeat in Scotland colours. He also sampled European football regularly with the Dons, most notably in the double header against Italian giants Torino in the 1993–94 European Cup-winners' Cup when Aberdeen took the lead in both the home and away legs before losing 3–2 and 2–1 after pushing the Serie A side all the way.

After eight years at Pittodrie, with 263 appearances and 22 goals, Connor was released by Miller after a long battle against an Achilles injury and returned west to hook up with Kilmarnock. He spent a further two years playing Premier Division football with Killie before winding down his playing days on a high with his first Championship medal, at the age of 36, after helping Ayr United to the Second Division title in 1997. Partick and Queen of the South were his final staging posts after 19 years of plying his trade on Scotland's football pitches.

Connor went on to become a freelance football writer and agent before returning to the coaching staff at Ayr. In 2005 he stepped up to become manager of the Somerset Park club, 28 years after first crossing the front door as a fresh-faced teenage signing, and he remained in charge until 2007.

Charlie Cooke

Date of birth: 14 October 1942, St Monance

Aberdeen record:
Appearances: League 125, Scottish Cup 14, League Cup 26
Goals: League 27, League Cup 3
Debut: League Cup, 13 August 1960 v Ayr United (h) won 4–3

Also played for: Scotland (16 caps), Port Glasgow, Renfrew, Dundee, Chelsea,
Crystal Palace, LA Aztecs, Memphis Rogues, California Surf
Managed: Wichita

Charlie Cooke is the first of two wildcards to make the final cut of 100 and is at the head of a duo of former Dons players within these pages who do not tick any of the boxes used to select the remaining 98.

Cooke never won anything with Aberdeen. He was never capped for Scotland when he was with Aberdeen. Yet he is the one name most fans of a certain vintage would place at the very top of their list.

Cooke was an entertainer, nicknamed The Cavalier by appreciative Chelsea supporters in his post-Pittodrie days as a tribute to his intricate runs and free-flowing attacking flair.

Despite being born in Fife he was a Greenock boy and first came to the attention of the Dons while playing for Renfrew in the junior ranks. He signed provisionally for Aberdeen in 1959 and by the time he made his reserve-team debut the following year it was clear the club had unearthed a gem.

With immaculate footwork and the ability to split a defence with an arrowed pass, Cooke was soon catapulted into the first team. He made his debut in a League Cup win at home to Ayr United at the start of the 1960–61 season and within weeks, word of his talents had spread south of the border. Newcastle United weighed in with an offer, Arsenal were on his trail and that was after just a single game.

Within months he was in the thoughts of the SFA selectors, a reserve for the Scotland Under-23 squad at the start of 1961 before stepping up to become a key player for the young Scots in the months that followed.

Cooke's talents illuminated Pittodrie during a difficult spell for the club, playing at a time when honours proved elusive. Two sixth-place finishes were the League highlights during his spell in the red of Aberdeen, during which time his esteemed talents on the ball were utilised both in the front line and, briefly, from deep as a right-half.

Frustrated by the failure to compete with the country's dominant clubs, Cooke asked for a transfer late in 1964 and before the year had ended his wish was granted. Dundee, champions of Scotland two years previously, weighed in with a Scottish record fee of £44,000 to trump Coventry City and Wolves. It shattered Aberdeen's previous record haul, which was the £32,500 profit on George Kinnell's move to Stoke in 1963.

Manager Tommy Pearson had stressed his desire to hold onto the player who had scored 32 goals in less than five full seasons and created many, many more. Yet the offer from Dundee was simply too good to refuse.

Cooke was promoted to the Scotland senior team within a month of his move to Dens Park, eventually making his debut for his country in a 4–1 win against Wales in November 1965 under Jock Stein. He went on to win 16 caps during a nine-year spell with the national team.

In the spring of 1966 he collected the Dundee Supporters' Club Player of the Year award. The next morning he was gone, transferred to Chelsea in a £75,000 deal. It was a record for the Blues but a shrewd piece of business, as their recruit went on to earn cult status.

It was at Stamford Bridge that Cooke's standing in the game was elevated to new levels, a masterful creative display in the London club's European Cup-winners' Cup victory over Real Madrid in 1971, having been a key player in the previous year's FA Cup win against Leeds United.

Cooke had two spells with Chelsea, wrapped around a season with Crystal Palace in 1972–73, before leaving England behind for a new life in America in 1977. He starred in the US indoors and outdoors before moving into coaching with Wichita.

His passion for coaching the arts which made him a darling of the terraces led Cooke to help with the creation of the Koerver Coaching empire, which became a global phenomenon in 1990 as countries across the world searched for a way of injecting the skills that made Cooke and his contemporaries household names. The former Scotland star, who released his biography *The Bonnie Prince* in 2006, remains based in the States.

Neale Cooper

Date of birth: 24 November 1963, Darjeeling (India)

Aberdeen record:

Appearances: League 133+16, Scottish Cup 27+2, League Cup 27+1, Europe 33+6

Goals: League 6, Scottish Cup 3, League Cup 1

Debut: League, 11 October 1980 v Kilmarnock (h) won 2–0

Also played for: Aston Villa, Rangers, Reading, Dunfermline, Ross County

Managed: Ross County, Hartlepool, Gillingham

Neale Cooper was still more than a month short of his 17th birthday when he was thrust into Premier League action for Aberdeen by Alex Ferguson. It turned out Sir Alex knew a good young player when he saw one.

That first game in 1980, a 2–0 win at home to Kilmarnock on 11 October, was the start of a special relationship with the Pittodrie crowd for a player born in India but an Aberdonian at heart. Cooper grew up in the city, plucked from school football and juvenile club King Street by the Dons and rapidly promoted to first-team duty. He explained, 'I was cleaning the manager's office as part of my duties around the club as one of the young players when Alex Ferguson came in and told me there was a problem with Alex McLeish and that I had to get myself home and prepare to play the next day.'

Cooper is, of course, one of the Gothenburg Greats, the 1983 European Cup-winners' Cup Final against Real Madrid in the Swedish city a defining moment for one of the club's great characters. He won a Scotland Under-21 cap by the time he pulled on the red number-four jersey in that landmark Final against the Spanish giants, a dynamo in the Dons midfield. Cooper featured in nine of the 11 ties in that famous run, a key component in the most famous side Aberdeen has ever produced.

That momentous triumph came when Cooper was still only 19, by which point he was already a regular in the Pittodrie first team and had a Scottish Cup medal safely tucked away.

The national Cup win was in the 1982 Final when Aberdeen sent out a message of intent to the Old Firm, hammering Rangers 4–1 and their emerging young midfielder was on the scoresheet. It was 3–1 when the opportunity presented itself, Gers 'keeper Jim Stewart's clearance bouncing off Cooper and presenting him with an open goal; he could have walked it home but chose to almost burst the net with a thunderous effort to round off a memorable day for the travelling Red Army. His forward roll and salute capped the occasion.

After European success in the 1982–83 season the following term added a Premier Division winners' medal to Cooper's rapidly expanding collection, Celtic beaten by seven points in the chase for the Scottish game's main prize. He also claimed a European Super Cup medal, having played in the first leg of Aberdeen's victory over SV Hamburg over two games in the same 1983–84 term that heralded a second Scottish Cup win – this time Celtic were beaten 2–1 in a Final which went to extra-time.

Cooper made 20 appearances in the 1984–85 Premier Division as Aberdeen retained the title for the first time in the club's history and the following year played a key role in both the 3–0 League Cup Final victory against Hibs and the Scottish Cup triumph against Hearts by the same margin.

That rout against the Jambos proved to be Cooper's final outing for the Dons. In the summer of 1986, just months before his manager headed south to Manchester United, he made the leap to English football with Aston Villa. A tribunal set a fee of £350,000 for a youth product who had played 220 games and scored 10 times.

Cooper spent two years at Villa, playing under Graham Turner and Billy McNeill before Taylor allowed him to move back to Scotland as part of the Graeme Souness revolution at Rangers in 1988.

He was part of the Premier Division winning team at Ibrox in his first season, featuring in 14 games as he helped ensure the Dons had to settle for second place at the start of the Govan men's nine in a row run. He was restricted to a handful of appearances under Souness the following term, returning to England for a short spell with Reading before finding a more permanent home with Dunfermline and smashing through the 100-game barrier with the Pars between 1991 and 1996.

Cooper called time on his spell in Fife when Ross County tempted him north to lead them as manager through the Scottish Football League, winning promotion from the Third Division and Second Division on his way to establishing the Dingwall side as an accomplished First Division outfit. He said, 'I was 16 when I played my first game for Aberdeen, 17 when I scored in the Scottish Cup Final win and 19 when we won in Europe. At the time I took it all in my stride but looking back now I appreciate most players will go through their whole career without those experiences.

'It meant a lot to me that someone like Alex Ferguson showed faith in me when I was starting out and I'll always be grateful for that. I took it into management with me – I've always believed in giving players a chance at 16 or 17 if they deserve it.'

After resigning from his County post after six years at the helm, Cooper returned to management with Hartlepool in 2003 and led them to the League One Play-offs in his first season. A stint in charge of Gillingham followed before he returned to his roots in the north east, where his connection with football continued with his appointment as Steve Paterson's assistant at Peterhead.

Willie Cooper

Date of birth: October 1909, Aberdeen
Died: May 1994

Aberdeen record:
Appearances: League 327, Scottish Cup 37, League Cup 9
Goals: League 2, Scottish Cup 1
Debut: League, 14 April 1928 v Cowdenbeath (h) won 3–0

Also played for: Mugiemoss, Forfar Athletic, Huntly
Managed: Huntly

The Scottish Football Association is not known as a sympathetic organisation. The governing body bends it rules for no man, or at least for very few men. One exception was Aberdeen legend Willie Cooper. The cool and composed right-back played in every single game leading up to the 1947 Scottish Cup Final before a pulled muscle in the semi-final forced him out of the showdown with Hibs.

The Dons, in Cooper's absence, defeated the Easter Road men 2–1 but the north-east fans who made the pilgrimage to Hampden to take their place in the 82,684 crowd were not happy. They, and the Dons team, refused to leave the turf of the national team until Cooper joined in the celebrations and took his bow.

Willie Waddell was the man taken into the Aberdeen team in Cooper's place but even he felt the injustice, insisting his winners' medal would be passed to the man he deputised for. In the end, that gesture was not necessary – the SFA made the unprecedented step of having an extra medal struck to ensure Cooper did not miss out. He had got the Cup run up and running with the winner against Partick Thistle in the first round, so it was only right that he was there at the end to join the triumphant squad.

By that time he already had a Southern League Cup win under his belt, part of the team that beat Rangers 3–2 in the 1946 Final. That made up for the pain of defeat in the 1937 Scottish Cup Final against Celtic, when a record 146,433 crammed inside Hampden and 20,000 were locked outside.

Cooper launched his career with Aberdeen junior side Mugiemoss, earning a trial for the Dons early in 1927 and signing in time for the start of the 1927–28 season at the tender age of 16. He was briefly farmed out on loan to Forfar Athletic before forcing his way into the first team and staying there for an incredible period of two decades.

Cooper made his first appearance in a 3–0 win at home to Cowdenbeath on 14 April 1928 and could not have predicted the way his career would unfold. His final game did not come until 31 January 1948, in a 3–1 defeat at Falkirk.

Despite his heroics for the Pittodrie side, international recognition escaped Cooper. He could console himself with two caps for the Scottish League against England in 1936 and 1937, though.

His full-back partnership with Charlie McGill was legendary, with the pair clocking up 161 consecutive games together in the 1930s. Cooper went one further, clocking up a record 162 consecutive games between September 1932 and October 1936.

He played 373 games in an Aberdeen career spanning 21 years, his considerable tally of course limited by the outbreak of war. Cooper also played under only two managers in his time with the club, Pat Travers and Dave Halliday, and found League success elusive. The closest call came in 1937 when he and his teammates were runners-up to Rangers in the First Division, missing out by seven points as they chased the club's first title triumph.

After leaving Pittodrie in 1948, following 373 appearances and three goals, Cooper spent two years as player-coach of Huntly in the Highland League before retiring from the game to concentrate on his career as a sales representative in the whisky industry. He died in 1994 at the age of 84.

Billy Dodds

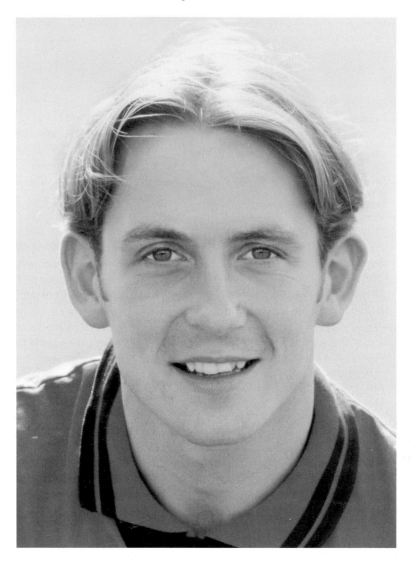

Date of birth: 5 February 1969, New Cumnock

Aberdeen record:
Appearances: League 131+8, Scottish Cup 6+3, League Cup 15+1, Europe 8
Goals: League 49, Scottish Cup 1, League Cup 14, Europe 4
Debut: UEFA Cup, 9 August 1994 v Skonto Riga (a) drew 0–0

Also played for: Dundee, St Johnstone, Dundee United, Rangers, Partick Thistle

In September 1998 Aberdeen Football Club and manager Alex Miller conducted a piece of business which baffled the Pittodrie faithful. Out went Billy Dodds, leading scorer in each of the four seasons he had spent at the club, to Dundee United along with £500,000 of the Dons' cash. In came Arabs striker Robbie Winters, a talented yet inconsistent young striker. It would prove to be either a masterstroke by Miller or one of the biggest miscalculations in the history of the club. Most would argue the latter applied and United completed the steal of the century.

Winters proved to be a decent performer for the Dons but he could not match Dodds as an out and out goalscorer. Miller was lambasted by furious supporters and lasted less than a year in the manager's chair.

The bubbly Glaswegian was a hero in Aberdeen's most recent trophy success – the 1995 League Cup victory against Dundee. Dodds was on target along with Duncan Shearer in the 2–0 win. For the success-starved Pittodrie regulars it was a moment to savour and one they hoped would herald a new era. Yet it proved to be a false dawn and the chances were limited by the departure of Dodds.

As a player, Willie Miller got to grips with a succession of top-class strikers. As a manager, he put that experience to good use when it came to identifying the man he wanted to spearhead his team, turning to St Johnstone's 25-year-old marksman. Dodds had started out as a trainee with Chelsea and had a loan spell with Partick before carving out a reputation as a goalscorer with Dundee and Saints. It cost Miller £800,000 to persuade the Perth side to part with their biggest asset but it proved to be a worthwhile investment.

Dodds made a low-key debut on 9 August 1994 in the first leg of the disastrous UEFA Cup tie against Skonto Riga, which saw the Dons crash out against the unfancied Latvia, but was on target in his first League match against Hearts.

It was the first of 17 goals in the 1994–95 season for the struggling Dons. Miller departed and was replaced by assistant Roy Aitken as the club narrowly avoided relegation in a season which also saw them dumped out of the Scottish Cup by Stenhousemuir. There was a marked improvement in the next term, when, in addition to the League Cup triumph, there was a third-place finish in the Premier Division to hearten supporters. Dodds tied with Scott Booth on 12 goals at the head of the club's scoring chart.

The 1996–97 season was the diminutive striker's most prolific in a red shirt as he bagged a 26-goal haul, which included hat-tricks against Raith and Morton. That form brought the first of 26 Scotland caps, claiming seven goals in the process, when Craig Brown pitched him in against Latvia. Dodds spent five years on the international stage.

Twelve goals followed the next year but the 1998–99 term spelled the end of a fruitful relationship. A League Cup hat-trick against Caley Thistle in August was not enough to persuade Alex Miller of the merits of a forward who hit 68 goals in 162 games.

It proved to be costly as in 15 months Dodds scored 25 goals in 44 Premier League starts for United and was whisked away by Rangers in a £1.3 million deal in December 1999. He proved a valuable squad man for the Ibrox side, netting 34 goals in just 46 starts and 38 appearances from the bench.

Dodds, now an established football pundit on television, returned to Dundee United in 2003, serving as player-coach for three years before a short spell on the Partick Thistle playing staff.

Frank Dunlop

Date of birth: 1914, Glasgow
Died: 1991

Aberdeen record:
Appearances: League 112, Scottish Cup 20, League Cup 14
Debut: League, 29 August 1936 v Falkirk (h) won 4–0

Also played for: Benburb

When Aberdeen clinched the Scottish Cup for the first time in 1947 with a hard-fought 2–1 win over Hibs at Hampden Park, there was no prouder man in the national stadium than Frank Dunlop. As captain he hoisted the famous trophy above his head in front of 82,140 and led the victorious team on their parade through the streets of the Granite City on their return. The win meant so much to the city, with 15,000 fans greeting their heroes when they returned by train.

Dunlop and goalkeeper George Johnstone had both been on the losing side 10 years earlier when the Dons fell at the final hurdle in the national Cup competition against Celtic. In 1947 they made up for that pain when despite losing a goal inside the first 30 seconds of the game, goals from George Hamilton and Stan Williams repaired the damage and saw the name of Aberdeen etched on the Cup.

By that stage Dunlop already had a Southern League Cup medal safely in the vault, playing in the side which beat Rangers in the 1946 Final. A crowd of 135,000 watched the Dons win that game 3–2, with goals from George Taylor, Stan Williams and Archie Baird. Dunlop was resplendent in the number-five shirt, which would prove to be his lucky charm in the Scottish Cup the following year.

Those senior prizes joined the Scottish Junior Cup-winners' reward he secured with Benburb in 1936, the earliest sign that the Glaswegian had a fruitful career in the game ahead of him. Dunlop was snapped up by the Dons after the junior Final and made his debut in a 4–0 win over Falkirk at Pittodrie on 29 August 1936.

War interrupted his career but the defender's record of 146 hard-fought games ensured legendary status. He played under Pat Travers and Dave Halliday and was an automatic pick for both managers. In the 1945–46 season he was the only man to play in each of the 45 games that term.

A 4–2 Scottish Cup defeat against Hibs at Easter Road on 21 February 1948 spelt the end of a long and illustrious playing career. It was the same season in which Willie Cooper called time on his 20-year association with the club.

In 1949 Dunlop emigrated to Zimbabwe, then under the flag of Rhodesia, to concentrate on his professional life as a chiropodist, but his football connection lived on as he went on to coach the national team in his adopted country.

He remained an avid Dons fan during his time in Africa, having local newspapers shipped out to his home to keep up to date with events at Pittodrie and made annual return trips to the city. In the 1960s he even called upon Eddie Turnbull to pick up coaching tips to help him in his duties as chairman of selectors with the Bulawayo Callies club.

Dunlop, who never recorded a senior goal for the Dons, came back 'home' to Aberdeen in 1979 and was a regular in the stands at Pittodrie until his death, at the age of 77, in 1991.

Jim Forrest

Date of birth: 22 September 1944, Glasgow

Aberdeen record:
Appearances: League 128+3, Scottish Cup 20, League Cup 27+2, Europe 11
Goals: League 44, Scottish Cup 8, League Cup 8, Europe 2
Debut: League Cup, 10 August 1968 v Clyde (a) lost 4–1

Also played for: Scotland (5 caps), Rangers, Preston North End, Cape Town City, Hong Kong Rangers

When the minnows of Berwick Rangers shocked their Ibrox counterparts with a 1–0 win in the 1967 Scottish Cup the fall-out was considerable, and for Jim Forrest the game proved to be his last in light blue as he was one of the players held accountable for the humiliating defeat. Rangers' loss proved to be Aberdeen's gain.

Forrest, a powerful and pacy forward who was just as adept on the wing, found his escape with Preston North End but by 1968 was back in Scottish football with the Dons following a £25,000 transfer. The Glaswegian returned with a point to prove and laid the Scottish Cup ghost to rest in grand style when he helped his new club to lift the trophy in 1970 with the 3–1 win over Celtic. It completed a full set of domestic honours for the player who had joined Rangers from school and went on to pick up a Championship medal and play in two League Cup wins for the Ibrox men.

Forrest did not score in the Scottish Cup Final of 1970 but was regularly on target for Eddie Turnbull and his successor Jimmy Bonthrone. Indeed, in his first season with the Dons he was the club's leading scorer with 23 goals and collected the Aberdeen Supporters' Club Player of the Year award for his efforts. He also captained the side before handing over that responsibility to Martin Buchan.

Forrest made his debut on 10 August 1968 in a 4–1 League Cup defeat at Clyde and scored the first of those 23 goals just four days later, with the winner against Dunfermline at Pittodrie in the same competition. Aberdeen avoided relegation by just eight points and two League places that season, and a series of vital goals from Forrest played a significant part in that mission.

In the seasons that followed the Dons improved steadily, climbing from that 15th place to finish the following campaign eighth before being runners-up to Celtic in both 1970–71 and 1971–72. With the Championship just outside their grasp, the Scottish Cup win of 1970 proved to be the crowning glory for Turnbull and his team.

In March 1971 Forrest confirmed his place as one of the best strikers of his generation when he smashed home his 200th senior goal in Scottish football in a 4–1 win against Ayr United. In five seasons with the Dons he notched 62 goals in 191 appearances and established himself as a fans favourite. He also won favour with Scotland managers after making his international debut under Jock Stein as a Rangers player in the 4–1 win over Wales in 1965, having already picked up two Under-23 caps.

By the time he was turning out for the Dons it was Bobby Brown who led the national team and he called on Forrest in January 1971, for the 3–0 European Nations Cup defeat against Belgium in Liege. He won further caps against Denmark and the USSR that year to complete his international career with five caps.

Forrest, who scored 62 goals in 191 games, was freed by Bonthrone at the end of the 1972–73 season after being troubled with injuries and rounded off his career in South Africa with Cape Town City and then in Asia with Hong Kong Rangers.

Willie Garner

Date of birth: 24 July 1955, Stirling

Aberdeen record:
Appearances: League 113+1, Scottish Cup 11, League Cup 31, Europe 6+1
Goals: League 1, League Cup 2
Debut: League, 17 January 1976 v Hearts (a) drew 3–3

Also played for: Celtic, Alloa, Keith
Managed: Alloa, Keith, Deveronvale

It was fitting that Willie Garner emerged from his most consistent season for Aberdeen with a winners' medal in his pocket. The powerful defender was the only ever present for Ally MacLeod in the 1976–77 season and a rock in the 11-game League Cup campaign which ended with a 2–1 win over Celtic in the Final.

In all, the 6ft 2in centre-half played in 50 games that term, all 36 in the League alongside the emerging talent of Willie Miller in central defence. The next season, with Billy McNeill at the helm following MacLeod's switch to the national team, Garner missed just a single game. Significantly, the man who deputised for him on that occasion was a youngster called Alex McLeish. Soon McLeish would take that place permanently, his chance coming when Garner broke his leg in a European Cup-winners' Cup tie against Marek Dimitrov in September 1978.

When he returned to fitness in the 1979–80 season there was still room for Garner in Alex Ferguson's side as they swept to the club's first Championship success since 1955, although McLeish was first choice by the time the term ended. The defender played in 21 of the 36 League games that season as well as all 11 League Cup ties, including the bitterly disappointing 3–0 defeat against Dundee United in the final replay after the first game had ended 0–0. That could not detract from the joy of winning the top flight, especially for a player who thought his dream of making it as a professional was over before it had even begun.

Garner had trials with Sheffield United as a youngster growing up in the Stirlingshire town of Denny and was connected to Airdrie while playing for juvenile side Campsie Black Watch, but neither club took a chance on him. It was in a Diamonds reserve game that scout Bobby Calder spotted the defender's potential and encouraged the club to snap him up. Garner grew to become an important defensive cog for the club and made 163 appearances over the course of six years, netting three times.

With first-team opportunities increasingly limited at Pittodrie, Garner switched to Celtic in the summer of 1981 in a £46,000 transfer, although two own-goals in a disastrous debut for the Hoops against St Mirren did not make it an easy passage. Garner was not fully fit when he played in that game and struggled to recover from a difficult start to his Parkhead career.

In 1982 he became Britain's youngest manager, combining playing duties with team control at Alloa, and he enjoyed success when he kept his side in the First Division following their promotion under predecessor Alex Totten. That early coaching promise was enough to secure a surprise return to Pittodrie in February 1984 as assistant

manager under his old mentor Ferguson, who had lost his right-hand man Archie Knox to Dundee.

Garner, now the manager of a communications team with Scottish Widows in Edinburgh, said 'When I got the call from Alex Ferguson to invite me to become his assistant it was a surprise and an honour. I'd actually spoken to Alex for advice when Alloa offered me the manager's job a couple of years earlier – he had told me to jump at the chance. I was 27 when I went out on loan from Celtic to Alloa. Alex Totten is a good friend of mine and offered me the chance to get some games under my belt at a better level than the Celtic reserves – I was in the right place at the right time when he left to move to Falkirk.

'Going back to Aberdeen as assistant manager was a real challenge and one I enjoyed. Obviously I had been a teammate of a lot of the players in the dressing room but it wasn't difficult because of the type of professionals we had at the club – people like Willie Miler, Alex McLeish and Gordon Strachan accepted that I had a job to do and helped me get on with it. The only thing I made a point of doing differently was not socialising with them as I had done when I was a teammate.

'I had good times alongside Alex, it was an experience that taught me a lot. When Archie became available again he came back to the club and there was no job for me but that's part and parcel of football. I can look back on some important trophy wins for the club during that period, not to mention the medals I won as a player. They were good times.'

Garner continued to turn out for the reserve team, charged with developing the young players around him while assisting Ferguson with the running of the first team despite the fact he had not yet celebrated his 29th birthday.

It was a profitable pairing, securing the Scottish Cup and Premier Division title in their first season and defending the League crown in the 1984–85 season. The following term brought a League Cup and Scottish Cup double for Ferguson and Garner but in June 1986 the ties were severed when Knox returned as co-manager at Pittodrie.

Garner went on to continue playing junior and Highland League football and also managed at that level with Keith and, briefly, Deveronvale, before concentrating on his career in the finance industry with Lloyds TSB – joining the company in 1988 and later switching to the Scottish Widows branch of the business.

Garner maintained his involvement in football through his role as assistant manager at leading junior club Tayport prior to the departure of boss Keith Burgess in February 2007. He then joined Forfar Athletic as assistant to Jim Moffat in time for the 2007–08 season.

Hans Gillhaus

Date of birth: 5 November 1963, Helmond (Netherlands)

Aberdeen record:
Appearances: League 78+6, Scottish Cup 6, League Cup 5, Europe 5
Goals: League 27, Scottish Cup 3, Europe 1
Debut: League, 18 November 1989 v Dunfermline (a) won 3–0

Also played for: Netherlands (3 caps), PSV Eindhoven, Vitesse Arnhem (both
Netherlands), Jaro Pietersaari (Finland), Gamba Osaka (Japan)

Aberdeen supporters would give anything to return to the heady days of the late 1980s, when the Dons were a match for any club on the continent in the transfer market. Arsenal star Charlie Nicholas was snapped up in a record £500,000 deal in 1988 but that deal was trumped in November 1989 when the club stumped up £650,000 for the services of a Dutchman who found himself behind Brazil star Romario in the pecking order at his club.

Hans Gillhaus had hit 19 goals for PSV Eindhoven in the 1988–89 season on their way to the title and won three caps for the Netherlands, the type of credentials which would put a striker well out of Aberdeen's reach in the current climate. But the prospect of travelling to the continent to pinch one of Holland's rising stars did not deter manager Alex Smith, who already had Theo Snelders and Willem Van der Ark on his books, and he got his man.

It proved to be a shrewd investment. Gillhaus did not stay for long in Scotland but his time at Pittodrie left a lasting impression. He announced his Premier Division arrival with a stunning double on his debut in a 3–0 win against Dunfermline at East End Park on 18 November 1989, which included a memorable overhead kick and a poacher's header from close range. It must surely rank as the most dynamic debut the club has ever seen.

For good measure Gillhaus chipped in with the winner against Rangers, an exquisite curling left-foot effort, at Pittodrie the following week to establish himself as the new darling of the stands. He and Charlie Nicholas proved to be a deadly combination and complemented each other with their mix of trickery, vision and goalscoring ability.

By his own admission, Gillhaus could not maintain the devastating form of his first two games but he was still a prolific player for the Dons, finishing that season with 11 goals in just 24 appearances and starring in the penalty shoot-out victory over Celtic after the 0–0 Scottish Cup Final draw to claim his first medal in Aberdeen colours.

In the dramatic 1990–91 season, when the Dons lost the title by two points to Rangers, he finished joint top scorer with Eoin Jess after bagging 15 goals and claimed his first hat-trick for the club in a 4–2 win at Hibs. It came on the back of his inclusion in the Dutch squad for the World Cup in Italy at the start of the campaign, when he served as Marco Van Basten's understudy. Not a bad inclusion on any CV.

Romario reportedly demanded that PSV brought his former strike partner back to Eindhoven that summer and Gillhaus did nothing to nip talk of a return in the bud, freely admitting his stop in Aberdeen was only temporary. The message to fans was enjoy it while it lasted, and thanks to his habit of scoring spectacular goals they did. Many were frustrated by the import's laid-back approach and lack of long-term commitment to the club, but nobody could deny his talent.

In the end, nothing came of the rumoured £1.2 million bid by PSV and in the summer of 1992 the Dutchman took matters into his own hands, taking advantage of his expired Dons contract and returning to Holland to look for alternative employment. By that time Willie Miller had replaced Alex Smith in the top job. He provided a return of 31 goals in 100 games.

It proved to be a long wait: Gillhaus trained with PSV but there was no prospect of a contract at his old club and he was picky about others on the table, despite interest from England and suggestions of a Rangers bid. He spent months in the wilderness before returning to action with Vitesse Arnhem and finishing his career in Japanese football.

Today Gillhaus continues his career at the very top level as chief scout for Chelsea under Jose Mourinho, having filled a similar role for PSV prior to his Stamford Bridge appointment.

Stephen Glass

Date of birth: 23 May 1976, Dundee

Aberdeen record:
Appearances: League 96+13, Scottish Cup 7+2, League Cup 10, Europe 3
Goals: League 9, League Cup 2, Europe 2
Debut: Competition, 29 October 1994 v Dundee United (h) won 3–0

Also played for: Scotland (1 cap), Newcastle United, Watford, Hibs, Dunfermline

A succession of home-grown Aberdeen players have been linked with moves to the promised land of the English Premiership but, to date, only two have successfully followed that path directly. Eoin Jess was the first and Stephen Glass became the second in 1998 when Kenny Dalglish, then manager of Newcastle United, homed in on one of the Scottish game's most promising talents.

Others have gone between the Pittodrie and the Premiership, including Craig Hignett and Dean Windass, but the elevation of Glass to that level was a vindication of Aberdeen's insistence that the famed Dons youth programme was still capable of delivering top-notch players.

There should have been pride when Glass made the move to what was emerging as the world's most entertaining League, but in fact there was a sense of injustice. He was out of contract and eligible for a Bosman transfer but was the first player to test what was then an unwritten rule that a British club would be liable to pay a compensation fee if taking a player under the age of 24 from another UK side.

Newcastle made a derisory £100,000 offer while the Dons wanted in excess of £1 million for a player they had taken through their youth ranks, blooding him in the man's world of north-east junior football when they farmed him out as a teenager to the now defunct Crombie Sports. In the end, a tribunal set a fee of £650,000 and Aberdeen had to settle for it.

The sense of disappointment at losing Glass at 21, coupled with the double blow of losing him at less than market value, did not detract from his achievements during four seasons in the first team. He got his big break as an 18-year-old when Willie Miller introduced him as a substitute in a 3-0 win over Dundee United at Pittodrie on 29 October 1994.

He had entered the team at a turbulent time, as Miller's reign came to an end and the Dons battled against relegation. Roy Aitken took over from Miller in February 1995, but shared his predecessor's judgement on Glass and kept faith with him as the fight to beat the drop intensified. Luckily, the teenager came into his own when the team was on the ropes, scoring on the final day of the regular League campaign in a 2-0 win over Falkirk to complete a run of three consecutive victories and ensure it was Dundee United in 10th place who fell through the trap door.

The work was not finished, as the Dons still had to endure a Play-off against Dunfermline, the First Division runners-up, to safeguard their top-flight status. Glass played and scored in both as his side recorded two 3-1 wins to end the season on a relative high.

The 1995-96 season saw the versatile left-sided youngster cement his place in the starting XI, missing only four League games and an ever present in the run to the League Cup Final against Dundee. He turned out at left-back in the Final and produced a Man of the Match performance as goals from Duncan Shearer and Billy Dodds landed the silverware.

It was the highlight of his Dons career but Glass continued to perform consistently, equally at home on the left side of defence or as an out and out winger.

Alex Miller was the manager by the time the Premiership scouts began to circle Pittodrie's rising star, with Arsenal reported to have joined Newcastle on the list of admirers, and the deal to take him to the north east of England was struck before the 1997-98 term was completed. He took his tally to 133 games and 13 goals before departing.

His new Newcastle leader Dalglish was replaced by Ruud Gullit just months after his arrival but Glass held his own in distinguished company, making 29 appearances in his debut season with the Toon and contributing match-winning goals against Leicester and Derby. He also experienced FA Cup Final day at a packed Wembley, although there was no happy ending as Manchester United lifted the trophy after a 2-0 win.

Glass spent three seasons on Tyneside, winning his solitary Scotland cap in a 2-1 win over the Faroes Islands in 1998 before dropping down to the Championship with Watford from 2001 to 2003. He came back to Scotland with Hibs in 2003 to play a key role in the Easter Road club's revival before being farmed out on loan to Dunfermline early in 2007.

Archie Glen

Date of birth:	16 April 1929, Coalburn
Died:	1998

Aberdeen record:

Appearances:	League 203, Scottish Cup 24, League Cup 42
Goals:	League 24, League Cup 3
Debut:	League, 19 February 1949 v Falkirk (a) won 2–1

Also played for: Scotland (2 caps), Annbank United

Aberdeen's captains will always hold a special place in the history of the club and Archie Glen booked his in emphatic style. It was the defender who scored the goal that clinched the first Championship in 1955 after a 52-year wait.

It was on 9 April 1955 that the Dons travelled to face mid-table Clyde, needing a win to secure the coveted prize. Failure to do that would hand the initiative back to second-placed Celtic, who would play host to the Pittodrie side the following week. It was a high-pressure occasion but that did not trouble Glen, a cool and composed defender who had formed a formidable partnership with Jack Allister and Alec Young.

In the 13th minute a handball inside the box gave Aberdeen a golden opportunity. Glen had missed from the spot already that season but he shouldered the responsibility for the most crucial penalty in the history of the club to that point and smashed the ball high into the postage-stamp corner. It proved to be the winner and the Dons made the journey back from Shawfield as champions of the country.

Glen, who died in 1998, led by example as skipper of the Dons and was one of only two ever presents in the League-winning term. Jackie Hather was the other.

The left-sided half-back, renowned for his timing and tackling accuracy, was never cautioned by a referee in 269 appearances for the club. His title-winning goal was one of 27 he scored in 13 years on the playing staff.

The defender signed for the Dons from junior side Annbank United in Ayrshire when he became one of the first recruits discovered by legendary scout Bobby Calder. His association began in 1947 but it was in the following decade that he made his mark on the club.

The Championship win was followed in the 1955–56 season by the club's first success in the League Cup, although it had been lifted in its previous guise of the Southern League Cup. The same season brought Glen his two Scotland caps, making his debut at Hampden in a 1–1 draw with England on 8 October 1955 and playing in a 2–1 away defeat against Northern Ireland six months later. The Lanarkshire-born player also represented the Scotland B team and the Scottish Football League. He turned out in 269 games for Aberdeen and scored 27 goals.

A Scottish Cup-winners' medal was all that was missing from Glen's collection but he did come close, losing in both the 1954 and 1959 Finals. That proved to be his final shot at completing the trophy hat-trick as a serious knee injury in 1959 forced him to retire from the game at the age of 30.

Glen's intelligence extended beyond the boundaries of the football pitch. As a graduate in pure science from Aberdeen University, he went on to become a managing director of an Aberdeen paint firm after hanging up his boots.

He remained in the north east until his death, serving as a church elder and active Rotary Club member in Aberdeen.

Arthur Graham

Date of birth: 26 October 1952, Glasgow

Aberdeen record:
Appearances: League 220+8, Scottish Cup 22+1, League Cup 44+1, Europe
11
Goals: League 34, Scottish Cup 1, League Cup 9, Europe 2
Debut: League, 21 March 1970 v Dunfermline (h) won 2–0

Also played for: Scotland (11 caps), Leeds United, Manchester United, Bradford

When most boys his age were just dreaming of winning the Scottish Cup at Hampden, Arthur Graham went out and did just that. The Glaswegian was only 17 when he lined up in the number-11 shirt in front of 108,434 supporters at Hampden as Eddie Turnbull's side tackled Celtic on their home turf in the 1970 showdown.

Not for the first time, and not for the last, it was the Dons who had the upper hand in Glasgow and the 2–1 win gave Graham a short and sharp introduction to the joys of the professional game. Up to that 11 April Final he had started just four games for his club, making his debut as a substitute on 21 March in a 2–0 win against Dunfermline at Pittodrie. Four days later he was in the first XI for the first time, scoring in the 2–1 win against the Hoops at Parkhead to announce his arrival in the First Division. He scored again in a 2–2 League draw against Kilmarnock five days before the Scottish Cup Final and there was no way Turnbull could leave his teenage protégé out for the Hampden showpiece.

Graham missed just three First Division games in the 1970–71 season as the Dons attempted to build on the Cup success. They emerged as the only team in Britain to keep an unbeaten home record in tact but it was not enough – Celtic won the title by two points. Second place was the club's highest finish since 1956.

Graham made the berth on the left wing at Aberdeen his own between 1970 and his departure in 1977, hardly missing a game. He had pace, trickery and an infectious character – all the ingredients to make him an idol for the Aberdeen fans.

In 1974–75 he was an ever present and it proved to be his most prolific season in a Dons shirt, his 11 goals putting him just two behind top scorer Drew Jarvie in the final Pittodrie chart. His form pushed him into the Scotland squad but his international career looked to be over before he had even made his debut when - along with Joe Harer, Billy Bremner and Willie Young - an incident in a Copenhagen nightclub after a victory over Denmark led to lifetime bans from the national squad for the trio. The decision was reversed by the SFA but by the time he made his first Scotland appearance, in a 1–0 defeat at the hands of East Germany in 1977, he was a Leeds United player.

Graham, who won 11 caps and scored two international goals over four years, made the switch to Elland Road in the summer of 1977 after 307 games

and 46 goals. He was a fixture in the Leeds team for six seasons, part of the side that was relegated from the English top division in 1982 but spent only a season in the Second Division before Ron Atkinson and Manchester United moved in to take him to Old Trafford in a £45,000 deal. At the age of 30 Graham helped the club to fourth place in the First Division but was edged out the following term by Jesper Olsen and moved to Bradford in 1985, staying south of the border and moving into coaching at senior and youth level following his playing retirement.

Brian Grant

Date of birth: 19 June 1964, Bannockburn

Aberdeen record:
Appearances: League 245+20, Scottish Cup 24+3, League Cup 18+7, Europe
11+4
Goals: League 27, Scottish Cup 2, League Cup 2, Europe 1
Debut: League Cup, 22 August 1984 v Airdrie (a) lost 3–1

Also played for: Stirling Albion, Hibs, Dundee

He was not showy or pretentious, but Brian Grant was certainly effective and consistent throughout his 12-year spell at Pittodrie in the 1980s and 1990s.

Grant was the type of midfielder every successful side requires: confident in the tackle and a neat passer, who always put in a full shift and was never afraid to take hold of the ball. He could even score goals, featuring as a striker in the reserves in his early days, and was the complete midfield player.

He played in three winning Dons side: the dramatic Scottish Cup Final penalty shoot-out victory over Celtic in 1990 and the League Cup triumphs against Rangers in 1989 and Dundee in 1995. The win against Rangers, when two goals from Paul Mason earned a 2–1 win, is the one Grant classes as the highlight of his career because it brought his first winners' medal. It also gave the Dons the upper hand against their fiercest rivals, with the two clubs dominating the Scottish scene while Grant was in his prime.

He cut his teeth with Stirling Albion in the early 1980s and played under Alex Smith for the Binos in the Second Division. After less than a full season the teenager was attracting interest from Celtic, Manchester City and Arsenal, but there would be only one winner in the race for his signature. Grant commented, 'Aberdeen were the best team in Scotland at the time, having won at home and in Europe, with the best manager in Alex Ferguson. It wasn't a difficult decision for me to make when I found out they wanted to sign me.

'It was made clear to me that I would have to bide my time and serve an apprenticeship with the reserves. In the game now there doesn't seem to be the same path for players from the lower Leagues now and that's a shame because there must be talent waiting to be found. The route I followed was fairly common when I was starting out in the game and every club, even the Old Firm, was willing to look within Scotland for fresh blood. That meant there was a flow of money around the game and it helped the smaller clubs like Stirling Albion survive.'

Alex Ferguson took him north to Pittodrie in 1984 in a £40,000 deal but it was not until Grant was reunited with Smith, following his appointment as Aberdeen manager in 1988, that his career with the club really took off. Under Smith and his co-manager Jocky Scott there was always a place for the Bannockburn-born midfielder, but under Ferguson and his successor, Ian Porterfield, first-team games were harder to come by, not helped by a broken leg in his early days on the playing staff.

He made his debut on 22 August 1984 at the age of 20 in a 3–1 League Cup defeat at Airdrie but had to bide his time in the reserves for four years before establishing himself as a regular, taking over from Neil Simpson and forming a partnership with Jim Bett in the middle of the park. Grant said 'I owe a lot to Alex Smith for the start he gave me at Stirling and the faith he showed in me at Aberdeen. We still live in the same part of the country and meet up now and again for coffee. Alex, Jocky Scott and Drew Jarvie were a great coaching team. It is hard to believe that it was considered failure for us to finish second to Rangers in any of the competitions but that was the way it was and it cost Alex his job. Under Willie Miller in his first year in charge we were runners-up in all three domestic competitions – that wasn't good enough and Willie set about changing the team, although it was difficult to replace the calibre of players who moved on.'

Under Smith and then Miller, Grant's skill in anchoring the midfield allowed Bett freedom to roam forward and it proved to be a productive pairing at the heart of the team but not enough to earn the international recognition his performances appeared to merit.

Grant made 329 appearances for the club, scoring 31 goals in the process and collecting three Cup-winners' medals as well as a League runners'-up badge four times in the space of just five seasons between 1989 and 1994. That more than anything is an indicator of how strong the club was in that period, only bettered by Graeme Souness and his multi-million pound Rangers squad. Grant recalled 'Rangers didn't win too many games up at Pittodrie then and we were competing with them for every trophy. The League Cup Final win against them in 1989 was good for me because I had been involved in two previous Finals as a substitute and lost, so to play from the start and pick up my first winners' medal was great.'

In August 1996 a crowd of 9000 turned out to honour Grant when he was awarded a testimonial match against Joe Royle's Everton, who hadn't read the script and beat their hosts 3–1. He moved to Hibs that year in a £75,000 deal and spent 15 months at Easter Road before moving to Dundee as the Edinburgh side were relegated in 1998 and then wound down his playing days back where it all started with a loan spell at Stirling in 1999.

Grant, living with his family in the central belt, now holds the flourishing McDonald's franchises in Forfar and Arbroath, combining his business commitments with youth coaching. He also worked briefly with Elgin City in 2006 but rejected the chance to become assistant manager to former Dons teammate Brian Irvine at Borough Briggs to concentrate on his other interests.

George Hamilton

Date of birth: 7 December 1917, Irvine
Died: May 2001

Aberdeen record:
Appearances: League 201, Scottish Cup 32, League Cup 48
Goals: League 102, Scottish Cup 18, League Cup 33
Debut: League, 13 August 1938 v Partick Thistle (a) lost 2–1

Also played for: Scotland (5 caps), Queen of the South, Hearts, Hamilton

Gentleman George Hamilton, as he will forever be remembered, has gone down in history as one of the finest players ever to pull on an Aberdeen jersey. His scoring record of 153 goals in 281 appearances makes him one of the most prolific strikers ever to grace the Scottish game, let alone Pittodrie.

Hamilton, who died in 2001 at the age of 83, spent a decade at Pittodrie either side of World War Two. He was 38 by the time he helped the club to the League title in 1955, playing a supporting role as the drama unfolded. He only played four times in that campaign but chipped in with two goals.

It takes a lot to make an Aberdonian part with his money, but the Dons had no hesitation in signing a cheque for £3000 to complete a record deal to bring the Irvine-born striker to the north east in 1938 from Queen of the South.

The dividends were rich and instant, with the new recruit netting 17 times in 37 League games, 18 in total, to finish leading scorer in his debut season. He made his first appearance in a 2–1 defeat at Partick on 13 August 1938 and grabbed the first goal of many 11 days later in a 3–0 win at home to the same side.

Post war Hamilton helped the side to a Cup double: part of the Southern League Cup-winning side in 1946 when Rangers were beaten 3–2 and a goalscorer in the Scottish Cup Final the following year when Hibs were dumped 2–1. His debut for Scotland followed that Hampden celebration, earning his first cap in November 1946 in a 0–0 draw against Northern Ireland. Hamilton returned to the national team with a bang in 1951 when he scored a hat-trick against Belgium in a 5–0 win. Three further caps followed up to 1954, when he scored the only goal of the game in a home win against Norway.

At club level, in the final weeks of 1947 Hamilton was surprisingly transferred to Hearts at his own request, having scored nine goals in 14 games for Aberdeen up to that point. Hearts finished ninth in the 1947–48 campaign, one place and one point above the Dons.

Hamilton later described the decision to move to Edinburgh as the biggest mistake he ever made, admitting he thought it would boost his career but soon discovering that the grass was not always greener on the other side.

The switch to Tynecastle proved temporary and within six months Hamilton was back in the fold at

Pittodrie under his old mentor Dave Halliday. This time the club paid £10,000 for his services. He topped the club's scoring charts in both the 1948–49 and 1950–51 seasons. The latter was his best for the Dons, with an incredible return of 29 goals in 40 League and Cup games.

Hamilton left again as the dust settled on the Championship success in 1955, playing for six months with Hamilton Accies before retiring due to injury.

At the end of his playing career he returned for a third stint at Pittodrie, serving as reserve-team coach before moving into the whisky industry as a sales rep. Hamilton, who was a church elder in the city, proved multi-talented and was crowned champion of Deeside Golf Club in 1967.

Joe Harper

Date of birth: 1 November 1948, Greenock

Aberdeen record:

Appearances: League 207+ 7, Scottish Cup 24+1, League Cup 53, Europe 16
Goals: League 125, Scottish Cup 15, League Cup 51, Europe 8
Debut: League, 4 October 1969 v Ayr United (a) won 2–1

Also played for: Scotland (4 caps), Morton, Huddersfield, Everton, Hibs
Managed: Huntly, Peterhead, Deveronvale

The undisputed king of the Beach End, Joe Harper holds a record unlikely ever to be bettered with 205 goals in 308 games for Aberdeen over two periods with the club and leads the all-time Dons scoring chart.

He was capable of finding the net from close range or long range, with tap-ins or spectacular net-bursting shots – wherever he was on the park, Harper knew the way to goal. That ability made him an idol to the Dons fans and the fact he played a part in success in every domestic competition cemented his place in Pittodrie folklore long before his record goal haul had been completed.

Harper was still in his first year as an Aberdeen player when the Scottish Cup was won in 1970 with a 3–1 win over Celtic. It was only the third time Celtic had been beaten at the national stadium in 26 appearances and the Hoops had started overwhelming favourites, rated 4–11 on by the bookmakers. In the pressure-cooker atmosphere the Dons won a 27th-minute penalty and it was Harper, aged just 22 at the time, who took on the responsibility and calmly slotted the spot-kick home to put his side on the way to success. A double from Derek McKay, either side of an 89th-minute Bobby Lennox goal for the Glasgow side, sealed victory.

Harper and his teammates were met by a crowd of 50,000 on their return to the north east, but it would not be the last time the stocky striker was centre of attention. He had arrived at Pittodrie from Morton in 1969 in a £40,000 deal as Eddie Turnbull pinned his hopes on the young striker from Greenock.

Harper had signed for the Cappielow men as a 15-year-old, scored on his debut in a Cup tie against Partick Thistle and never looked back, establishing himself as one of the best goalscorers in the Scottish game. In 1967, after finishing as the country's leading scorer with 28 strikes to his credit, he was plucked from Morton by Huddersfield. The move to England was short, with Morton bringing him back north in 1968 before selling him on to Aberdeen at a profit the following year.

Harper's debut for the Dons was in a 2–1 win away to Ayr United on 4 October. The first of those 205 goals came seven days later in a 2–1 win against Partick. Davie Robb won the Pittodrie bragging rights in the 1969–70 season with 19 goals to the newcomer's nine, but the tables soon turned. The next term Harper led the scoring charts with 27 goals, the best return since Ernie

Winchester seven years earlier. Yet that was nothing compared to what followed.

In 1971–72 Harper hit a rich vein of form and became the first Dons player since Benny Yorton in 1930 to smash through the 40-goal barrier in a single season. Yorston hit 46 that year and Harper was just four away from equalling that achievement, his 42-goal tally making him the third-highest scorer in Europe.

The King made an explosive start to that season with 19 goals in the first 23 games, including three in just four UEFA Cup ties against Celta Vigo and Juventus. At home, luckless Ayr United felt the full force of the Harper steamroller as he smashed four in a 7–0 League win on the way to earning a First Division runners'-up medal.

That devastating form over the course of an entire season tempted Everton to part with £180,000 and Harper was an instant hit on Merseyside, forging a partnership with Joe Royle which made the Scottish import the leading scorer at Goodison. Within 18 months he was reunited with Eddie Turnbull, who had moved to Hibs by that point, but by 1976–77 he was back in action with his beloved Dons after returning north from Easter Road.

He picked up where he left off, scoring on his first game back in red as Kilmarnock were brushed aside 2–0 in the League Cup. Harper went on to net nine goals in that competition as Aberdeen marched to the Final to face Celtic again. This time the result was 2–1 and Harper had helped the Dons to another Cup success.

The striker won four caps for Scotland between 1972 and 1978, punctuated by his ban after the Copenhagen nightclub incident which also disrupted Arthur Graham's international career, and was part of the Scotland squad at the 1978 World Cup in Argentina.

His top-flight club career ended two years later. Despite again topping the scoring table at Pittodrie in Alex Ferguson's first season in charge with 33 goals, he was hampered by a knee injury and restricted to eight starts and three appearances from the bench in the 1979–1980 Championship-winning side as he completed his collection of domestic honours.

Harper went on to manage Huntly, Peterhead and Deveronvale in the Highland League before carving out a career in after dinner speaking and the media as a football columnist and broadcaster. He currently writes for the *Evening Express* and is a radio regular with Northsound.

Tony Harris

Date of birth: 1920s, Glasgow
Died: 2000

Aberdeen record:
Appearances: League 188, Scottish Cup 31, League Cup 54
Goals: League 18, Scottish Cup 5, League Cup 7
Debut: League, 10 August 1946 v Third Lanark (a) won 3–0

Also played for: Queen's Park Rangers, Airdrie

Tony Harris, or John Robert Harris to give him his full Sunday name, liked the club so much he tried to buy it. You don't get commitment like that too often in football.

A Scottish Cup winner in 1947 with Aberdeen, he and former Pittodrie teammate Don Emery returned in 1969 to try and overthrow the Dons board but the takeover bid failed to get off the ground and Dick Donald went on to take over as chairman. Nobody will ever know if the Harris and Emery partnership would have been a success, but Donald most certainly was and the outcome of the 1960s power struggle proved to be the right one for the club's long-term prospects.

Harris first moved to Aberdeen in 1946 after emerging as a centre-forward with Queen's Park Rangers. He was an amateur international and won a senior cap in 1945 in a Wartime tie against England.

Dave Halliday added him to the Pittodrie playing staff for the 1946–47 season and he marked his debut with a goal in a 3–0 win at Third Lanark on 10 August 1946. The Dons finished third behind champions Rangers and Hibs that term, but it was in the Scottish Cup that Halliday's men came to the fore.

Harris, still playing in attack, netted a hat-trick in the 8–0 second-round victory over Ayr United and played in every one of the seven ties in the national Cup competition up to and including the 2–1 Final victory against Hibs. By that time he had switched from number nine to number seven, the start of a new career as a wing-half. He was moved initially to the right side of the Dons team before settling down to become a regular on the left.

Harris was renowned as a grafter, a 90-minute man who gave his all for the Aberdeen cause every time he pulled on the jersey. That type of spirit made him popular with his fellow professionals, who accepted his whole-hearted approach to the game. He was a great friend of Dundee's Billy Steel, but that did not transfer on to the pitch and in one encounter at Pittodrie he put Steel out of the game with a crunching challenge inside the first minute. There were no hard feelings – the first name signed on Steel's plaster cast was John R. Harris.

For seven full seasons he was unmovable from the side, missing just a handful of games each term, but in 1954 Harris made a £1,500 move to Airdrie. An ankle injury he suffered while playing for the

Diamonds forced him out of the game. He had played 273 times for Aberdeen and scored 30 goals.

Harris concentrated on his career as a dentist after his playing days and returned to practice in his King Street surgery in Aberdeen in 1956, moving on to Glasgow shortly after his attempt to seize power at Pittodrie in 1969.

He returned to the city in 1973 to continue his work, retiring to the Lake District before his death in 2000.

Jack Hather

Date of birth: 1927, Annfield Plain
Died: 1996, Peterlee

Aberdeen record:
Appearances: League 264, Scottish Cup 34, League Cup 53
Goals: League 78, Scottish Cup 10, League Cup 16
Debut: League, 1 January 1949 v Dundee (h) lost 3–1

Also played for: Annfield Plain, Horden Colliery

He had pace, precision, a left foot as good as any in the game and an uncanny knack of scoring at the end of his surging runs down the wing. In the modern game Hather would be worth millions.

The Flying Englishman, as he was known, was recruited by Dave Halliday in 1948 from non-League club Annfield Plain for a nominal fee at the tail end of 1948. He was tasked with replacing the veteran Tommy Pearson at outside-left and won the seal of approval from his successor.

In 1955 Pearson, in his new career as a sports writer, voted Hather as Dons Player of the Year at the end of their historic Championship-winning campaign. Hather and captain Archie Glen were the only two ever presents in the title-winning term, but what the Aberdeen fans did not know at the time was that the winger was battling against illness. He required an internal operation at the end of the season to restore him to full fitness, having soldiered on for a year without being able to train properly and needing extra recovery time due to the fatigue the illness caused in the aftermath of match action.

Triumph in the face of adversity was nothing new for Hather. He broke his leg at the age of nine, leaving him with one leg shorter than the other, but defied doctors who told him he would never play football again. As a teenager he was dumped by Newcastle United but bounced back to carve out a career for himself in Scotland.

That season he and Harry Yorston, both on 15 goals, were second only to Paddy Buckley in the scoring stakes. Hather had the habit not only of scoring but of scoring vital goals – on the way to the title trophy his haul included single strikes in a 1–0 win against Falkirk, a 4–3 win at Stirling Albion, a 2–1 win against St Mirren and a 2–1 win in the rematch against the Bairns. The League was won by just three points and those particular wins were crucial.

In the 1955–56 season he scored a double in the 4–2 quarter-final win against Hearts in the League Cup to ease Aberdeen's passage towards a Final, which they won 2–1 against St Mirren to earn the Englishman his second winners' medal. Three Scottish Cup Final appearances proved fruitless.

Hather appeared frequently on the scoresheet throughout more than 11 years at Pittodrie and his record of 104 goals in 351 games puts him among the all-time leading Aberdeen goalscorers. Many were

spectacular long-range efforts courtesy of the powerful punch he packed in his left boot.

He made his debut on New Year's Day 1949, in a 3–1 defeat at home to Dundee and was on target for the first time on 26 February to help his side to a 4–2 win against Partick Thistle.

Goalscoring was only a small part of his game – the major asset was Hather's searing pace down the wing. He was regarded as the fastest sprinter of his football generation and proved a nightmare for defenders up and down the country. Before signing for Aberdeen, Hather had been offered the chance to become a professional sprinter but opted against a life in athletics.

He was eventually released by the club in August 1960, to allow him to accept a job offer in his native north-east England. He played on with Horden Colliery in non-League football before hanging up his boots.

Hather returned to the Aberdeen area in the 1960s but by the time of his death in 1996 he was back home south of the border. His love of the Dons never left him and passed down through the generations, his son John becoming an Aberdeen fan and even ending up on the Pittodrie books as a promising player in the 1970s when he made two appearances for the first team.

Jim Hermiston

Date of birth: 30 September 1947, Edinburgh

Aberdeen record:
Appearances: League 195+2, Scottish Cup 15, League Cup 45, Europe 15
Goals: League 10, League Cup 5, Europe 1
Debut: League, 15 October 1966 v Ayr United (h) won 2–0

Also played for: Bonnyrigg, Grange Thistle, Brisbane City, Brisbane Lions

It is impossible to imagine any of the current Aberdeen squad tearing up their Pittodrie contract to switch from parading their skills on the pitch to policing its perimeter, but that is exactly what Jim Hermiston did in 1975.

The captain made the decision to ditch professional football in exchange for the security of life as a PC with Grampian Police. It was a bold, headline-grabbing move which did not lead to any regrets later in life for the Edinburgh-born defender.

Hermiston had been sickened by Willie Ormond's decision not to include him in Scotland's squad for the 1974 World Cup. That made him desperate to get away from it all and when a proposed move to Chelsea broke down when Aberdeen held out for £5,000 more than the £75,000 the Londoners had offered, he turned his back on the game altogether. At least for a while.

Shortly after his stunning decision the Hermiston family upped sticks and emigrated to Australia, where he returned to playing before once again entering the police system. In recent years he was honoured by his adopted country with a bravery award after tackling an armed robber outside a bank in Brisbane, with the same type of vigour he applied to wingers in Scotland's top flight in his playing prime. He was off duty at the time.

Hermiston believes his football career stood him in good stead for life in the police force, particularly when it came to his 1999 valour award. He said 'The determination and fitness I learned under Eddie Turnbull and Teddy Scott came to the fore that day.'

Hermiston, who retired from the police force in 2003 after 24 years, has had both his right hip and knee replaced in the past three years. Unable to run, he keeps fit instead with daily boxing workouts and by cycling on the roads around his Queensland home.

Of his fitness, he says 'The surgeon who carried out both operations was Dr Robert Cooke, who was the chief registrar for Aberdeen and the north east from 1969 to 1974. He remembers me playing and reckons it must have been all those 80-yard passes I used to put up to wee Joe Harper that did the damage!

'After leaving the force I worked in the hospitality industry in an Italian deli and cafe called New Farm Deli, the Italian fellow was football daft. It was great fun but now Maureen and I, who celebrated our 40th wedding anniversary recently, are working at living, not living at work.'

Hermiston and his wife, who have eight grandchildren, are now enjoying their retirement, but he retains a link to his Aberdeen days through regular contact with Harper, Drew Jarvie, Bobby Clark and Henning Boel among others.

He added 'The Scottish Cup win was one of the great highlights but, in saying that, I consider the main highlight to be the fact I was coached and thought highly of by the men who mattered most, namely the boss Eddie Turnbull, Teddy Scott and my teammates. It is so good to be in contact with some of them after all these years - the friendships are still there and the memories come flooding back.'

Hermiston was signed from Bonnyrigg by Eddie Turnbull in 1965 and made his debut as an 18-year-old in a 2–0 win at home to Ayr United on 15 October the following year. Over the course of the next three years he was gently introduced to the first team but by 1969–70 he had replaced Jim Whyte as the first-choice number three.

That rise to prominence came in time for Hermiston to savour his finest moment in the Dons shirt he wore in 270 first-team games as he helped his side to the 3–1 Scottish Cup Final victory against Celtic in 1970. He and Henning Boel became a rock-steady full-back pairing for Aberdeen as they challenged for the Championship the following year and Hermiston went on to skipper the side as his career drew to a close.

Even after moving to Australia he maintained his interest in the club by having tapes of key games posted from Scotland and has been an occasional visitor on returns to the north east. His links to the game extended beyond spectating in Australia, reviving his playing career when he emigrated in 1977 and becoming one of the most-respected players in the game in his new homeland. He even released a coaching manual to cater for the growing army of young followers he had.

His first club in Australia was Grange Thistle, but he went on to carve out a distinguished playing career with Brisbane City and the Brisbane Lions, starting in the inaugural year of the country's national League.

He twice won the Philips Cup in Australia and was voted Player of the Year by the country's football writers in 1980. His outstanding performances, in central defence and midfield, led to clamour for him to play for the Australian national team and manager Rudi Gutendorf agreed – going as far as to claim the Scot would be his first pick as Socceroos captain. There was a flaw in the plan, though, with a 45-minute appearance for Scotland's Under-23 team during his time as an Aberdeen player preventing Hermiston from turning out for any other international team. The SFA had to break the bad news that the brief, injury-curtailed appearance had scuppered his hopes of playing in the 1982 World Cup for Australia.

He admits 'It was so disappointing not to be able to not only represent Australia but also to have captained them, which was the plan. Every avenue was tried, but the rules were set in stone back then. Because I had represented Scotland at Under-23 and League level it could not happen.'

Hermiston retired from playing in the early 1980s to concentrate on reviving his ambitions of a career in policing and continued to rise up the ranks in the Queensland force.

John Hewitt

Date of birth: 9 February 1963, Aberdeen

Aberdeen record:
Appearances: League 201+65, Scottish Cup 30+10, League Cup 41+11,
                   Europe 41+14
Goals: League 52, Scottish Cup 8, League Cup 13, Europe 12
Debut: League, 15 December 1979 v St Mirren (h) won 2–0

Also played for: Celtic, Middlesbrough, St Mirren, Ross County, Cove Rangers
Managed: Dundalk

Peter Weir to Mark McGhee, a cross and then bang – John Hewitt was a legend. The Aberdonian's headed winner in the 112th minute of the European Cup-winners' Cup Final against Real Madrid on 11 May 1983 was the defining moment in Hewitt's career.

Wherever he went from that moment on, whatever he did, there would be no escape from the glory of Gothenburg. As the only Aberdeen-born player to feature on that momentous occasion, it was fitting that it was Hewitt who had the last word.

Without that man there would not only have been no ECWC win, but there would not even have been a Final to savour. Hewitt had popped up in the 77th minute of the quarter-final second leg against Bayern Munich to score the winner in the 3–2 win to edge his side into the last four and spark the biggest night of celebration ever seen at Pittodrie.

For a man who had dreamed of gracing the stadium as a youngster growing up playing football in the city's public parks, it surely could not get any better.

Hewitt was a product of Middlefield Boys' Club and became a schoolboy international after starring for Hilton Academy. He was still only 17 when Alex Ferguson handed him his big break, thrown the number-11 shirt for a 2–0 win against St Mirren at Pittodrie on 15 December 1979. He started two games and made two cameos from the bench in that title-winning season.

Hewitt was eased into the first team over the course of the next year, scoring his first goal in a 4–1 League Cup win over Berwick Rangers at Shielfield – upstaged by goalkeeper Marc de Clerck who marked his Dons debut with a goal.

By 1981–82 Hewitt was a permanent fixture in Ferguson's team, with 19 goals in 34 starts including a hat-trick against Rangers in front of an appreciative home crowd in the final League match of the season. A winners' medal from the 4–1 Scottish Cup Final

victory against the Ibrox side 10 days later capped it all, having set a record earlier in the competition for the fastest-ever goal when he netted the winner after just 9.6 seconds in the first-round tie against Motherwell.

On top of the European medal in 1983–84 there was a Premier Division Championship badge to add to the collection. This was accompanied by another title success the following year as the Dons dominated, with Hewitt a key player in both legs of the European Super Cup triumph against SV Hamburg for good measure.

A third consecutive Championship medal was collected in the 1984–85 season before a Cup double the following year. Hewitt played in both Finals, bagging a double in the Scottish Cup showdown as Ferguson's troops defeated Hearts 3–0. The Man of the Match award joined the other accolades on the Hewitt mantelpiece.

He topped the Pittodrie scoring chart for the first time in 1986 as the club entered a transitional period following Ferguson's departure and Ian Porterfield's arrival, scoring 14 to draw level with Billy Stark in the club standings.

After 10 years, 364 appearances and 90 goals, Hewitt moved to Celtic in 1989 to link up with Billy McNeill as the Hoops tried to break the dominance Rangers and the Dons were enjoying.

He struggled to break into the Parkhead team, though, and had two periods on loan at Middlesbrough before signing for St Mirren in 1992. A short spell with Ross County followed before a stint as a manager with Irish side Dundalk. He also featured as a player and assistant manager to former teammate Doug Rougvie with Highland League club Cove Rangers in the late 1990s. Hewitt carved out a career in the north-east business community after hanging up his boots.

Frank Hill

Date of birth: 21 May 1906, Forfar
Died: 1970

Aberdeen record:
Appearances: League 98, Scottish Cup 8
Goals: League 9, Scottish Cup 1
Debut: League, 1 September 1928 v St Mirren (a) lost 5–2

Also played for: Scotland (3 caps), Forfar Athletic, Arsenal, Blackpool, Southampton
Managed: Crewe, Burnley, Preston, Notts County, Charlton

In 2006 the football bandwagon was briefly rocked as it thundered through another season when allegations of a multi-million pound betting culture among managers in the English Premiership were made. Suggestions that coaches were gambling on the outcomes of games involving their own teams caused consternation among the paying public but it was far from the first time the game had been embroiled in that type of controversy. One of the earliest cases came in Aberdeen in the 1930s and caused the premature end of a player who looked set for a long and prosperous career with the Dons.

Frank Hill made a sharp exit along with Benny Yorston, Jimmy Black, Hugh McLaren and David Galloway in 1932. The decision to allow the group to leave was shrouded in mystery but Yorston, decades later, confirmed that they were accused of betting on Aberdeen to draw the first half of a series of games before winning after the break. Suspicions arose when Yorston missed an easy chance in a game and the striker never denied the allegations levelled at him and his teammates.

Nobody can tell what might have been had it not been for the forced exit, but it is clear Hill was already well on his way to proving himself as one of the finest performers the club had had in its brief history. He had joined from home-town club Forfar Athletic in 1928, making his debut in a 5–2 defeat at St Mirren on 1 September that year.

Hill featured 14 times in his first season but missed just three in 1929–30 as Aberdeen's stock began to rise, climbing from seventh in the First Division the previous year to third in the table.

It is easy to become complacent about international recognition but in Hill's era appearances by Aberdeen players in Scotland colours were few and far between. When he made his debut for the national side in 1930, in a 2–0 win against France in Paris, he became only the fifth Dons star to make it to the top level.

His promotion to the national stage earns him a place in the club's list of legendary players, following in the footsteps of early Scotland trailblazers Willie Lennie, Alex Cheyne, Jock Hutton and Donald Colman.

He was capped again that year in a 1–1 draw against Wales at Hampden and made his third and final international appearance in a 0–0 draw against Northern Ireland in Belfast.

Hill had made 106 appearances for Aberdeen by the time he played his last game, a 1–1 draw against Kilmarnock on 14 November 1931, but the half-back line of Black, McLaren and Hill was considered the strongest in Scotland before its unfortunate demise.

Leaving Pittodrie under a cloud did not spell the end of Hill's top-flight career and with Arsenal, who paid the Dons £3,000 for the player's services, he took English football by storm, winning three consecutive Championships in the 1930s.

Hill, who died in 1970, rounded off his playing days at Blackpool and Southampton before moving into management with Crewe, Burnley, Preston, Notts County and Charlton. The London club did not renew his contract in 1965 after a four-year stint in charge and, at the age of 60, he retired from the front line of the game. Manchester City continued to utilise Hill as a scout until his death in 1970.

Jock Hutton

Date of birth: 29 October 1898, Dalziel

Aberdeen record:
Appearances: League 241, Scottish Cup 39
Goals: League 13, Scottish Cup 4
Debut: League, 16 August 1919 v Albion Rovers (h) won 2–0

Also played for: Scotland (10 caps), Hall Russells, Bellshill Athletic, Blackburn
Rovers

The exploits of Aberdeen's tank-like defender became the stuff of legend on both sides of the border in the 1920s. Standing just 5ft 8in tall, Jock Hutton was built like an ox. His weight was officially logged at under 14 stone, but that was considered a gross underestimate by the reporters of the time. He is said to have wowed teammates with amazing feats of strength, once picking up a Blackburn Rovers teammate at training. Nothing too staggering in that, until you consider Hutton used his teeth for that particular party trick.

Despite his bulk, the Glaswegian also had tremendous pace and was a feared opponent both in Scottish and English football. He first caught the eye of the Dons while turning out for junior side Hall Russells in the city during his service with the Gordon Highlanders. Aberdeen began rebuilding their team when World War One ended and in 1919 turned to Hutton, signing him from Bellshill Athletic.

He spent his first season as an inside-forward, making his debut in a 2–0 win at home to Albion Rovers on 16 August 1919. The following term manager Jimmy Philip switched him to defence and the number-two shirt became Hutton's property for seven seasons. In that time he emerged as one of Scotland's finest defenders, captaining the Scottish League select side four times and capped for the first time in a 1–0 win in Northern Ireland in 1923.

Hutton played 10 times over the course of five years, skippering the national team to a 2–0 win at home to Northern Ireland a year after his debut and scoring his solitary Scotland goal in a 2–2 draw against Wales in 1927. His cap haul, seven appearances as a Dons player, was an Aberdeen record for more than four decades. To catch the eye of international selectors was not easy for Aberdeen players of Hutton's era. In his time at the club they never finished above fifth place in the First Division, battling just to get out of the bottom half of the table.

He was more than just a star in Scottish football and his unique physique and consistent performances drew attention from England, with Blackburn Rovers stumping up £5,000 in 1926 to take him to Lancashire after 282 games and 17 goals for the Dons. It was a record-breaking deal for the club and a considerable sum of money – in the 1920s you could have the house of your dreams built for £850.

It proved to be a fruitful relationship and within two years he had helped Rovers to lift the FA Cup with a 3–1 win over Huddersfield under the twin towers of Wembley.

A larger than life character who played the game with a smile on his face, Hutton retired from the senior game in 1933 before moving to Northern Ireland.

Brian Irvine

Date of birth: 24 May 1965, Bellshill

Aberdeen record:
Appearances: League 294+14, Scottish Cup 29+1, League Cup 23+3, Europe 19
Goals: League 30, Scottish Cup 4, League Cup 4, Europe 2
Debut: League, 3 May 1986 v Clydebank (a) won 6–0

Also played for: Scotland (9 caps), Falkirk, Dundee, Ross County
Managed: Elgin City

Brian Irvine's boots have long been cast to one side, but he is a man who retains a burning ambition in football. A huge favourite with the Aberdeen fans as a player, Irvine yearns for a return to the Pittodrie staff one day.

He cut his managerial teeth with Elgin City in 2006, having taken his first steps on the coaching ladder with Ross County, but left the club in the same year and returned to his media role as a summariser with BBC Radio Scotland. Already a frequent visitor to his old stomping ground in that capacity, Irvine makes no secret of his passion for the Dons. In fact, he still pays through the gate to take his Dons-mad family to Aberdeen games when he is not on active duty at the ground.

Broadcasting is proving Irvine's forte at present, but a return to coaching appears a certainty for a man with a wealth of experience and the same measure of integrity. That dream ticket back to the Dons is the incentive.

As a coach he adopted the same honest approach to the game he did as a central defender. Irvine was the epitomy of the no-nonsense centre-half and played the game in a simple but effective manner.

Dominant in the air, he posed a threat in attack and his haul of 40 goals in his 338 Aberdeen appearances is an illustration of that. His most important strike did not come with his head but from his boot in the most dramatic of circumstances. The 1990 Scottish Cup Final against Celtic had ended locked at 0–0 after extra-time. The penalty shoot-out also struggled to find a winner, with the teams tied at an amazing 8–8 when Irvine stepped up to bury the decisive spot-kick and take the trophy back to Pittodrie. The towering defender's wild celebrations told their own story.

Challenging the Old Firm, and getting the better of them, was part and parcel of life at Pittodrie for a player who signed during the Ferguson era and went on to play a key role in Alex Smith's powerful side. He added 'That season we won the Scottish Cup and the League Cup and we were expected to compete with Rangers, who were the dominant half of the Old Firm at that point, in every competition. We came close in the League a few times and the rivalry between the clubs was fierce, there were some tremendous games and exciting Cup Finals in that period.

'When I was a young supporter it was classed as an amazing achievement for Aberdeen to beat Rangers or Celtic. That all changed in Alex Ferguson's era and the expectation carried on throughout my time at Pittodrie. They were good times to be at the club and I was fortunate to play a part in it.'

Irvine had to wait his turn to take centre stage, as understudy to the legendary figures of Willie Miller and Alex McLeish, but when his time came he grasped it with both hands.

The Bellshill-born player was recruited from Falkirk in 1985 by Alex Ferguson after establishing himself in the Bairns first team as a teenager. He had just turned 20 when he arrived at Pittodrie and found himself rubbing shoulders with the stars of the Scottish game, joining a team who had just been crowned champions of Scotland for the third year in succession.

The Dons surrendered their crown that term but Irvine at least achieved a personal goal, making his first start for the club in the final League game of the season when Clydebank were humbled 6–0 on 3 May 1986. He had to wait patiently behind Miller and McLeish, but that did not limit his opportunities in the first team.

He stepped in to fill the number-five or number-six shirt close to 100 times over the course of just four full seasons, before Miller's retirement at the start of the 1990–91 season paved the way for a permanent role in Alex Smith's team. Prior to that he had been a substitute in the 2–1 League Cup Final win over Rangers in 1989–90, before standing in for Miller in the Scottish Cup Final to collect his second winners' medal after the penalty shoot-out.

As first-choice central defender, Irvine was promoted to the Scotland scene and made his debut under Andy Roxburgh in a 2–1 win over Romania in September 1990. He retained his place when Craig Brown took charge of the national team and went on to earn eight further caps up to his last appearance in 1994 in a 3–1 defeat against Holland in Utrecht.

His international career coincided with an almost unbroken run of appearances in the Aberdeen first team, missing just eight League games over the course of three seasons between 1991–92 and 1993–94. Loosening the domestic stranglehold Rangers had established proved impossible, but in 1995 the on-field struggles took a back seat when Irvine was diagnosed with multiple sclerosis.

Strong Christian beliefs helped Irvine through his darkest days and he amazed doctors by reviving his football career, playing on with the Dons until his transfer to Dundee in 1997. He made 79 appearances for the Dens Park side over two seasons before Ross County took him north in 1999 to marshall their defence. Irvine played 143 games for County before joining the coaching staff following his final appearance in May 2003, when he was just three weeks from his 38th birthday.

His appointment at Elgin at the start of 2006 sparked an upturn in fortunes and he steered the club to the Third Division Play-offs, although promotion proved a bridge too far.

Irvine also branched out into the world of publishing when he released *Winning Through* in 2006, an innovative book designed at developing readers which received a seal of approval from adult literacy experts. It came a decade after his more traditional autobiography, *What a Difference a Day Makes*, was released.

Drew Jarvie

Date of birth: 5 October 1948, Annathill

Aberdeen record:

Appearances: League 275+35, Scottish Cup 28+3, League Cup 66+14, Europe
                   17+1
Goals: League 85, Scottish Cup 6, League Cup 29, Europe 10
Debut: League Cup, 12 August 1972 v Queen of the South (a) won 4–0

Also played for: Scotland (3 caps), Kilsyth Rangers, Airdrie, St Mirren

Under the stewardship of Dick Donald, Aberdeen was a club which prided itself on prudence and a solid fiscal approach. There was no place for extravagance and a dislike of risky gambles, so when manager Jimmy Bonthrone went knocking on the boardroom door in 1972 looking for a transfer fee larger than anything the club had ever spent previously, he must have presented a good case.

The target was Drew Jarvie and the £70,000 the Dons paid to wrest him from Airdrie's grasp proved to be a bargain. It was a record buy for Aberdeen, using the proceeds from Martin Buchan's £125,000 switch to Manchester United two years previously.

For Jarvie it continued an upward spiral in the game which started when he helped Kilsyth Rangers to the Scottish Junior Cup in 1967, earning caps for the junior international side along the way. Airdrie snapped him up after that Cup triumph and he continued his football apprenticeship with the Diamonds. His performances won Scotland Under-23 recognition before he stepped up to the full national team in 1971 when he played in three internationals under Bobby Brown, surprisingly the only caps he collected in a long career at the top level.

He was recruited to form what Bonthrone expected to be a lethal partnership with Joe Harper, and those hopes were boosted when the new boy made a scoring debut in a 4–0 League Cup win against Queen of the South on 12 August 1972. The budding pairing got off to a solid start in the 1972–73 season but Harper's move to Everton within four months ripped it apart. Harper had thrived on Jarvie's creativity and unselfishness, but it was after he had left to move to Goodison that his former strike partner came into his own.

Jarvie bagged 28 goals to finish leading scorer in his first season at Pittodrie, haunting his former club Airdrie when he hammered home his first Aberdeen hat-trick along the way, and again topped the chart in 1973–74 with a haul of 24 which included four in a single game against Falkirk. He made it a hat-trick the following term when his tally of 13 put him one ahead of Arthur Graham on the Dons scoring list.

While those personal triumphs flowed thick and fast, Jarvie had to wait until the 1976–77 campaign for the team glory he craved. When it came, he proved to be a key player. He scored two goals in the League Cup run, which ended when the Dons lifted the trophy with a 2–1 win against Celtic and both came against the Old Firm. He opened his account in the competition with a screaming volley from outside of the box in the semi-final against Rangers to help his side to a memorable 5–1 victory, but the real trump card came in the Final against Celtic.

The Hoops were old hands, having appeared in every one of the previous 12 League Cup Finals, but for Aberdeen it was the first time since 1955. Celtic looked to be putting their experience to good use when Kenny Dalglish put them ahead from the spot in the 11th minute, but Jarvie hit back within 13 minutes when he headed home the equaliser. Davie Robb snatched the winner in extra-time for Ally MacLeod's side and Jarvie had his first senior medal tucked in his pocket. The next came in 1980 when a Premier Division Championship badge joined the Jarvie collection and his contribution to that first title success for a quarter of a century should not be underestimated.

Steve Archibald was leading scorer overall for Alex Ferguson's team that season, but in the League he and Jarvie shared the workload with 12 goals each. That included a run of six in eight games for Jarvie as the season entered a crucial stage in February and March.

Alex Ferguson's young guns began to edge the seasoned campaigner out of the first team in the following seasons but Jarvie remained a hero to the Dons fans, who turned out to honour him in a testimonial match against Ipswich in 1982 to put a cap on his career with the club.

In October 1972, at the age of 34, he switched back to Airdrie with a glowing tribute from Ferguson ringing in his ears and spent a year at Broomfield before his appointment as assistant manager to Alex Miller at St Mirren. It marked the first step on a long road in coaching, which continued at Dundee before he arrived back at Pittodrie as assistant to co-managers Alex Smith and Jocky Scott in 1988.

Jarvie helped to mastermind the Scottish Cup and League Cup double of the 1989–90 season and continued, alongside Roy Aitken, as one of two right-hand men to Willie Miller when he took over from Smith in the manager's office. In 1995, following Aitken's promotion to the top job, Jarvie switched roles to take charge of Aberdeen's youth system and remained on the coaching staff until parting company with the club in 2002 following Steve Paterson's appointment.

He is now back in Aberdeen after a spell as assistant manager to another Pittodrie old boy, Ian Porterfield, at Korean side Busan Icons.

Eoin Jess

Date of birth: 13 December 1970, Aberdeen

Aberdeen record:

Appearances: League 275+36, Scottish Cup 21+2, League Cup 29+5, Europe
                              9+2

Goals: League 79, Scottish Cup 4, League Cup 5, Europe 6

Debut: League, 6 May 1989 v Motherwell (h) drew 0–0

Also played for: Scotland (18 caps), Coventry City, Bradford City, Nottingham
                              Forest, Northampton Town

For Aberdeen supporters there are few greater pleasures than getting one over on Rangers and in the case of Eoin Jess, the Dons certainly had the last laugh. Released by Rangers as a schoolboy, Jess went on to torment the Light Blues time and time again as the two clubs became locked in a fierce battle for supremacy in the late 1980s and early 1990s.

Despite his childhood connection to Ibrox, Jess falls very much into the category of home-grown talent for Aberdeen. Born and raised in the north-east town of Portsoy, he has commanded in excess of £3 million in the transfer market.

Alex Smith gave the Dons fans a taste of what was to follow when he introduced Jess as an 18-year-old on 6 May 1989, in a 0–0 draw against Motherwell at Pittodrie. One week later he played as a substitute in a 3–0 League win against champions Rangers at Ibrox and the seeds for a love of the big stage were sown.

That was confirmed in October 1989, when Jess played from the start in the 2–1 League Cup Final win against the club who had released him just two years earlier. It was a sweet victory for the rising Dons star. He had scored his first goal in a red shirt earlier that season, hitting the only goal in a game against Dundee, but it was in the 1990–91 season that he truly established himself as one of Scottish football's biggest threats.

He tied with Dutch international Hans Gillhaus on 15 goals at the top of the scoring chart and proved a valuable match winner, scoring all of the goals in a 4–1 win against Dunfermline at East End Park and shattering Dundee United with a hat-trick in a 3–2 win at Pittodrie.

Late in 1992 the first of 18 caps for Scotland was won in a 0–0 draw with Italy at Ibrox when he came off the bench to replace Gordon Durie. Jess, who featured fleetingly in the Euro '96 thriller against England at Wembley, scored against the Czech Republic and San Marino in a seven-year stint with the national team.

Just months after his Scotland debut the versatile attacker, who was equally at home in midfield as he was leading the forward line, broke his leg in a Scottish Cup tie against Clydebank, but he bounced back quickly and rediscovered his best form. He gained his second winners' medal in the 1995 League Cup when the Dons defeated Dundee 2–0 but less than three months later was off the Pittodrie pay-roll.

Coventry City tempted Aberdeen with a £1.7 million offer and that record-breaking fee was too good to turn down, although it didn't turn out to be pure profit. After just one full season with the Sky Blues, Jess returned to Aberdeen in a £700,000 deal in the summer of 1997 to team up once again with manager Roy Aitken.

Bred on a diet of Cup success and title challenges, he found himself at a club now classed as perennial strugglers. In 2000 it was only Falkirk's inability to meet SPL stadium standards which prevented a relegation Play-off against the Bairns after Ebbe Skovdahl's Dons had finished 10th in the 10-team division. Jess spent the second half of that term on loan at Bradford City and joined the Bantams permanently at the end of the campaign before going on to turn out for Nottingham Forest and add Northampton Town to his list of clubs in 2005, before retiring two years later with the aim of embarking on a coaching career.

George Johnstone

Date of birth: 1910s, Uddingston
Died: 1974, Kirkcaldy

Aberdeen record:
Appearances: League 151, Scottish Cup 25, League Cup 24
Debut: League, 6 February 1937 v Motherwell (a) lost 1–0

Also played for: Benburb, Dunfermline, Morton, Cowdenbeath

In the first 100 years of the club's existence only six goalkeepers collected League or Cup-winners' medals. George Johnstone was the first in a group which included Fred Martin, Bobby Clark, Jim Leighton, Theo Snelders and Michael Watt.

Johnstone left Pittodrie with two coveted badges tucked in his pocket, the first coming from the 1946 Southern League Cup Final against Rangers when his side won 3–2. The competition was the forerunner to the League Cup and represented Aberdeen's first triumph on the national stage.

The following year Johnstone was again the number one as the Scottish Cup was claimed with a 2–1 victory over Hibs – when the Dons 'keeper feared he had made the most costly error of his career within 30 seconds of kick-off at Hampden. Johnstone allowed a harmless-looking backpass from George Taylor slip past him and into the net, but he recovered from that nervous start to keep the Leith side at bay as his outfield colleagues hit back with two first-half goals.

Johnstone was not a Scottish Cup Final rookie in 1947, as he was a survivor from the club's appearance at the same stage in 1937. On that occasion it had ended in a 2–1 defeat against Celtic. A year before that game he had played in goal for the Benburb side that won the Scottish Junior Cup, recruited from that victorious side by Aberdeen alongside Frank Dunlop. He took over from Steve Smith on 6 February 1937 and, despite a 1–0 defeat at Motherwell, never looked back as he played the final nine First Division games in a Dons team which finished runners-up to Rangers.

Johnstone went on to become an ever present in his first full season at Pittodrie, keeping 11 clean sheets. In 1947, the same year as the Scottish Cup was won, Johnstone was part of the team that shipped four goals without reply against Rangers in the League Cup Final, but it did not dent his reputation. A fierce wind and driving rain ensured it was not a day to judge goalkeepers.

A succession of men tried and failed to dislodge Johnstone from the first team during his 12 years at the club, including Pat Kelly and Tom Rennie, but he always bounced back to win favour with Dave Halliday until his departure in 1949.

A 2–0 defeat at home to St Mirren on 29 January proved to be the death knell for Johnstone's position as Aberdeen's number one. He was replaced by John Curran and never played another first-team game. The result saw the club rooted at 15th in the 16-team League and confirmed their status as favourites for relegation. It came just a week after the Dons had been dumped out of the Scottish Cup in the first round by Third Lanark.

Johnstone played in 200 games for Aberdeen before his switch to Dunfermline and then Raith Rovers. In the twilight of his career, after turning to coaching, he also pulled the gloves back on to come to the aid of Morton and Cowdenbeath. He went on to coach Newburgh juniors in Fife before becoming trainer of Darlington in 1963. He died in Kirkcaldy in 1974.

Stuart Kennedy

Date of birth: 31 May 1953, Grangemouth

Aberdeen record:
Appearances: League 223, Scottish Cup 29, League Cup 55+1, Europe 26+1
Goals: League 3, League Cup 5, Europe 1
Debut: League Cup, 14 August 1976 v Kilmarnock (h) won 2–0

Also played for: Scotland (8 caps), Falkirk

The European Cup-winners' Cup Final in 1983 brought amazing highs and terrible lows for defender Stuart Kennedy, as the Scotland international's career came to a shuddering end on one glorious night in the most tragic of circumstances.

Not fit enough to take his usual place at right-back against Real Madrid due to a knee injury, Kennedy was named among the substitutes and leapt from the bench to celebrate John Hewitt's winner, catching his studs between the track and pitch and aggravating the knee injury which kept him out of the game in the first place, ending his playing career in the process. Up to that point Kennedy had been a shining light for the Dons and established himself as one of Scotland's leading defenders thanks to blistering pace and impeccable timing.

In the build-up to the European Cup-winners' Cup Final he had played in nine of the previous 10 ties, scoring in the opening game against Sion, but his dream of playing in the big one was dealt a cruel blow when a challenge from Roy Aitken in the Scottish Cup semi-final against Celtic left him crumpled on the turf. He answered Alex Ferguson's plea to haul himself back into the team for the European semi-final ties against Waterschei but twisted his already damaged knee against the Belgian side and the chance was gone.

Kennedy, now back living in his home town of Grangemouth, did not play again and chose to sever his ties with the club and football after brief stints coaching and scouting for Ferguson. The pair's relationship went back beyond their time together at Pittodrie, with Kennedy a part-time player for Falkirk and apprentice electrician in the shipyards of the Clyde when Ferguson was part of the same Bairns squad as his own playing career was winding down in the early 1970s.

Kennedy was 18 when he first played for Falkirk in 1971. Five years later Ally MacLeod took him to Aberdeen on the back of the club's desperate, but successful, fight against relegation in the 1975–76 season.

There was an instant and dramatic upturn in fortunes as MacLeod led his team to third in the Premier Division and to the League Cup with a 2–1 victory over Celtic in the Final. Kennedy, who had made his Dons debut in a 2–0 win against Kilmarnock at Pittodrie in the first game of that Cup run on 14

August 1976, was an automatic pick and wore his traditional number-two shirt in the Hampden showdown. He had missed just a handful of games, notching 43 appearances in his first term at Pittodrie. Between then and his retirement in 1983 he made in excess of 40 starts in all but two seasons.

Just as he had given Kennedy his big break with Aberdeen, it was MacLeod who thrust the defender into the international limelight. He made his first Scotland appearance in a 1–1 draw with England at Hampden in May 1978, in time to book his place on the plane to the World Cup Finals in Argentina. His number-13 shirt proved unlucky in the 3–1 defeat against Peru on the game's biggest stage, but Kennedy experienced the other end of the spectrum when he made his second, and last, appearance in football's showpiece in the 3–2 win against Holland.

He collected eight caps between 1978 and 1981 but could well have added to the collection if his career had not been cut short by injury.

Domestically Kennedy completed a clean sweep, missing just a single game in the Championship win of 1980 and adding the Scottish Cup to his honours list when he starred in the 4–1 extra-time win over Rangers in 1982.

He took a conscious decision to walk away from the prospect of a career in coaching as he reeled from the abrupt end to his playing days after 335 Dons appearances and nine goals, moving into the hospitality trade in the central belt.

Graham Leggat

Date of birth: 20 June 1934, Aberdeen

Aberdeen record:

Appearances: League 109, Scottish Cup 16, League Cup 26
Goals: League 64, Scottish Cup 7, League Cup 21
Debut: League, 12 September 1953 v Stirling Albion (a) lost 1–0

Also played for: Scotland (18 caps), Banks o' Dee, Fulham, Birmingham, Rotherham, Toronto Metros
Managed: Toronto Metros

In his 67th game as a professional football player for his home-town team, Graham Leggat won the prize hundreds of Aberdeen players before him had fought so hard for over the course of more than half a century.

The former Woodside Primary School and Central Secondary School pupil was still only 20 when the Dons clinched the 1955 First Division Championship and in only his second season in the first team, having signed as a 17-year-old from junior outfit Banks o' Dee. In that time he had made the right-wing berth in Dave Halliday's team his own and missed just four games in the victorious League run, weighing in with 11 goals in his 26 First Division appearances.

His contribution to the League Cup triumph the following season was just as telling, bagging a hat-trick in the 5–3 win over Hearts in the first leg of the quarter-final and scoring again in the 4–2 second-leg win to complete the job. Rangers were the semi-final opposition and Leggat was again on target, opening the scoring in a 2–1 win before being rushed to hospital with a shoulder injury. He overcame that pain to take his usual place in the side for the Final against St Mirren and it was a good thing for the Dons that he did – popping up in the 80th minute to score with a bizarre shot from the right flank, which looked harmless until it was missed by the Saints goalkeeper and nestled in the net to secure another trophy for the Pittodrie boardroom display. He finished as leading scorer for his club that term with 29 goals.

International honours soon followed for a player who had already been capped at Youth and Under-23 level. Leggat, who had taken his bow for the Dons in 1953 in a 1–0 defeat at Stirling Albion on 12 September, made his debut for Scotland on 14 April 1956, against the Auld Enemy at Hampden. It was a happy afternoon for the player, who marked his milestone with a goal in the 1–1 draw against England in front of 132,817 supporters.

The Aberdonian went on to win 18 caps and score eight vital goals – on target in another 1–1 draw against England and earning the same result for Scotland in games against Wales and Northern Ireland, as well as scoring in a 2–1 win against Holland and a 3–2 win against West Germany among others. He also earned the distinction of playing in the 1958 World Cup Finals in Sweden as Scotland drew 1–1 with Yugoslavia and fell to a 3–2 defeat against Paraguay.

At club level, Leggat enhanced his growing reputation when he once again topped the Pittodrie scoring chart in the 1956–57 season. In July 1958 Fulham got themselves a bargain when they took one of Scotland's greatest talents to London for a fee of just £15,000. The Aberdonian was an instant hit, scoring on his debut and in the next six games he played for the Craven Cottage side.

He spent eight seasons with Fulham before switching to Birmingham City in 1966. He stayed for two seasons with the club before a stint as a youth coach with city rivals Aston Villa.

In 1971 Leggat began a new chapter in his life when the Toronto Metros tempted him to Canada with a player-coach role in the North American Soccer League. Within a year his expertise was being put to good use in an entirely different way, with the Scotsman appointed to CBC's commentary team covering the NASL. His broadcasting career has taken in World Cup Finals, Olympic games and a host of other top-level events as he established himself as one of the best-known faces in Canadian sports television.

In 2001 Leggat won a place in Canadian football's hall of fame, but his legend still lives on across the other side of the world. In 2006 he joined Martin Buchan as the only two former Dons players in the city of Aberdeen's sporting hall of fame.

Jim Leighton

Date of birth: 24 July 1958, Johnstone

Aberdeen record:
Appearances: League 382, Scottish Cup 49, League Cup 54, Europe 43
Debut: League, 12 August 1978 v Hearts (a) won 4–1

Also played for: Scotland (91 caps), Manchester United, Dundee, Hibs

Never before had an Aberdeen player represented Scotland as often as Jim Leighton, and there is no sign on the horizon that the club's most-decorated player's record will ever be broken.

Leighton made 91 appearances for his country and could have passed the magical 100 mark had he not decided to call time on his international career in controversial circumstances in 1998, when he rejected manager Craig Brown's plea to continue and stood by his decision to retire due to a troubled relationship with Scotland's goalkeeping coach Alan Hodgkinson.

His amazing run in the national team ended on his own terms and with Leighton holding the record as the most-capped goalkeeper the country has ever seen.

The Scotland journey began in October 1982, when he made his debut in a 2–0 win against East Germany. It spanned a staggering 16 years, to his final appearance in a 3–2 win over Estonia. In between, the Johnstone-born 'keeper had played in three World Cup Finals, savouring that experience for the first time in Mexico in 1986 when he was an ever present. It was the same story in Italy four years later and again in France in 1998.

It was an amazing adventure, mirrored by a club career which had more than its share of twists, turns and fairytale moments. Leighton was an Alex Ferguson protégé, thrown into the melting pot at the tender age of 20 when he made his debut in a 4–1 win against Hearts at Tynecastle on 12 August 1978, in place of the veteran Bobby Clark. Clark returned to see out the season and remained number one until Leighton emerged from his considerable shadow in the 1980–81 campaign, when he missed just two games in a marathon 48-match season.

That was nothing compared to the following season, when he and Willie Miller were the only two men to play in every single one of the 58 games the Dons played in all competitions. The reward at the end of that gruelling effort was a Scottish Cup-winners' medal after the 4–1 Final win against Rangers.

Leighton made another 58 appearances the next season, sitting out just one fixture (a 1–1 League draw against Hibs) and shut out Rangers in the Scottish Cup Final to earn another domestic prize. He was an ever present in the run to victory in the European Cup-winners' Cup, conceding just six goals in 11 matches in the most famous sequence of encounters in the history of the club.

Aberdeen's steely defence, with Leighton as its anchor, was renowned. Despite finishing third behind Dundee United and Celtic in 1983, they conceded a miserly 12 goals in 36 games to finish the season as Scotland's meanest rearguard.

In the 1983–84 season that amazing resolve was strengthened even further as Aberdeen, with Leighton as their only ever present, lost just nine goals in 36 games on their way to the Premier Division Championship. A 2–1 win against Celtic in the Scottish Cup rounded off a memorable term for the club and its goalkeeper, who had turned out 63 times between 20 August 1983 and that Final against the Hoops on 19 May the following year.

Success came thick and fast for Leighton in that glorious period, with another League-winners' medal secured in 1985 to join the League Cup and Scottish Cup double of the 1985–86 season. Alex Ferguson's departure upset the rhythm at Pittodrie but Leighton remained a rock-solid fixture under his successor Ian Porterfield, an ever present in 1987–88 and set a new Dons record with a remarkable 35 clean sheets in 55 games.

In the summer of 1988 he was reunited with Ferguson in a £750,000 transfer to Manchester United. The Scotland international took over as United's first-choice 'keeper but within two years the dream had turned to a nightmare and Leighton's relationship with his manager hit an all-time low. The root cause was Ferguson's decision to drop him from the 1990 FA Cup Final replay against Crystal Palace, after being held up as a scapegoat for the shock 3–3 result in the first Final and left in the wilderness at United after that.

He got the chance to rebuild his career when Dundee took him back to Scotland in 1992 in a £200,000 deal. A First Division Championship medal was added to the Leighton collection with the Dark Blues, courtesy of 13 League games after his arrival from Old Trafford, before his 1993 switch to Hibs where the comeback was completed when the 'keeper returned to the Scotland team in 1994 after a four-year absence.

He made 178 appearances for the Easter Road club before his homecoming to Pittodrie in 1997, when Roy Aiten took him back to Aberdeen.

Leighton made 100 appearances in his second spell at Pittodrie, his playing career ending in the agony of a severe facial injury which forced him out of the 2000 Scottish Cup Final against Rangers in the opening minutes. He was 41 when he played that game, his 531st and last match. Leighton remains on the staff as goalkeeping coach.

Willie Lennie

Date of birth: 26 January 1882, Glasgow

Aberdeen record:
Appearances: League 227, Scottish Cup 24
Goals: League 62, Scottish Cup 5
Debut: League, 19 August 1905 v Partick Thistle (h) lost 1–0

Also played for: Scotland (2 caps)

In 2008 Aberdeen Football Club will hope to celebrate a century of international representation in style. The dream scenario would be for Scotland to clinch qualification to the Euro 2008 Finals, with the Dons contributing to the team.

It would be a fitting tribute to the man who launched the Pittodrie side's relationship with the national team in fine style in 1908. Willie Lennie was Aberdeen's first tartan foot soldier and he announced the club's arrival on the big stage with a bang. He made his debut against Wales in the British International Championship on 7 March that year, at Dens Park in Dundee.

He and his teammates trailed 1–0 at the interval but a goal from Alec Bennett on the hour gave the home fans in the 18,000 crowd hope of victory – and it was Lennie who delivered with an 87th-minute winner.

It was only four years and seven months since Aberdeen had played their first competitive match and Lennie's inclusion was an indication of his club's rising status in the game after humble beginnings. The Dons had played the 1903–04 season in the Northern League but could only finish third behind Montrose and Arbroath, crashing out of the Scottish Cup in a first-round tie against Alloa. It was not the dream start the founding fathers had hoped for.

Aberdeen went national the following season, finishing seventh in the Second Division, and by the time Lennie arrived in 1905 they were a First Division side. He was installed as manager Jimmy Philip's first-choice number 11 at the start of the 1905–06 season, making his debut in a 1–0 defeat at home to Partick Thistle on 19 August. He was sidelined only once that term as the Dons found their feet in their new League, 12th in the 16-team competition.

The following season Lennie was joint top scorer with Henry Low, both hitting nine as the club moved up one place on Scottish football's ladder. He was goal king in his own right in 1908–09 with 14 strikes, but surprisingly had fallen out of the Scotland reckoning by the time he hit his peak with his club side. Lennie gained his second and last cap seven days after making his international debut, playing in a 5–0 win against Northern Ireland at Dalymount Park.

His career with Aberdeen ended in 1913, by which time he had made another unique claim for a place in the club's history books. In the 1909–10 season he became the first Dons player to earn a benefit game and 3,000 supporters turned out for his moment in the spotlight, when Dundee provided the opposition.

The highlight of Lennie's time with the club was undoubtedly the 1910–11 campaign, when he and his teammates were just four points behind champions Rangers as they collected runners'-up medals.

The Glaswegian was only 31 when he played his last game for the club. Lennie emigrated to America but later returned to the north east and ran a newsagent's shop in Aberdeen.

Andy Love

Date of birth: 26 March 1905, Renfrew
Died: 1962

Aberdeen record:
Appearances: League 215, Scottish Cup 22
Goals: League 79, Scottish Cup 4
Debut: League, 21 November 1925 v St Johnstone (h) lost 1–0

Also played for: Scotland (3 caps), Kirkintilloch Rob Roy, Aldershot, Montrose

Andy Love was another of the Dons who wore the dark blue of Scotland with pride in the early days of the club. His international career was a whirlwind affair, lasting just eight days but including three games and one goal.

His first cap came in Vienna in a 5–0 defeat against Austria on 16 May 1931. Four days later he was in the touring side which lost 3–0 to Italy in Rome. By 24 May he and his teammates were in Geneva to face Switzerland and the Dons man had the last word, scoring an 89th-minute winner as Scotland returned home with a 3–2 win to atone for at least some of the disappointment caused by the first two results.

Love, a powerfully-built winger adept on either flank, arrived at Pittodrie from Kirkintilloch Rob Roy in 1925, and his committed approach and powerful two-footed shooting drew favourable comparisons with star Alex Jackson.

The Pat Travers signing made his debut on 21 November 1925, in a 1–0 defeat at home to St Johnstone. He was used sparingly the following campaign but did score in one of the most dramatic games Pittodrie has ever seen, his goal making it 1–1 against Hearts on the first anniversary of his debut in a First Division game which ended 6–5 in Aberdeen's favour.

In the 1927–28 season Love finally established himself as a regular in the first team and his scoring ratio of one goal in every three games from the wings made him a valuable weapon in the Dons armoury.

The next term he improved on that, notching 15 goals in 30 League games, and he remained a potent scoring threat until the end of his career with the club. In all, between 1925 and 1934 he scored 83 goals in 237 games and finished leading scorer in the 1931–32 campaign. He had picked up where he left off the previous term, when he had scored his one and only Aberdeen hat-trick in an 8–1 demolition of Clyde on the last day of the season.

The Pittodrie fans appreciated Love's fearless approach to the game as much as they did his goals, but it was that attitude which eventually proved his downfall. He left the Dons in 1935 and spent two years in England with Aldershot before returning for a short spell with Montrose in 1937, where a knee injury forced him out of the game. It was the last in a long line of scars inflicted in his duels with opposition defenders on both sides of the border.

His last game for the club, at which he made his name as an international, came in a 0–0 draw at home to St Mirren on 14 March 1934, without getting his hands on any domestic prizes. The closest call was in 1929–30, when he and his Pittodrie teammates streaked ahead early in the First Division before slipping to third, despite boasting the only unbeaten home record in British football.

After his playing retirement Love accepted a job as a groundsman at Kings College, where he coached the Aberdeen University football team. The Renfrew-born player died in 1962 at the age of 57.

Frank McDougall

Date of birth: 21 February 1958, Glasgow

Aberdeen record:
Appearances: League 54+5, Scottish Cup 6, League Cup 6, Europe 3+1
Goals: League 36, Scottish Cup 3, League Cup 4, Europe 1
Debut: League, 18 August 1984 v St Mirren (a) won 2-0

Also played for: Clydebank, St Mirren

Achieving legendary status can take some players an entire career, but for Frank McDougall it happened in the space of 90 minutes during his first season at the club. A hat-trick in a 5–1 rout against Rangers at a packed Pittodrie early in 1985 did the trick, the Pittodrie fans revelling in their team's demolition of the Light Blues and their new recruit's goalscoring knack.

It was a sweet moment for McDougall, who was a Celtic fan as a boy, but he did not reserve his most devastating displays for games against the Ibrox men. Later that year he destroyed the Hoops with a four-goal blitz in a 4–1 win at Pittodrie to become the first player since 1975 to score hat-tricks against both halves of the Old Firm, and there has yet to be a repeat. They were heady days for the player and fans alike, and the bond remains strong on his rare returns to the north east.

McDougall played for just two full seasons but picked up more honours and scored more goals than many players do in a lifetime, including a sought after Premier Division winners' medal from the 1984–85 season. He completed the clean sweep in his second season with matching 3–0 wins against both Edinburgh sides in the League Cup and Scottish Cup Finals, Hibs steamrollered in the first competition and Hearts in the second.

In both his seasons as Aberdeen's number nine the striker finished leading scorer, bagging 24 in his first term and 20 in his second. He scored three hat-tricks in the space of those two seasons, with Hearts sunk by a McDougall treble at the end of the 1984–85 season to join Celtic and Rangers on the list of victims.

McDougall made his debut on 18 August 1984, back on his old haunt at Love Street as the Dons beat his former St Mirren teammates 2–0. The first of many goals came a fortnight later in a 4–1 win against Hibs at Pittodrie. He was prolific and consistent, going on a run of seven consecutive games on target between 6 October and 24 November that year to help the team to 12 points from a possible 14.

After one year and 360 days, 75 games and 44 goals, it was all over. A serious back injury cut McDougall down in his prime, with a solitary appearance from the bench at the start of the 1986–87 season in a 4–0 win at home to Hibs marking the end of his career at the age of 28.

By his own admission he was not what would be classed as a model professional in modern terms – his favourite meal on the eve of a big game was vindaloo washed down with lager – but he was a model goalscorer.

The Glaswegian was a Schoolboy international and was picked up by Hearts at the age of 16. Homesickness led to a return to the west coast with Partick Thistle and spells with Glasgow Perthshire and Clydebank followed.

It was with the Bankies that McDougall's reputation was built, netting 40 goals in his only season at Kilbowie. That led to a record-breaking £180,000 switch to St Mirren in 1979, with the Paisley side out-bidding Celtic to complete the deal.

In 1984 Aberdeen paid £100,000 to add McDougall to Alex Ferguson's illustrious squad and his goals proved vital to the success the club enjoyed in the short time he was on the books. In the League-winning season of 1984–85 he was the golden boot winner in the Premier Division with 22 League goals, yet that form was still not good enough to earn international recognition, with not a single cap to the striker's name by the time he was forced out of the game.

Following his injury McDougall relocated to England and for a spell ran a pub in Bury, where he still lives.

Ernie McGarr

Date of birth: 9 March 1944, Glasgow

Aberdeen record:
Appearances: League 43, Scottish Cup 7, League Cup 8
Debut: League, 21 October 1967 v Hearts (h) lost 2–1

Also played for: Scotland (2 caps), Kilbirnie Ladeside, Dunfermline, East Fife, Cowdenbeath, Airdrie, Berwick Rangers

Ernie McGarr is a legend of football trivia. He did not win medals, he did not play many games, but the goalkeeper did win two international caps to make Aberdeen the answer to a favourite question with pub quiz comperes everywhere: which club provided Scotland with two international goalkeepers in one season?

McGarr and Bobby Clark both forced their way into Bobby Brown's first team within months of each other, in a bizarre series of events sparked by a dip in form Clark suffered in the 1968–69 season. After shipping 11 goals in just two games, six against Hibs and five against Dunfermline, he found himself banished to the touchlines by Eddie Turnbull. That opened the door for McGarr, who had made his one and only appearance for the club up to that point in a 2–1 home defeat at the hands of Hearts on 21 October 1967.

His reintroduction to the Dons team came in December the following year but he was again on the losing side, with Airdrie winning 2–0. Despite the result the new number one did enough to persuade Turnbull to keep the faith and he kept the gloves for the remaining 25 games of the season, 19 in the League as the Dons steered clear of the relegation places and six in a Scottish Cup run that ended with a shattering 6–1 semi-final defeat against a Rangers side inspired by a Willie Johnston hat-trick.

McGarr was not held responsible for the dramatic collapse and won the affection of the Aberdeen fans over the course of the season with a flamboyant style and habit of producing spectacular saves. When Aberdeen started the 1969–70 season he retained the goalkeeper's jersey and caught the attention of the Scotland manager. Brown handed McGarr his first cap on 21 September 1969, against the Republic of Ireland in Dublin.

The national team was gearing up for a vital World Cup qualifier against West Germany, but injury wrecked McGarr's hopes of securing a place in that game. He went into the game against Ireland carrying a thigh strain and lasted just 35 minutes before he had to be replaced by James Herriot, who retained his place for the clash with the Germans a month later with McGarr as his understudy.

He did make it into the starting XI for the World Cup qualifier against Austria in Vienna in November 1969. A 2–0 defeat in that game was the latest blow to the qualification hopes of the struggling national side.

Any hopes McGarr had of making it back into the Scotland team were shattered when he lost his club place to Clark in February 1970. Clark took McGarr's jersey at Aberdeen and completed his rapid return to favour when Brown fielded him as the country's number one against Northern Ireland in the British International Championship just two months later.

The whirlwind promotion to the national team, and taste of first-team football with the Dons, had given McGarr confidence in his own abilities to hold his own as a first-choice 'keeper .

No longer content to serve as a support player, and resigned to the fact that Clark would keep his place in Turnbull's team at Pittodrie, he asked for a transfer in 1970 and won a move to Dunfermline early the following year. He had spent more than five years with Aberdeen, arriving in October 1965 as a 20-year-old recruited from Kilbirnie Ladeside and went on to play 58 games.

There were no hard feelings between the rival Dons 'keepers, with McGarr later returning to play in Clark's testimonial game in 1978. That match more than anything served to prove he was right to believe Clark would be impossible to shift from the side.

After just half a season at East End Park he was voted Player of the Year by Pars fans in 1971 as their club escaped relegation from the top flight by virtue of a better goal difference. In 1972 he made the short hop to East Fife, playing out his senior career with Cowdenbeath, Airdrie and Berwick before hanging up his gloves in 1980. McGarr made fleeting returns to action in the years that followed as emergency cover for the junior sides he went on to coach.

Mark McGhee

Date of birth: 25 May 1957, Glasgow

Aberdeen record:

Appearances: 164+12, Scottish Cup 20, League Cup 34+1, Europe 31+1
Goals: League 61, Scottish Cup 7, League Cup 18, Europe 14
Debut: League, 1 April 1979 v Morton (a) won 1–0

Also played for: Scotland (4 caps), Morton, Newcastle, SV Hamburg, Celtic
Managed: Reading, Leicester City, Wolverhampton Wanderers, Millwall, Brighton

John Hewitt scored the winner in Gothenburg but it was Mark McGhee who finished the European Cup-winners' Cup campaign as Aberdeen's top scorer in the competition. His cross for Hewitt's match winner in the Final against Real Madrid was his decisive contribution to that stunning run, but his six goals in the 10 games prior to Gothenburg were as important.

McGhee got off and running with a strike in the first leg of the preliminary round against Sion at Pittodrie as the Dons brushed their Swiss opponents aside with a 7–1 win and notched a double in the 4–1 victory in the return leg. His second-round goal at Pittodrie in the first leg against Polish outfit Lech Poznan was crucial, breaking the deadlock against stuffy opponents with the opener in a 2–0 win. His double in the first leg of the semi-final against Belgian side Waterschei at home gave Aberdeen a 5–1 cushion to take across the channel and virtually guaranteed the Final berth.

McGhee proved he could score in European competition but he was equally emphatic on the domestic scene, with 16 goals in the League on top of four in the League Cup and one in the Scottish Cup to make him leading scorer, with 27 in total, as the club won both the European prize and the Scottish Cup.

He led the way in the Pittodrie stakes three times in just five full seasons to make the £80,000 fee Alex Ferguson paid to sign him from Newcastle United in 1979. He was just 21 at the time and claimed his main aim was simply to establish himself in the first team.

McGhee need not have worried about that. He made his debut in a 1–0 win away to Morton, the club where he launched his career, on 1 April just days after signing and was a permanent fixture for the remaining 10 games of the season.

He opened his Aberdeen scoring account in his third game with the only goal of the game away to Partick and made the healthy return of four goals in 11 appearances.

In 1979–80 McGhee made 21 League appearances to earn a Premier Division winners' medal and was leading scorer for the first time the following season with 17 goals, although the Dons ended up empty handed.

His first Scottish Cup medal came in dramatic circumstances in the 1982 Final. Rangers and Aberdeen were locked at 1–1 going into extra-time but McGhee's 93rd-minute header put them on their way to success. Ten minutes later he turned provider, flicking the ball back for Gordon Strachan to make it 3–1 before Neale Cooper added a fourth in the 110th minute. McGhee had also opened the scoring in the 3–2 semi-final replay win against St Mirren.

After the double celebration of the 1983–84 campaign he remained bang in form the following term with 24 goals, including 13 in the Premier Division as Aberdeen stormed to the title. The west-coast striker added another Scottish Cup goal to his collection, along with another medal, when he scored the only goal of extra-time from a Strachan assist to secure a 2–1 victory against a Celtic side reduced to 10 men when Roy Aitken was dismissed for an assault on McGhee after just 40 minutes.

It proved to be the striker's final game in the red of the Dons as he secured a lucrative and life-changing move to German club SV Hamburg in the summer of 1984. He used the freedom of contract rules as they stood at the time to secure a £280,000 move.

Injuries wrecked the Scotsman's hopes of making it big on the continent and in 1985 he returned to home soil with Celtic. He rounded off his playing career with Newcastle before moving into coaching as manager of Reading in 1991.

As a player McGhee won four caps, all while on the Dons staff, in the space of a year. He marked his June 1983 debut with a goal in a 2–0 win at Canada and scored his only other international goal on his final appearance in dark blue when he hit the net in a 1–1 draw against England at Hampden in May 1984.

McGhee quickly established himself as a promising boss and his ruthless ambition led to quickfire moves firstly to Leicester in 1994 and then Wolves from 1995 to 1998. He managed Millwall between 2000 and 2003 before a three-year stint in charge of Brighton, which ended in 2006.

Derek McKay

Date of birth: 13 December 1949, Banff

Aberdeen record:
Appearances: League 15+3, Scottish Cup 3, Europe 1
Goals: Scottish Cup 4
Debut: Scottish Cup, 4 October 1969 v Ayr (a) won 2–1

Also played for: Deveronvale, Dundee, Forres Mechanics, Barrow, Siu Fong, Durban United, Keith, Kiev, Ross County

Derek McKay played football on three continents and for an array of clubs, but one place will always have a special place in his heart. That place is Hampden Park, the scene of the far-travelled player's legendary heroics.

The date was 11 April 1970 and more than 108,000 were shoehorned into the national stadium to watch champions Celtic tackle Eddie Turnbull's unfancied Aberdeen side. Joe Harper's 27th-minute penalty gave the Dons the initiative but one goal was never likely to be enough to keep the Hoops at bay. When McKay tucked home the rebound after a Jim Forrest shot had been parried in the 83rd minute the impossible dream looked almost probable. Bobby Lennox looked to have set-up a tense final minute when he reduced the deficit to 2–1 in the 89th minute, but within seconds McKay had completed his double and won the trophy for the Dons with a neat left-footed goal.

Without McKay's goals the club would not have even reached the Final, let alone won it. A close range 66th-minute goal in the quarter-final, part of a Man of the Match performance, secured a 1–0 win against Falkirk. In the semi-final he scored the only goal of the match against Kilmarnock in the 22nd minute to take the Dons through to the Celtic showdown.

And so the legend of Cup tie McKay was born, with the Scottish Cup return of four goals in his only three games in that season's competition a stunning contribution from a player who only mustered 15 League starts and not a single First Division goal in his Pittodrie career.

The player had moved to Dens Park as a 16-year-old, having caught their eye playing as a winger for Deveronvale in his native Banffshire, but was freed by the Dark Blues less than four years later.

After stealing the show in the Cup Final McKay completed the League season with two top-team starts and looked set for a key role in the 1970–71 campaign, in the first XI for two of the three League openers and in the 3–1 European Cup-winners' Cup first-round first-leg victory against Honved at Pittodrie.

That proved to be the final appearance of a short but very sweet stay with the Dons, with McKay freed by Turnbull in April 1971. He returned to the Highland League with Forres that summer but within weeks, and after three appearances, he had switched to English Fourth Division side Barrow.

In 1972 McKay accepted his first foreign assignment, joining Hong Kong side Siu Fong and sampling Australian football briefly before joining Durban United in South Africa late in 1973.

Within a year he was back in the north east with Keith but before long was back on his travels, adding Australian club Kiev to his growing list of attachments. Ross County, in 1978, became the 15th club on his playing CV. McKay soon returned to Australia, where he still lives.

Pat McKenna

Date of birth: 26 April 1920, Glasgow

Aberdeen record:
Appearances: League 134, Scottish Cup 17, League Cup 30
Debut: League, 1 September 1945 v Celtic (a) drew 1–1

Also played for: Blantyre Celtic, Plymouth Argyle, Arbroath, Fraserburgh

Only four players were ever present in both of Aberdeen's victorious runs in consecutive seasons in the Southern League Cup and Scottish Cup in the 1940s. Frank Dunlop, Billy McCall and Stan Williams were three and Pat McKenna completed the quartet.

The Glaswegian was an unspectacular player but totally dependable, and his record of two trophy wins in seven seasons at Pittodrie stands up to scrutiny. The full-back played 181 games for the Dons without scoring a single goal, but his forte was defending. Despite a lack of height, he proved to be a formidable member of the rearguard.

Speed was central to McKenna's role within the team and one of the qualities which persuaded Dave Halliday to gamble on the Blantyre Celtic player in 1944, taking him north as a 24-year-old.

He made his post-war debut in a 1–1 draw at Parkhead on 1 September 1945, in a team which was proving to be capable of mixing with the big guns of the Scottish game. That season the Dons lost just one game at home, when Clyde escaped with full points, and went on to finish third as Celtic won the League and Hibs took the runners'-up spot.

Aberdeen could console themselves with the Southern League Cup to grace the Pittodrie trophy cabinet at the end of the 1945–46 season, with McKenna playing in each of the 10 games in the competition. That included the 3–2 win against Rangers at Hampden and McKenna was no stranger to the national stadium during his time with the club.

The next visit ended in disappointment, with a 4–0 defeat in the 1946–47 League Cup Final against Rangers. Fourteen days after that shattering blow McKenna was back in his number-three shirt for the Scottish Cup Final against Hibs, to play his part in the famous 2–1 victory.

The Dons had once again finished third in the League, the best they could do during McKenna's seven-year stay. When he was hospitalised for an appendix operation in the summer of 1950 he missed

the start of the season and struggled to force his way back into Halliday's plans as Dave Shaw established himself in the left-back berth.

In August 1952 McKenna moved from the north-east coast of Scotland to the southern shore of England when he linked up with Plymouth Argyle at the age of 32. He spent a season with Argyle as they finished fourth in the Second Division before returning to Scotland with Arbroath in Division Two. McKenna wound down his playing days in the Highland League with Fraserburgh.

Stewart McKimmie

Date of birth: 27 October 1962, Aberdeen

Aberdeen record:
Appearances: League 430+1, Scottish Cup 46, League Cup 47, Europe 39+1
Goals: League 9
Debut: League, 17 December 1983 v Hibs (h) won 2–1

Also played for: Scotland (40 caps), Dundee, Dundee United

When it comes to Aberdeen legends, Stewart McKimmie ticks every box. An Aberdonian born and bred, the defender was a loyal servant and captain as well as winner of every domestic honour and a star on the international stage. McKimmie also has continental success on his list of honours, courtesy of the European Super Cup medal he won in only his second game as an Aberdeen player.

A product of Aberdeen juvenile club Deeside, he clocked up more than 100 appearances for Dundee before being taken home to Aberdeen by Alex Ferguson in December 1983, in a £90,000 deal.

At the age of 21 McKimmie made his Dons debut in a 2–1 home win against Hibs on 17 December and three days later retained his place for the second leg of the Super Cup showdown with Hamburg. After a 0–0 draw in Germany, a 2–0 home victory secured the title.

It was an early taste of what was to follow in a trophy-laden 14-year stay with the club for McKimmie, with a Premier Division medal collected in his debut season thanks to 17 appearances and another joining it when the Championship was retained in 1984–85 after he missed just two League games. It was an appearance record only beaten by Willie Miller and matched by Jim Leighton that term.

Despite his tender years the player smashed through the century mark of games for the Dons in the 1985–86 campaign on his way to adding League Cup and Scottish Cup-winners' medals to his burgeoning collection.

Ferguson, who had considered buying Tosh McKinlay before opting for the McKimmie signing, had once again proved a shrewd judge in the transfer market and a succession of managers benefited from his neat piece of business.

Under Ian Porterfield and then the team of Alex Smith and Jocky Scott, the right-back proved to be an automatic selection. McKimmie was an ever present in the two runs, which brought both the League Cup and Scottish Cup in the 1989–90 season for Smith and Scott's team. By that time he was a fully-fledged member of the Scotland squad, having made his debut in May 1989 in a 2–0 defeat against England in the Rous Cup. Days later Andy Roxburgh gave the Pittodrie player his second cap in a 2–0 win against Chile in the same event, but it was against the world champions Argentina early in 1990 that he sealed his place in the international party for the World Cup in Italy that summer.

McKimmie scored the most famous goal of his career at Hampden Park when he ventured forward in the 32nd minute to rifle home a spectacular winner. He played against Brazil and Costa Rica in Italia '90, adding to his big-stage experience in Euro '92 and Euro '96. He played all three group games in Sweden and in the huge ties against Holland and hosts England in 1996.

The Euro '96 adventure, which brought his 40th and final cap, came just months after one of McKimmie's proudest moments as an Aberdeen player when he joined a select band of trophy-winning Dons captains to lead his side forward to collect the League Cup in the 1995–96 season after the 2–0 victory over his former club Dundee. He had taken over the skipper's armband from Alex McLeish following his departure for Motherwell in 1994, the same year in which McKimmie was honoured with a testimonial against Blackburn.

Like Ferguson, Porterfield, Smith and Scott and Willie Miller before him, Roy Aitken relied on McKimmie as a defensive mainstay. Having launched his career as a full-back, he became adept as a central defender in the second half of his Pittodrie career and his versatility proved valuable.

The League Cup proved to be the last of his many Cup Final appearances for the club. He was released in March 1997 and made the short move to Dundee United, where he remained for a further season before retiring at the age of 35. McKimmie, who made 564 appearances for Aberdeen and scored nine goals, retains his involvement in football through his role as a newspaper columnist with the *Evening Express*.

Alex McLeish

Date of birth: 21 January 1959, Barrhead

Aberdeen record:
Appearances: League 493+2, Scottish Cup 68+3, League Cup 74+1, Europe
56+1
Goals: League 25, Scottish Cup 2, League Cup 2, Europe 1
Debut: League, 2 January 1978 v Dundee United (h) won 1–0

Also played for: Scotland (77 caps)
Managed: Scotland, Motherwell, Hibs, Rangers

Never let it be said that there is no room for humour in football. During a 0–0 draw at Ibrox, with Aberdeen inflicting more pain on Alex McLeish and his toiling Rangers team in 2005, the Dons fans unfurled a banner with a cutting message. Signed off with Willie Miller's name, it simply read: Agent McLeish, mission accomplished, return to base.

While the Pittodrie faithful revelled in the fall from grace their arch rivals suffered under the one-time playing hero, in truth most would welcome him back with open arms if he were to decide to test his managerial skills in Scottish club football at some point in the future.

Most, but not all. Moving to Rangers is an unforgivable act in the eyes of some Aberdeen fans, as many who have made the switch have found in the past, but for the majority McLeish will always be considered a Don first and foremost.

Before the prospect of a return to the club game even looms on the horizon he has far bigger fish to fry as manager of the national side, a job inherited from Walter Smith. For one of Scotland's most revered and respected players, it truly is the dream job.

This football journey started almost 30 years ago, with the first glimpse of the McLeish-Miller partnership coming two days into 1978. Willie Garner had broken the team's curfew and manager Billy McNeill thrust a flame-haired 17-year-old into action in his place.

It was a one-off move that season but the birth of one of Scottish football's greatest defensive partnerships. For the record, it also marked the first clean sheet for the duo as the Dons defeated Dundee United 1–0.

It was under Alex Ferguson that the Barrhead-born central defender truly blossomed, bedded in over the course of the 1978–79 season before cementing his place the following term as Ferguson claimed the Premier Division Championship for the first time. He relied heavily on McLeish, who turned 21 mid way through the season, and nobody played more games than he did in that nail-biting League race which went right to the final match.

His list of honours with Aberdeen is phenomenal. The Scottish Cup in 1982 and again in 1983 and 1984, the European Cup-winners' Cup and the European Super Cup, two further League Championships, another Scottish Cup in 1986 and then a Cup double in the 1989–90 season. That double-winning season also saw him recognised as Scotland's Player of the Year.

McLeish outlasted every one of his Pittodrie contemporaries during his career. By the time he left in 1994, Miller had graduated to become team boss.

In 17 years as a first-team player he played in 696 games and scored some vital goals among his career total of 30. Among the most memorable goals was the sublime, curling equaliser against Rangers in the 1982 Scottish Cup Final, one facet of a Man of the Match performance in a game his side went on to win 4–1 after extra-time.

Against Bayern Munich in the second leg of the European Cup-winners' Cup semi-final in 1984, McLeish once again moved forward from the heart of the defence to level the scores at 2–2 with a typically-imperious header from a Gordon Strachan free-kick. A minute later John Hewitt made it 3–2 and the Dons were on their way to the most famous victory Pittodrie has ever seen.

Of course, it was as a defender of international standing that McLeish made his biggest mark on the game. He and Miller took their vaunted partnership into the world arena with Scotland throughout the 1980s. McLeish made his debut for the national team in March 1980, in a 4–1 win against Portugal under Jock Stein. A further 76 caps followed to catapult him into the SFA's hall of fame.

His international career coincided with a purple patch for Scotland and allowed him to play in the World Cup Finals in 1982, 1986 and 1990. He was booked only once in those 77 internationals, a measure of his talents as a defender who did not have to rely on muscle to compete at the top level.

In 1994 it took an offer McLeish could not refuse to break his bond with the Dons. The chance to follow Miller onto the managerial ladder with Motherwell tempted him south and he got his coaching career off to a promising start when he led the Steelmen to second place in his rookie season as a manager. He switched to Hibs in 1998 to join a club in turmoil and could not prevent their relegation. The First Division Championship in 1999 followed and in 2001, with Hibs chasing the Old Firm at the head of the SPL table, Rangers made their move.

McLeish enjoyed tremendous success initially, winning the Championship in 2003 and 2005 as well as the Scottish Cup twice and the League Cup three times. Even as his exit loomed after a run of poor domestic form, McLeish became the first manager to lead a Scottish team into the last 16 of the Champions League. He left Ibrox at the end of the 2005–06 season to be replaced by Paul Le Guen and rejected several approaches from English clubs before accepting the role of Scotland manager at the start of 2007.

John McMaster

Date of birth: 23 February 1955, Greenock

Aberdeen record:
Appearances: League 205+32, Scottish Cup 29+5, League Cup 54+7, Europe
28+3
Goals: League 20, Scottish Cup 4, League Cup 9
Debut: League Cup, 24 August 1974 v Dunfermline (h) won 3–0

Also played for: Peterhead, Morton

Aberdeen supporters do not suffer fools gladly and when 16,500 of them turned out to pay tribute to the sophisticated skills of John McMaster in his 1985 testimonial against a Billy McNeill select XI, it served a significant gauge of the regard in which he was held by the paying public in the Granite City.

He was a hero to the masses and nobody begrudged him a lucrative benefit game to recognise his dedication to the Dons cause. It was fitting that Liverpool manager Kenny Dalglish made a contribution – since it was one of the Merseyside club's players who came close to ending McMaster's career prematurely.

Five years prior to his testimonial, in a European Cup tie against the Anfield club at Pittodrie, he was scythed down by Ray Kennedy. He had a knee operation within hours and surgeons informed the Pittodrie hierarchy that their player, cut down in his prime, would never play again. McMaster, however, defied the odds to return to the game he loved and after almost a year on the sidelines it was business as usual for the versatile left-sided player.

By the time he suffered that injury setback McMaster was already the proud owner of a Premier Division Championship medal, having played in all but three of Aberdeen's League games on the way to the 1980 title. He was also knocking on the door of the Scotland squad but his hopes were dashed by Kennedy's rash challenge and in the end he never won the cap he craved.

At club level, his return to action in the 1981–82 season allowed him to take his place in the side for the 4–1 Scottish Cup Final win against Rangers and he again played in the 1983 Final against the Ibrox men when the Dons recorded a 1–0 win. By then, McMaster and his teammates were champions in the European Cup-winners' Cup. He started seven of the 11 games in that campaign, making two additional contributions from the bench – with his substitute's appearance against Bayern Munich in the 3–2 success in the second leg of the quarter-final particularly telling.

McMaster turned from player to play actor as he and Gordon Strachan feigned a mix-up over who was to take an attacking free-kick as Aberdeen trailed 2–1. After pretending to collide, Strachan turned swiftly to swing in the free-kick which provided Alex McLeish with the chance to head home the equaliser and set up John Hewitt's winner. The audacious McMaster and Strachan move bamboozled the German defenders.

He forced his way back into the starting XI for the second leg of the semi-final against Waterschei and was handed the number-three shirt for the tumultuous 2–1 Final win against Real Madrid in Gothenburg. McMaster was 28 at the time of the Final and, not surprisingly, it proved to be the peak of his career. He played a third of the 1983–84 League campaign to earn another Championship medal, adding a European Super Cup badge to the collection, but a serious ankle injury kept him out of the successful defence of that title.

After struggling to regain his place in the side, Ian Porterfield granted McMaster a free transfer as a thank you for his service to the club which had spanned 15 years. He had signed as a 17-year-old from Port Glasgow, making his debut on 24 August 1974 in a 3–0 League Cup win against Dunfermline at Pittodrie, and went on to appear 363 times and score 33 goals. He spent a period on loan at Peterhead in the early part of his career but other than that had never ventured away from the club he joined as a teenager.

When McMaster left the Dons he switched to his home-town club Morton, where he served as player-coach and then assistant manager.

Tommy McMillan

Date of birth: June 1944, Paisley

Aberdeen record:
Appearances: League 172, Scottish Cup 23, League Cup 45, Europe 8
Goals: League 1, Europe 1
Debut: League Cup, 21 August 1965 v Rangers (h) won 2–1

Also played for: Neilston, Falkirk, Inverness Thistle
Managed: Inverness Thistle, Fraserburgh

Martin Buchan played the captain's role in the 1970 Scottish Cup Final victory against Celtic but playing a key supporting role was his defensive partner Tommy McMillan. Both men were given their big break by Eddie Turnbull in the second half of the 1960s and both were at the heart of the defining moment of that era, when the Dons collected the club's first piece of silverware for 15 years with a 3-1 win against the Hoops.

The McMillan and Buchan partnership which served Turnbull so well in every one of the five Scottish Cup ties in 1970 never had the chance to flourish, with the skipper's departure after the Hampden Final taking him on to bigger and better things in England. While Buchan's career was still in its infancy when the trophy was claimed, McMillan was an experienced campaigner. He was a robust centre-half but having played as an inside-forward as a schoolboy, was also prone to attacking excursions up field.

Aberdeen came within a whisker of missing out on their target when Turnbull moved in for McMillan, who had been starring for Neilston Juniors, in the mid 1960s. He was preparing to board a plane bound for a new life in Australia, when he got the call from Pittodrie. Without hesitation he ditched his plans to emigrate and travelled north, leaving behind his job as an electrician to become part of the vision for a new-look Aberdeen team.

McMillan made his debut in a League Cup tie against Rangers on 21 August 1965 and got off to a winning start, as goals from Jorg Ravn and Billy Little earned a 2-1 victory. He went on to miss only two League games in his debut season, quickly establishing himself as a key player for his new club. His arrival coincided with an improvement in form for the club, finishing eighth in the First Division compared to 11th the previous term.

The 1966-67 season proved even more fruitful. McMillan played 48 times, missing just a single game, and helped the Dons up to fourth in the table. His form at the heart of the defence ensured his first taste of international football, called up by the Scotland Under-23 team in November 1966 for a game against Wales and again in March the following year. They were his only caps at any level and brought two victories.

A month after his last appearance in dark blue he tasted Cup Final football for the first time. He was an ever present in the run to the 1967 Scottish Cup Final but was powerless to shut out the Celtic side, who ran out 2-0 winners. Sweet revenge was gained three years later when he won a winners' medal to go with his runners'-up badge.

Despite the disappointment of the 1967 Final it did win McMillan and his teammates the chance to compete in the European Cup-winners' Cup Final due to the Parkhead side's passage to the European Cup through their latest Championship success. It was a landmark event for a club that had never sampled continental competition up to that point. McMillan played in all four ties against KR Reykjavik and Standard Liege and had the distinction of scoring in Aberdeen's first European tie, when 14,000 turned out to quench their curiosity. His 44th-minute goal was the fourth in a 10-0 win against the Icelandic amateurs. A 3-2 aggregate defeat against the Belgians in the next round ended the campaign.

McMillan played in all four of the Fairs Cup ties the following season, against Slavia Sofia and Real Zaragoza as he continued to play an important part in Turnbull's ongoing effort to establish his team as a force in the Scottish and European game. After the 1970 Cup success there was another continental sortie to look forward to, but McMillan would have no part to play due to injury. That 1970-71 season marked the beginning of the end of his Pittodrie career, with Willie Young emerging to take over as the defensive pivot Turnbull's side revolved around.

The Paisley-born former Under-23 cap moved to Falkirk in a £10,000 deal in 1972 and spent 15 months at Brockville before switching to the Highland League with Inverness Thistle in 1973. He went on to become a successful manager of the north side, winning a succession of Cups before resigning to take a job in the North Sea oil industry. A stint in charge of Fraserburgh followed for McMillan in 1978.

Kevin McNaughton

Date of birth: 28 August 1982, Dundee

Aberdeen record:
Appearances: League 165+10, Scottish Cup 13, League Cup 9, Europe 5
Goals: League 3
Debut: League, 5 August 2000 v St Mirren (h) won 2–1

Also played for: Scotland (3 caps to 2007), Cardiff City

When a home-grown player rejects a new contract in favour of searching for greener grass on the other side of the border, the traditional feelings of outrage and betrayal from the supporters in the stand are understandable.

The fact that Kevin McNaughton left with the blessing of both his management team and the fans despite exiting Pittodrie in those circumstances hints at the regard in which he was held at the club that nurtured him on his path from schoolboy to fully-fledged international. Jimmy Calderwood desperately wanted to retain McNaughton's services when his Aberdeen deal expired in the summer of 2006, but there was no bitterness when the final decision was made and the versatile Dundonian moved on to Cardiff City to help the Welsh club in its quest for a Premiership place.

Despite uncertainty over his future for the last five months of his final season, there was never any question among the management team or the fans that he would continue to give his all to the cause.

McNaughton was part of a crop of youngsters blooded within the space of two seasons by Ebbe Skovdahl. Jamie McAllister, Darren Mackie, Kevin Rutkiewicz, Phil McGuire, David Lilley, Calum Bett, Fergus Tiernan, Ross O'Donoghue and Scott Michie were all catapulted into the first team as the Danish coach raided the youth ranks in an attempt to boost the club's flagging fortunes. McNaughton, to date, is the only one of that group to have gone on to play for Scotland's national team and truly thrive in the club game.

He came into the team at the start of the 2000–01 season. The previous season the club had finished rock bottom of the SPL and only avoided a relegation Play-off because First Division promotion hopefuls Falkirk could not meet top-fleet stadium criteria.

It was a gloomy time for the club but McNaughton's introduction as a substitute in a 2–1 home win against St Mirren on 5 August 2000 provided a spark to give hope of brighter times ahead.

From that point on he was assured of a starting place, fitness permitting, and as an 18-year-old made 38 appearances in his rookie season. McNaughton, who had come through the coveted Pittodrie youth system, began his career as a left-back but went on to become a victim of his own versatility – playing on both sides of the defence, as a sweeper and in every position across the midfield during his six years of first-team duty.

In only his second season McNaughton was crowned Scotland's Young Player of the Year, the accolade coming on the back of his selection for the international side. He took his Scotland bow in front of an appreciative Pittodrie crowd on 17 April 2002, in a friendly against Nigeria. McNaughton, who was the first Dons player to turn out for the national team since 1999, played 90 minutes in a 2–1 defeat against the powerful and talented Africans.

Berti Vogts was the coach who gave McNaughton his big break and heaped praise on his new boy following his first appearance – but the German did as much to damage his career at that level as he did to aid it. Vogts withdrew McNaughton from his starting XI the day before he was due to make his debut against World champions France in Paris a month before the Nigeria game. Vogts claimed the Dons player was too nervous to play, a bizarre explanation and one of the first of the blunders which would become familiar as Vogts's tenure progressed.

The national coach criticised McNaughton for a second time following his second appearance for the team, in a 1–0 defeat against Denmark in 2002, after withdrawing him at half-time. Not surprisingly, it damaged the relationship between the pair further and McNaughton did not appear again under Vogts.

He returned for his third cap, a 4–1 defeat against Sweden, when Tommy Burns took control on a temporary basis and returned to the international fold under Walter Smith in 2006.

At club level McNaughton, who played 202 games and scored three goals, was unfortunate to arrive at Aberdeen during troubled times and domestic honours proved only a dream as the Dons toiled under Skovdahl, Paul Hegarty and Steve Paterson, before Calderwood's arrival sparked a revival.

His decision to leave at a time when the club was on the up was bold but paid off when Cardiff mounted an immediate challenge for promotion to the Premiership and the Scottish recruit emerged as a valued defensive cog.

Tommy McQueen

Date of birth: 1 April 1963, Glasgow

Aberdeen record:
Appearances: League 53+4, Scottish Cup 6+1, League Cup 3, Europe 3
Goals: League 4, League Cup 1
Debut: League, 11 August 1984 v Dundee (h) won 3–2

Also played for: Clyde, West Ham, Falkirk, Dundee

Ever since David Robertson's departure to Rangers in 1991, Aberdeen have searched in vain for a long-term solution to the traditionally difficult to fill left-back berth. In sharp contrast, the 1980s brought an embarrassment of riches in that department.

Robertson was the most famous Dons number three of that era, but his predecessor also played his part in the club's success. Tommy McQueen was an Alex Ferguson signing in the summer of 1984, going from an electrical salesman who combined his day job with his football commitments with Clyde under Craig Brown to a member of Scottish football's most-feared squad of players.

The Glaswegian was just 21 when Ferguson clinched the deal with a £40,000 cheque, nipping in to scupper the hopes of Hibs after the Easter Road club had agreed a fee with the Bully Wee. With Doug Rougvie off the books and John McMaster sidelined after surgery, there was an immediate passage to the first team for the new boy and he made his debut on the opening day of the season in a 3–2 win at home to Dundee on 11 August.

McQueen started 33 of the 36 Premier Division games that season on the way to Aberdeen's seven-point Championship win over Celtic. He made the transition from part-time football to life with the elite with ease, even assuming penalty duty for the Dons and eventually leaving with a record of seven goals from seven spot-kicks.

In a lightning introduction to life at football's top table, McQueen made his European Cup debut just a month after his first game as a Dons player. Aberdeen and Dinamo Berlin ended locked 3–3 on aggregate after two legs and despite McQueen converting his effort, the Germans won in a penalty shoot-out.

There was consolation in knock-out competition in the 1985–86 season when he won a place in Ferguson's side for the Scottish Cup Final against Hearts. The Jambos, who had suffered the crushing disappointment of being pipped to the League title on goal difference by Celtic just days earlier, had their misery compounded when John Hewitt's double and a Billy Stark goal took the trophy back to Pittodrie thanks to a 3–0 win.

It was another winners' medal for McQueen and it looked certain to be just the start of a long and profitable relationship between him and the Dons. Instead, he found himself battling with Brian Mitchell

for the number-three jersey in the 1986–87 campaign before suffering a leg fracture in training just three months into the season. By the time he returned there had been two crucial changes at the club: Ferguson had left and been replaced by Ian Porterfield, while David Robertson had established himself as one of the country's emerging talents and first choice in McQueen's position for Aberdeen.

In March 1987 a £125,000 offer from West Ham was accepted by Porterfield and McQueen, still only 23, linked up with the London club in the English top flight.

After 36 appearances for the Hammers he returned to Scotland with Falkirk in 1990 in a £60,000 transfer. In August 1995 he moved to Dundee but had his hopes of ending his career on a high dashed when Aberdeen defeated his new club 2–0 in that season's League Cup Final.

Fred Martin

Date of birth: 13 May 1929, Carnoustie

Aberdeen record:
Appearances: League 206, Scottish Cup 33, League Cup 52
Debut: League, 14 April 1950 v East Fife (a) lost 3–1

Also played for: Scotland (6 caps), Carnoustie Panmure

Fred Martin was the man behind the rock-solid defence that helped Aberdeen to the club's first Championship success. But it could all have been so different if his career had not taken a dramatic twist during national service.

Martin was signed by the Dons from Carnoustie Panmure in 1946 as an inside-forward, but national service followed and while turning out as a striker for Woolwich Royal Artillery an injury to the Woolwich 'keeper forced Martin between the sticks and it became a permanent transformation.

It took until the final games of the 1949–50 season for Martin to establish himself as Aberdeen's number one. He made his debut in a 3–1 defeat against East Fife at Bayview on 14 April 1950, but the result did not count against him.

By the start of the next campaign he was the first name on Dave Halliday's team sheet and came close to his first club honour when the Dons took Rangers to a replay in the 1953 Scottish Cup Final before falling to a 1–0 defeat in the second game. Aberdeen returned to Hampden for a second bite at the Scottish Cup in 1954 but this time it was Celtic who inflicted pain in the Final, winning 2–1.

The Pittodrie men refused to lick their wounds and inflicted revenge on both halves of the Old Firm with League success the following year. Rangers, Celtic and Hibs had dominated for more than two decades but Martin helped upset Scottish football's traditional pecking order.

In the 1954–55 season he and his defensive colleagues conceded just 17 goals in 30 League games as they pipped Celtic to the prize by just two points. The Hoops proved to be more of an attacking threat that year but could not match the Pittodrie side's resilience and that proved telling.

Martin recorded 11 shutouts in his 28 appearances in the League and that proved as valuable as the exploits of the famous goalscorers Paddy Buckley and Harry Yorston. By then he was also a star on the international stage, becoming the first Scottish goalkeeper to play in the World Cup Finals. The 1954 tournament in Switzerland was a harsh introduction for Martin and his teammates, who were beaten 1–0 by Austria in the opener and then 7–0 by Uruguay. In all the Dons 'keeper made six appearances for his country, including a painful 7–2 defeat against England at Wembley in 1955 which proved to be his final game for the national team.

Martin's career with Aberdeen lasted until 1961, when a series of injuries took their toll. Filling his gloves would not be easy, with six different replacements tried by the club in his final season at Pittodrie. It was John Ogston who eventually won the battle to become the next number one.

After 291 games Martin retired from football, becoming a sales manager in the whisky industry in Perthshire. His final appearance came in a 2–2 draw against Airdrie at Pittodrie on 16 January 1961.

Paul Mason

Date of birth: 3 September 1963, Liverpool

Aberdeen record:
Appearances: League 138+20, Scottish Cup 11+1, League Cup 13+2, Europe
7+1
Goals: League 23, Scottish Cup 1, League Cup 8, Europe 1
Debut: League Cup, 17 August 1988 v Arbroath (h) won 4–0

Also played for: Gronigen, Ipswich Town

Behind every great manager lies tactical awareness, masterful motivational skills and an aptitude for man management. On top of that the best bosses need an almighty slice of luck and Alex Smith had that good fortune handed to him on a plate in 1988 when he unearthed a player who went on to become an Aberdeen legend.

Smith was on a scouting mission in Europe to watch future Pittodrie goalkeeper Theo Snelders in action. While Snelders lived up to his expectations, an opposition winger by the name of Paul Mason also caught the wylie manager's eye.

Mason, a Liverpudlian, was turning out for Groningen in the Dutch League and it took an offer of £200,000 to snatch him from their grasp. His path to the Netherlands was a winding one, rejected by Everton and Tranmere as a youngster he played non-League football in England before a leg break and job loss forced him to rethink his future. Mason moved to Holland to join his brother, relaunched his football career in the amateur Leagues and finally made his mark on the professional game.

He became one of Smith's first signings at the start of a successful era for the club and despite being far from the most high profile, he was certainly one of the most effective.

Mason, a versatile player most at home on the right wing, was the main man when Smith clinched his first trophy as boss at Pittodrie. The magic date was 22 October, the year was 1989. A crowd of 61,190 had gathered at Hampden to watch Aberdeen attempt to beat Rangers in the Final of the League Cup and end a run of 19 straight wins over three years in the competition. Aberdeen had been the runners-up to Graeme Souness and his men in each of the two previous Finals, but thanks to Mason the unwanted hat-trick was avoided.

He got Aberdeen off to the perfect start when he headed a Robert Connor cross past Gers 'keeper Chris Woods, but Mark Walters levelled with a minute penalty. A tense Final was settled by the Englishman in the second half when he swept home the winner from a Charlie Nicholas flick-on to clinch the first trophy of the Scottish season.

The Dons also won the last trophy of the campaign when Mason and his teammates collected the Scottish Cup win – a penalty shoot-out victory against Celtic.

Mason was an ever present and instrumental in both Cup runs. In the League Cup he scored a double in the 4–0 second-round win over Airdrie and again in the 3–1 victory against St Mirren in the next round before his Final heroics. In the Scottish Cup he was on target in the opening round's 6–2 success against Partick, but his goals were just a tiny part of his overall contribution to the team of the late 1980s and early 1990s.

Mason made his debut from the bench in a 4–0 League Cup canter against Arbroath on 17 August 1988, and went on to make 22 starts as the Dons ran Rangers close in the Premier Division race.

The order at the top of the League was the same in 1990 and again in 1991, the year of the famous last-day decider at Ibrox which Rangers won 2–0 to win the title by two points.

Mason missed that game through injury but he consistently racked up more than 30 appearances in each of his five seasons with the club and went on to make 193 appearances, scoring 37 goals, for the Pittodrie side. One of those strikes came in the European Cup-winners' Cup, on target in a 2–0 win against Salamina in 1990.

After a Cup double in the 1989–90 season Mason played in two further Finals for the club but found himself on the losing side in the League Cup and Scottish Cup showdowns against Rangers in the 1992–93 campaign.

The Scottish Cup Final of 1993, when the Light Blues won 2–1, proved to be Mason's final appearance in a red shirt. The Dons, by that time managed by Willie Miller, doubled their money when they sold their talented midfielder to Ipswich Town for £400,000 soon after. He spent five seasons at Portman Road, the first two in the Premiership, before retiring from the game to concentrate on a new career in the hospitality trade in Suffolk.

Joe Miller

Date of birth: 8 December 1967, Glasgow

Aberdeen record:

Appearances: League 184+31, Scottish Cup 14+8, League Cup 19+5, Europe 12+2

Goals: League 32, Scottish Cup 3, League Cup 10, Europe 2

Debut: League, 22 December 1984 v Dundee United (h) lost 1–0

Also played for: Celtic, Dundee United, Raith Rovers, Parramatta Power, Clydebank, Clyde

Managed: Clyde

At the tender age of 16, Joe Miller was billed as Scotland's answer to Roy of the Rovers by Andy Roxburgh. The comparison came after the youngster had waltzed past six England defenders to earn a 2-1 win for his country in a Youth international.

Roxburgh was bowled over by the promise of a young player who was likened to George Best from the Scotland Youth coach at the time, thanks to his fluent style and ability to ghost past defenders. Alex Ferguson did not share Roxburgh's passion for dramatic comparisons, but the two coaches did share a common appreciation of Miller's ability and at club level Ferguson showed his faith when he thrust the player into first-team action just 14 days after his 17th birthday in 1984, introduced to the Pittodrie crowd as a substitute in a 1-0 defeat against Dundee United on 22 December.

Having been thrown on the scrapheap by his boyhood heroes Celtic as a schoolboy, Ferguson was quick to offer him another chance to hit the big time. Miller, having suffered one crushing blow already, was not about to let that opportunity pass him by.

His debut was his only taste of first-team action in his first season in the top squad but by the 1985-86 season Miller was a key squad man. He started 18 games, including the 2-2 European Cup quarter-final draw against IFK Gothenburg, but it was one of his four cameos from the bench which brought him his first winners' medal.

Miller came on for John Hewitt in the Scottish Cup Final against Hearts as his side coasted to a 3-0 win; the occasion whetted his appetite and further success followed both with the Dons and Celtic. The Hoops pulled off a stunning transfer coup when they beat Liverpool, who had a substantial bid rejected, as well as Manchester United and Tottenham in a hotly-contested signing race late in 1987. Billy McNeill broke the record for a transfer between two Scottish clubs with his £650,000 swoop for the Scotland Under-21 international.

The new recruit won a Premier Division winners' medal with the Parkhead club that season and added another Scottish Cup badge to his collection when Celtic defeated Dundee United in the Final. His love affair with the national Cup competition continued in 1989 when he was part of the Hoops side which defeated Rangers 1-0 to lift the trophy again – with Miller scoring the winner.

That proved to be the shining moment of his Celtic career and brought his last winners' medal with the club, although not the last of his playing career. In 1993, at the age of 25, Miller returned to Aberdeen when manager Willie Miller invested £300,000 to land his first choice for the right-wing berth vacated by Paul Mason.

His decision to return to the north east was vindicated in the first season of his second stint at Pittodrie when Aberdeen finished two places above Celtic and came within three points of champions Rangers.

In 1995-96 the flying winger won his second Dons winners' medal when he starred in the 2-0 League Cup Final win against Dundee and he remained with the club until May 1998.

Miller's 14-year association with the club was brought to an end when he signed for Dundee United on a free transfer, but it proved to be only a short stop at Tannadice. After two seasons with United he played a handful of games for Raith and Clydebank, as well as enjoying two stints in Australia, before his surprise appointment as assistant manager to former Old Firm rival Graeme Roberts at Clyde in 2005.

After a year he was promoted to manager following the club's acrimonious split with Roberts and Miller led the Bully Wee to the Scottish Football League's Challenge Cup Final in November 2006, but even after the player-manager's introduction from the bench in the second half, his side slipped to defeat against Ross County.

Willie Miller

Date of birth: 2 May 1955, Glasgow

Aberdeen record:
Appearances: League 560+1, Scottish Cup 66, League Cup 109, Europe 61
Goals: League 19, Scottish Cup 6, League Cup 3, Europe 2
Debut: League, 28 April 1973 v Morton (a) won 2–1
Manager: February 1992–February 1995

Also played for: Scotland (65 caps)

In 2004 the Dons needed a saviour and the man they turned to was Willie Miller, the player affectionately referred to as God by fans old enough to have lived through the glorious years in which he lifted more than any other Pittodrie captain.

He returned as a director and was given free reign to run the club as he saw fit. One of his first acts was to replace manager Steve Paterson with former Glasgow schools select teammate Jimmy Calderwood, and it proved to be an inspired decision as the new boss breathed new life into the Dons and restored them to the top half of the SPL. Miller's appointment to the board also completed a full set of responsibilities for the Glaswegian, having served as player and captain as well as coach and manager up to that point.

Awarded an MBE for his services to football, Miller is one of the game's rarities – a one-club man. His Pittodrie connection spans four different decades and will soon enter a fifth.

He was a product of the vast Dons scouting network and taken north from Glasgow in the early 1970s. Miller spent the 1971–72 season farmed out to Peterhead in the Highland League and sparkled as a 16-year-old striker for the Blue Toon, a prolific scorer at Recreation Park.

He made his debut for the Aberdeen first team on 28 April 1973, in a 2–1 win at Morton. It was the final game of the 1972–73 campaign and when the next season began, Miller was at its heart – transformed from attacker to defender in Jimmy Bonthrone's side.

The teenager missed only three League games in his rookie season and for 17 full seasons he was the Aberdeen bedrock. In that time he was ever present five times and made a staggering 797 appearances, to set a record which is unlikely ever to be equalled.

Miller played under Bonthrone, Ally MacLeod, Billy McNeill, Alex Ferguson and Ian Porterfield before retiring while Alex Smith and Jocky Scott were at the helm. Every one of those managers depended upon him more than any other player.

Miller had a relatively long wait for his first taste of success, at least compared to the frequency in which honours would follow. By the time Celtic were beaten 2–1 in the 1976 League Cup Final he was captain of the side. What followed was an amazing run which earned the defender a total of three Premier Division Championships, four Scottish Cup and three League Cup winner's medals and the European Cup-winners' Cup and European Super Cup.

The image of Miller holding aloft the club's first European trophy is the most iconic in the history of the Dons and more than two decades on is still being snapped up by supporters desperate for a lasting reminder of that famous night in Gothenburg when Real Madrid were humbled by Miller and his troops.

He scored 30 goals during the course of his distinguished playing career, by far the most important coming in 1985 when on 27 April a 1–1 draw against Celtic at Pittodrie clinched the Championship. A Roy Aitken penalty had given the Hoops a first-half lead but Miller's typically-powerful header from a 61st-minute Ian Porteous free-kick smashed off the post and flew into the net to leave the visitors shattered.

It took a serious knee injury to force Miller out of the team. At the age of 35 he attempted to battle on despite the pain but after playing in a 2–1 League Cup win at Hampden against Queen's Park Rangers on the opening day of the 1990–91 season, he was forced to concede defeat and concentrate on his role as a member of Smith and Scott's coaching team.

He retired having established himself not just as a legend at club level, where he was Scotland's Player of the Year in 1984, but also on the international stage. Miller made 65 appearances for Scotland between 1975 and 1989, captaining the national team 11 times and taking part in the World Cup Finals of 1982 and 1986. His solitary goal in dark blue was the winner against Wales in 1980.

In 1992 a new chapter was opened when Miller replaced Alex Smith as manager at Aberdeen and in his first season they finished runners-up to Rangers in all three domestic competitions.

After again finishing second to the Light Blues in the Premier Division in 1994 Miller embarked on a radical overhaul of the playing staff, but his form dipped and he made an emotional exit from Pittodrie in 1995, going on to carve out a career in radio and as a newspaper columnist before his return to the club in 2004 as director of football. He continues to write for the *Evening Express*.

Willie Mills

Date of birth: 28 January 1915, Alexandria
Died: 1990, Aberdeen

Aberdeen record:
Appearances: League 182, Scottish Cup 28
Goals: League 102, Scottish Cup 12
Debut: League, 20 August 1932 v Motherwell (h) drew 1–1

Also played for: Scotland (3 caps), Bridgeton Waverley, Huddersfield Town, Huntly, Keith, Lossiemouth

The names Harper and Jarvie struck fear into the heart of defences in the 1970s, while in the 1980s it was Hewitt and McGhee. Before either of these latter players had even been born, the mention of Armstrong and Mills sent a shiver down the spine.

Armstrong's scoring exploits are well documented but the all-round contribution of Willie Mills was another reason to cheer for the Pittodrie fans. Long after his retirement, Mills was still being lauded as the finest inside-forward the Dons ever had on their books. His legendary status was confirmed by the Scotland selectors, who handed him three full caps as well as a place in the team for touring matches in his heyday.

Mills took his Scotland bow on 5 October 1935, in a 1–1 draw against Wales in Cardiff and went on to help the national side to a 2–1 win against Northern Ireland later that year. He made his final appearance in dark blue in a 2–1 home defeat at the hands of the Welsh in 1936 – wearing number 10 and lining up alongside clubmate Matt Armstrong at number nine.

The outbreak of war halted competitive football but did not stop Mills in his tracks. He teamed up with Sir Stanley Matthews in a select side to tackle the Scottish Command during the conflict and outshone the English legend, scoring once to help his team to a 2–1 win in 1941.

Nine years earlier he had turned up for a trial at Pittodrie as a raw 17-year-old who had been starring for Bridgeton Waverley. His chance to impress came in a reserve game against Celtic and manager Pat Travers was left with little option when the new boy scored the winner against the Hoops. He was signed on the strength of that performance and played just one further reserve game before being promoted to the starting XI for his debut in a 1–1 draw against Motherwell at Pittodrie on 20 August 1932. Four days later, he scored his first goal in a 7–1 win against Kilmarnock. Within three months he completed another landmark when he notched his first hat-trick in an 8–1 victory against Clyde. The teenager could play.

A ratio of 18 goals in just 31 games made him a key ally to leading scorer Paddy Moore, but the tables were turned in 1933–34 when it was Mills who topped the goal chart with an incredible 28 strikes in 35 League games, including hat-tricks against Airdrie and Cowdenbeath.

The following season the Mills and Armstrong dream team truly came into its own, Mills grabbing 16 to add to the 38 scored by his strike partner. Between them they scored 54 of the club's 83 goals that season.

It was that type of form that captured the imagination of the Scotland selectors and allowed the two men to join the ranks of Aberdeen's international stars.

A shock Cup exit at the hands of Second Division side East Fife in 1938 prompted a changing of the guard at Pittodrie and Mills found himself on the way out, joining Huddersfield Town in a £6,500 deal soon after. He had scored 114 goals in 210 games.

Post-war the Dumbartonshire-born forward returned to the north east and became a familiar figure on the Highland League playing circuit during spells with Huntly, Keith and Lossiemouth. In 1957 he continued his association with the League when he was appointed trainer to Fraserburgh's contingent of Aberdeen-based players. Mills died in Aberdeen in 1990.

Jimmy Mitchell

Date of birth: 1924, Glasgow
Died: 2004

Aberdeen record:
Appearances: League 129, Scottish Cup 21, League Cup 34
Debut: League Cup, 9 August 1952 v Motherwell (a) lost 5–2

Also played for: Queen's Park Rangers, Morton, Cowdenbeath
Managed: Cowdenbeath

At number 66 in the list of Aberdeen legends is a player with the unique distinction of conceding three penalties in one game and missing four in another after an unexpected twist in his sporting career.

Mitchell's series of fouls came while playing for Aberdeen in 1953, leading to a 3-0 defeat against Celtic as Bobby Collins scored a hat-trick from the spot. His combination of misses came in 1961 – after switching to rugby with Bellahouston FPs in his home city. This time it was an Aberdeen side, Gordonians, who took advantage of his misfortune.

For a man who built his reputation as a sturdy and reliable defender, failing to score a single goal as he stuck to his duties with discipline and tenacity, Mitchell's career was far from dull. The highlight was the 1955 League Championship success with the Dons, when the number two missed just a single game in the gallop to the title flag.

He also suffered heartbreak in three Scottish Cup Finals at Hampden, once with Morton in 1948 and then twice with Aberdeen in 1953 and 1954. That pain was offset by the glory of the 1955-56 League Cup Final when Mitchell skippered the Dons to a 2-1 triumph over St Mirren to lift the trophy.

Mitchell was no stranger to the national stadium, having launched his life in football in Mount Florida with the amateurs of Queen's Park Rangers in 1943. After serving his time in the Royal Navy, the defender turned professional in 1947 with Morton and spent five years at Cappielow before Pittodrie manager Dave Halliday came calling as he ended his search for a right-back to take over from Don Emery.

His first appearance came in a 5-2 defeat at Motherwell in the League Cup on 9 August in the 1952-53 campaign and from that moment he became a mainstay for the Dons, making more appearances than any other player in his first season at the club.

Mitchell, who helped the Scottish League select to victory against England in his only representative appearance, was a loyal and dedicated servant throughout his time with the club. He made 184 appearances in just five full seasons at Pittodrie before a broken rib at the start of the 1957-58 season sidelined him and allowed Dave Caldwell to retain the jersey he had won at the tail end of the previous term.

He left to take charge of Cowdenbeath in the summer of 1958, playing on for a further year before turning his back on management to launch a new career in the insurance industry in Glasgow. It was back on home turf in 1959 that he revived his sporting ambitions by turning to rugby with Bellahouston, where he had played the oval ball game as a schoolboy. Mitchell died in 2004.

George Mulhall

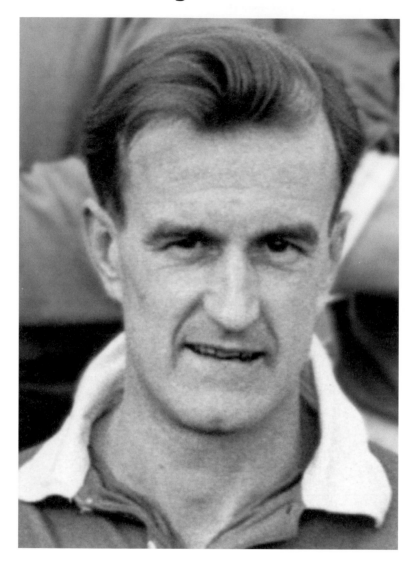

Date of birth: 8 May 1936, Falkirk

Aberdeen record:

Appearances: League 110, Scottish Cup 9, League Cup 31
Goals: League 30, Scottish Cup 2, League Cup 10
Debut: League Cup, 13 August 1956 v Hibs (a) won 1–0

Also played for: Scotland (3 caps), Kilysth Rangers, Sunderland, Cape Town City,
      Morton
Managed: Halifax Town, Bradford City, Bolton Wanderers

Aberdeen have rarely missed a trick in the transfer market, but in the case of George Mulhall the English press were in doubt and believed that the Pittodrie club had made a grave error of judgement when they sanctioned his 1962 transfer to Sunderland.

The Roker Park club paid £25,000 for the winger and it was classed as a stroke of genius on the part of manager Alan Brown. Three months into his career south of the border, Mulhall was described in reports as the finest left-winger in British football after a succession of flawless performances and glittering displays.

Mulhall played for the Dons in an era when success was thin on the ground, but he confirmed his place among the club's greats when he made his international debut on 3 October 1959, against Northern Ireland in Belfast.

It was a proud day for Aberdonians as home-grown talents Denis Law and Graham Leggat lined up in the same team as Pittodrie starlet Mulhall. The winger was a product of Kilsyth but he was Aberdeen's own, at least for a spell. He marked his Scotland debut with the fourth goal in a 4–0 win, finishing the job Fulham striker Leggat had started with the opener at Windsor Park.

By the time Mulhall made his second and third appearances for the national side in 1962 and 1963, he was a Sunderland man. Andy Beattie and Ian McColl were the men who handed him his caps.

He signed for Aberdeen under Dave Shaw and joined a club on the crest of a wave, a regular in the reserves as the first team clinched the 1955 Championship. The young recruit went on to play 12 games in the 1955–56 season and made an early contribution to the League Cup success the Dons enjoyed that term.

His first appearance was in that competition when he helped the Dons defeat Hibs 1–0 on 13 August 1956. He played five of the six Section Three games in the League Cup as Shaw's side topped the

group and scored his first goal for the club when he broke the deadlock in a 3–2 victory over Dunfermline in the second tie.

The experienced Jackie Hather reclaimed the number-11 shirt for the knock-out stages, including the Final victory against St Mirren, and Mulhall's hopes of a medal were dashed. He would never have predicted it would be his best opportunity to help the club claim some silverware.

After four seasons as a squad man he stepped up to become a regular in the 1959–60 campaign and remained camped in the first XI until his switch to Sunderland in 1962. For the Dons he played 150 games and scored 42 goals. He scored three goals in his first two games for the English side, who had Brian Clough to lead the line, and was an ever present in his first full season. In all he played 289 games and scored 66 goals for Sunderland.

He stayed at Roker until 1969, when he switched to South Africa to play for Cape Town City and helped the club to its first-ever Castle Cup success.

In 1971 Mulhall had a short spell with Morton before embarking on a long career in management, starting with his appointment as boss at Halifax in 1974. He moved on to become assistant manager at Bolton Wanderers and helped the club to promotion to the First Division before leaving to take the top job at Bradford in 1979. The former Dons winger returned to Bolton as manager soon after but departed in 1982, when the club claimed it wanted Pele to replace the departing Scot.

The Brazilian never did arrive at Burnden Park but Mulhall continued his career in management and in 1996, at the age of 60, he went back to where it all began, spending two seasons at Halifax Town and helping the club win promotion back to the Football League as Conference champions in 1998.

George Murray

Date of birth: 1940s, Glasgow

Aberdeen record:
Appearances: League 89+3, Scottish Cup 11, League Cup 20, Europe 7+2
Goals: League 4
Debut: League, 9 December 1967 v Kilmarnock (a) lost 3–0

Also played for: Drumchapel Amateurs, Motherwell
Managed: Odds-Ball, Canberra Arrows

In 1970 the famous double from Derek McKay and Joe Harper's goal won the Scottish Cup for Aberdeen. While the goalscorers deservedly stole the headlines, in a quiet corner of Hampden one man said a quiet thank you to an unsung hero in the Dons ranks as the Pittodrie playing staff celebrated.

Goalkeeper Bobby Clark cut through the euphoria in the aftermath of that glorious day in Glasgow to single out one moment which helped the club realise its dream. It came in the first half of the semi-final against Kilmarnock at Muirton Park in Perth, a game settled by another McKay Cup goal. A man who had a smaller but equally significant part to play was George Murray, who popped up on the line after Killie defender Jackie McGrory had beaten Clark with a powerful header from a corner. Murray cleared and the Dons sailed through to the Final.

The 3–1 Scottish Cup win against Celtic came at the end of a landmark season for Murray, who had started life as a midfielder with Motherwell and continued in the centre of the park after being brought to the Dons in 1967 in a swap deal involving Jimmy Wilson. He had spent seven years at Fir Park.

The Drumchapel Amateurs youth product was capped by Scotland at Under-23 level and for the Scottish League select as a midfielder, but found it difficult to break into an Aberdeen side well covered in that department as he made just 23 appearances in his first two seasons. He made his debut as a substitute in a 3–0 defeat at Kilmarnock on 9 December 1967, just

days after signing but made only 12 further appearances that term.

In 1969–70 Eddie Turnbull converted him into a left-back and Murray's Pittodrie career took off. He was the only player to start every single one of the 34 First Division games that term, missed just three League Cup ties and was an ever present in the Scottish Cup campaign.

He was a key man in 1970–71 for Turnbull and his side as they finished agonisingly just two points behind champions Celtic, but in 1972 he hung up his boots to concentrate on a new role as coach under Turnbull's successor Jimmy Bonthrone. He had first taken on coaching duties at Pittodrie as a 29-year-old the previous year and proved a valuable asset on the training ground, eager to innovate but with a firm approach to discipline at work.

In 1975 he took charge of the Dons team as caretaker manager following Bonthrone's departure, but the club opted not to promote from within and recruited Ally MacLeod instead.

He continued to serve on MacLeod's coaching staff and under Billy McNeill before resigning less than three weeks into 1978 to seek a fresh challenge after a decade with the Dons. That challenge took the form of a coaching post with Norwegian club Odds-Ball four months after his resignation from Aberdeen.

In 1980 he swapped the hostile weather conditions of Norway for the heat of Australia when he was appointed coach to the Canberra Arrows in the country's fledgling National League.

Steve Murray

Date of birth: 9 October 1944, Dumbarton

Aberdeen record:
Appearances: League 101, Scottish Cup 10, League Cup 22, Europe 7
Goals: League 20, Scottish Cup 1, League Cup 1, Europe 3
Debut: League, 18 March 1970 v St Mirren (h) drew 1–1

Also played for: Scotland (1 cap), Dundee, Celtic, Dundee United
Managed: Forfar, Montrose

Three months into 1970 Eddie Turnbull rocked the north east when he set a new Aberdeen transfer record. Dundee captain Steve Murray was the man the Dons boss was forced to dig deep for and it took £50,000 to convince the Dens Park club to part with their midfield star.

Murray, who took over the record signing tag from Joe Harper, made his debut on 18 March in a 1–1 draw at home to St Mirren. It was less than a month before the Scottish Cup Final win against Celtic but having played in the competition for Dundee in the earlier rounds, he was forced to sit out the biggest game the club played during his three years in the north east.

Turnbull heralded his new big-money buy as the man who would make his Pittodrie team tick and installed him as captain following Martin Buchan's departure early in 1972. By that time Murray was a Scotland international, having played alongside Buchan and Dons teammate Bobby Clark in a 1–0 European Championship qualifying group win over Belgium in November 1971. That game was played at Pittodrie and it proved to be Murray's solitary cap, with Tommy Docherty preferring to rely on his clutch of English-based players instead of home-based stars. John O'Hare scored the winner after five minutes to give Murray a short but perfect Scotland record.

Following his arrival at Pittodrie he played out the seven League games remaining on the card and missed just two games in the 1970–71 season as he made his mark on his new club, with 44 appearances and nine goals in domestic and European competition. Aberdeen finished second and the future looked bright as Turnbull attempted to break Celtic's dominance.

It proved to be an impossible task, with the Dons runners-up to Jock Stein's Hoops again in 1972 as Murray played out what proved to be his final full season at Pittodrie.

Murray, who had spent his entire senior career with Dundee and three years as skipper prior to signing for the Dons as a 25-year-old, was aware of the importance of his all-action displays to a club who were splitting the Old Firm. The Dumbarton-born player was also aware of his value and refused to accept the re-signing terms tabled by Dick Donald and his board at the start of the 1972–73 season. The club refused to give up hope of convincing him to stay and even rejected a £100,000 offer from Sheffield United before conceding defeat and accepting a deal worth half as much.

Celtic's £50,000 offer was approved in May 1973 and came three months after the player had asked to be relieved of the Dons captaincy as his unrest at the club grew. He made 140 appearances and scored 25 goals for Aberdeen.

After two years at Parkhead, winning the League in 1974 and the Scottish Cup, a foot injury forced his retirement from the game. Murray's involvement in the game was revived in 1979 when he was appointed as a scout by Dundee United and he made a short playing comeback with the Tannadice club within weeks of taking up the role, at the age of 33. He made five first-team appearances, winning a League Cup medal in the process, before retiring from playing permanently.

His first spell in management, with Forfar in 1980, was cut short after just five days due to business commitments, but he returned at the helm of Montrose two years later for a season. He was tempted back into football from a career as a bank manager in 1989 when he was appointed assistant manager at Dundee United under Jim McLean, but parted company with the Arabs less than a season later after a break down in the relationship between the two men, who had been teammates at Dundee. Murray was awarded a substantial settlement when the dispute went to court, returning to banking after his departure from Tannadice.

Murray combined his football and professional commitments with a love of art, first studying the subject while on Dundee's books and becoming a published cartoonist before branching out into painting and sketching everything from still life compositions to street scenes and portraits.

Charlie Nicholas

Date of birth: 30 December 1961, Glasgow

Aberdeen record:
Appearances: League 75+2, Scottish Cup 16, League Cup 8, Europe 3
Goals: League 30, Scottish Cup 5, League Cup 1
Debut: League, 9 January 1988 v Hibs (a) drew 0–0

Also played for: Scotland (20 caps), Celtic, Arsenal, Clyde

Charlie Nicholas is a Celtic man through and through. He grew up idolising the Hoops players of the 1960s and 1970s, made his name as a teenage starlet at Parkhead in the 1980s and left Aberdeen behind in the 1990s to return for a second spell with his boyhood heroes.

Despite his unbreakable ties to the Glasgow club, his final act as a Dons player was one which underlined his claim for a place in Pittodrie folklore. In the build up to the 1990 Scottish Cup Final between Aberdeen and Celtic, the worst-kept secret in the game was that Nicholas was ready to leave the north east to sign up at Parkhead.

Before then he had a game to take care of and when it ended tied at 0–0 after extra-time, the spectre of a penalty shoot-out loomed. Nicholas, never one to shirk his responsibility, was nominated as a penalty taker and struck a crippling blow against the men who would soon be his teammates when he rifled home his contribution to the shoot-out on the way to Aberdeen's 9–8 victory.

In 30 months with the Dons he collected two winners' medals: one from the Scottish Cup showdown with his future employers and the other in the 2–1 1989 League Cup Final victory against Rangers.

Nicholas cost £500,000 when Ian Porterfield swooped to take him back to Scotland from Highbury in January 1988. Arguably, he is the biggest signing the club has ever made. Paul Bernard is the record signing, but his arrival was put in the shade by the Nicholas deal.

The Glaswegian had been the darling of Celtic and Scottish football after bursting onto the scene in 1980 as a 19-year-old for the Hoops. The cultured attacker was named Scottish Player of the Year in 1983 and also collected the Scottish Professional Footballers' Association Award in the same year.

He was coveted by the English giants Arsenal and Liverpool, but it was the Londoners who won him over and in 1983 Nicholas switched to the Gunners in a £800,000 deal. He won a League Cup-winners' medal when he scored a double against Liverpool in the 1987 Final but under George Graham his free-flowing attacking style did not fit. The result was his shock move to Aberdeen and a brief but entertaining glimpse of his star quality for the Dons fans.

Nicholas made his debut in a 0–0 draw against Hibs at Easter Road on 9 January 1988. One week later a crowd of over 20,000 turned out to see their new hero on home turf for the first time, a staggering turnout considering lowly Dunfermline were the opposition. To put it in context, just over 11,000 had paid through the gate to watch the same fixture at Pittodrie in the first half of the same season.

Within months Porterfield had been replaced by Alex Smith and Jocky Scott, but Nicholas was still in the thick of things. Under Smith the gifted striker struck up a lethal partnership with Hans Gillhaus, another high-profile recruit. Between them they scored 17 goals in the 17 Premier Division matches they played together in the 1989–90 season. Opponents soon realised that if one didn't get you, the other certainly would.

Following his return to Celtic in 1990, Nicholas spent five years at Parkhead. In two spells with the Hoops he won the League title twice and the League Cup once.

The last of 20 Scotland caps was won while he was on the Pittodrie payroll, a 2–1 win against Cyprus at Hampden in 1989 under Andy Roxburgh. His international career brought five goals and spanned six years, including the 1986 World Cup in Mexico in which he made two appearances.

At club level, Nicholas was reunited with Alex Smith at Clyde in 1995 when he made the move with a view to launching a coaching career but played on for a year before making a change in direction.

He retired from playing in 1996 and quickly forged a new career in the media industry as a football analyst with Sky television and a newspaper columnist. His first taste of life in front of the lens came as the result of the biggest disappointment of his Dons career, when his performances in helping Aberdeen to the runners'-up spot in the Premier Division were not enough to earn him a place in Roxburgh's squad for the World Cup in Italy in 1990. Almost two decades of the on-field achievements are a fading memory, but now Nicholas is playing to a larger audience than ever before.

Dave Robb

Date of birth: 15 December 1947, Broughty Ferry

Aberdeen record:

Appearances: League 251+14, Scottish Cup 27+2, League Cup 51+4, Europe 16

Goals: League 78, Scottish Cup 10, League Cup 8, Europe 2

Debut: Scottish Cup, 28 January 1967 v Dundee (a) won 5–0

Also played for: Scotland (5 caps), Newburgh, Tampa Bay Rowdies, Norwich City, Dunfermline Athletic

In a split second inside extra-time in a Hampden Cup Final, Dave Robb had the chance to make himself a legend and, as he did 98 times for the club in the space of 12 years, he hit the back of the net without a second thought.

That was the most important goal in his career and came in the 93rd minute of the 1976 League Cup Final, as a match which had enthralled a crowd close to 70,000 moved into extra-time. Celtic were the opponents and it was the Hoops who drew the first blood. Kenny Dalglish was judged to have been fouled by Drew Jarvie inside the Dons box and the Celtic striker dusted himself down before converting the opener from the spot in the 11th minute. It was Jarvie who made it 1–1 just 13 minutes later with a header from a Joe Harper assist and the tie remained in the balance until Robb struck the killer blow, with his first goal in eight appearances in that season's Cup run.

It was the second winners' medal Robb had claimed with Aberdeen, having been at the beating heart of the team which had won the Scottish Cup in 1970. Again Celtic were the defeated finalists, falling to a 3–1 defeat on that occasion, and Robb had played his part in the Final and in the run to Hampden, having played in four of the five ties and scored a double in the 4–0 first-round victory against Clyde to set the ball rolling.

When he first savoured that winning feeling Robb was in his fourth season as a Pittodrie player. The Dundonian, signed in 1965 from junior side Newburgh, spent a season and a half learning his trade in the Dons reserves in five different positions, before being handed his senior debut by Eddie Turnbull in a 5–0 victory against Dundee in the first round of the Scottish Cup at Dens Park on 28 January 1967.

At 19 he had taken his bow as a right-winger, but his combative style and full-blooded approach ensured he would have a more central role to play in the seasons ahead, both in midfield and attack.

His goalscoring ability was demonstrated when he scored the first hat-trick of his Aberdeen career in a 6–0 mauling of Clyde at Pittodrie at the start of the 1969–70 season by which time he was an established first-team player, having made 42 appearances the season before and 20 in 1967–68 as he built on his introduction to the first team the previous term.

Between 1969 and 1972 he played in excess of 40 games a season for four consecutive campaigns.

The Cup win in 1970 provided an early Cup highlight and the following year there was cause for celebration on the international stage. Robb made his Scotland debut against Portugal in Lisbon in April 1971 as Bobby Brown's side fell to a 2–0 defeat. Each of his five caps came in the same year as his debut was followed by defeats against England, Denmark and the USSR, as well as a draw with Wales.

While his international career ended at the age of 24, Robb's work with his club was far from over and he remained at Pittodrie until 1978, playing under Eddie Turnbull as well as Jimmy Bonthrone, Ally MacLeod and Billy McNeill.

In addition to two Cup-winners' medals, Robb collected League runners'-up badges in 1971, 1972 and 1977. He overcame a serious injury in 1974 and battled to reclaim his first-team place. In his final campaign in 1977–78 he played 13 games and scored a hat-trick in a 4–1 win at home to Motherwell just over a month before his final outing in a 2–1 victory against Celtic in January 1978. There was no chance of going out with a whimper.

When Robb left it was for the glitz and glamour of the North American Soccer League, signing a three-year deal with the Tampa Bay Rowdies early in 1978. He combined his US commitments with a stint at Norwich City before a brief spell with Dunfermline in 1981. That year he retired from playing to take up a new career in the oil industry and has also been involved in the licensed trade in the north east.

David Robertson

Date of birth: 17 October 1968, Aberdeen

Aberdeen record:
Appearances: League 133+2, Scottish Cup 10, League Cup 21+1, Europe 9+1
Goals: League 2, League Cup 1
Debut: League, 16 August 1986 v Hamilton (h) won 2–0

Also played for: Scotland (3 caps), Rangers, Leeds United, Montrose
Managed: Elgin City, Montrose

At the end of his debut season David Robertson arrived at Pittodrie to find a new four-year contract awaiting his signature. The teenage defender was one of the hottest properties in British football and the Dons were sending out a clear warning to the big guns, who had set their sights on the speedy left-back.

The Aberdonian did not need time to think about his next move, agreeing to a deal which would see him spend his key developing years in the north east.

Robertson was signed from local juvenile side Deeside by Alex Ferguson and launched his Aberdeen career as the legendary manager was winding down his days in Scotland. Robertson was introduced gently by Ferguson, in front of home fans as a substitute against Premier Division underdogs Hamilton, on 16 August 1986. The Dons won 2–0 and the 17-year-old rookie's initiation had gone to plan. It would be rapidly intensified, however, under new manager Ian Porterfield following his arrival at the end of the year.

Robertson made his first start less than two months later and by the end of that 1986–87 season he had 42 appearances under his belt across all three domestic competitions and the European Cup-winners' Cup. He was also being fast-tracked at international level, with a Scotland B cap at the tender age of 18 after less than a season in the club game.

A knee injury in a match against Celtic at Hogmanay in 1988 proved to be only a temporary setback and in the 1989–90 season Robertson enjoyed his finest spell in the red of his home-town team. The Dons completed an Old Firm Cup double, with a 2–1 victory over Rangers in the League Cup Final followed up with the dramatic penalty shoot-out win against Celtic in the Scottish Cup showpiece. A Premier Division runners'-up medal completed an impressive haul for the emerging talent and he was a key part of the 1991 side which ran Rangers even closer in the League, only missing out on the title on the final day of the season when a 2–0 defeat to Rangers kept the flag at Ibrox by virtue of two points.

That heartbreak proved to be the catalyst for Robertson's switch to the champions in a £970,000 deal in the summer of 1991. He had been courted by a string of English clubs since making his breakthrough in the Aberdeen team, with managers attracted by his searing pace and attacking instincts from his berth on the left side of defence.

Robertson never hid the fact he was an Aberdeen supporter from childhood, but his ambition was to win major honours and he saw Ibrox as the best place to do that, despite the tension between two bitter rivals caused for him off the field. He and his family learnt to deal with abuse from the Dons fans who had once sung his praises from the stands of Pittodrie.

The defender was 22 when he switched to the Govan club and an established Scotland Under-21 international. It proved an astute move, as he went on to become a main man in the dominant Light Blues side of that period.

Between 1991 and 1997 he won the League Championship every year and added Scottish Cup and the League Cup medals as well as playing European football year in and year out. With Rangers he also realised his Scotland ambitions, but his tally of three caps, including his 1992 debut in a 1–0 home win against Northern Ireland, did not do justice to his standing in the club game

In 1997 he was on the move again and his availability prompted talks with Italian Serie-A side Torino before Robertson eventually opted for a lucrative move to the English Premiership with a £500,000 transfer to Leeds United, led by George Graham, at the age of 28.

Injury restricted his appearances for the Elland Road side and he retired in March 2000. Two years later he moved back to the north east and joined the coaching staff at Montrose, combining his training ground duties with a brief playing comeback. He launched his management career with Elgin City in 2003 and returned to Montrose to take the top job at Links Park in 2006, before leaving the following year to coach in America.

Doug Rougvie

Date of birth: 24 May 1956, Ballingry

Aberdeen record:

Appearances: League 181+19, Scottish Cup 26, League Cup 45+7, Europe
                   28+2
Goals: League 19, League Cup 2
Debut: League Cup, 9 August 1975 v Celtic (a) lost 1–0

Also played for: Scotland (1 cap), Keith, Chelsea, Brighton, Shrewsbury, Fulham,
                   Dunfermline, Montrose, Huntly, Cove Rangers
Managed: Montrose, Huntly, Cove Rangers

In 12 years on the Aberdeen staff Doug Rougvie became a playing legend, feared opponent and cult hero during the glory days of the late 1970s and early 1980s.

On the pitch the Rougvie name went hand in hand with heart-on-the-sleeve performances and a steely defensive resolve, while off the park he was synonymous with some of the more bizarre incidents of the time, all of which endeared him to the Pittodrie faithful.

Tales of the European Cup-winners' Cup hero's exploits are the stuff of legend, including his dispute over his decision to swap the safety of four wheels for the high-speed thrills of a motorbike during Alex Ferguson's reign. The manager was not amused, to put it mildly, but Rougvie's passion for bikes lives on to this day.

During the 1984 Scottish Cup victory parade the towering stopper lost his false teeth from the top deck of the open-top bus as it made its way along Union Street, prompting a comical scramble among the adoring fans below. They were eventually launched back onto the bus to a grateful Rougvie, but what price would those gnashers fetch in the world of internet auction sites today?

Rougvie's larger-than-life character in the dressing room did not disguise his fearsome reputation and formidable appearance once he crossed the white line, with the 6ft 2in defender no stranger to suspensions in a lengthy playing career.

The Fifer signed for the Dons from juvenile football in 1972 and was farmed out to Keith for an early introduction to the man's game, winning a Highland League Cup-winners' medal to whet his appetite for what was to follow with the Dons.

He made his breakthrough under Jimmy Bonthrone in 1975 in a 1–0 League Cup defeat against Celtic on 9 August but had a patient three-year wait to truly establish himself in the first team as an Alex Ferguson player, sharing the duties of partnering Willie Miller at the heart of the defence with Alex McLeish and Willie Garner in the 1978–79 campaign.

That season he had his first taste of controversy, becoming the only player in the history of the League Cup to be red carded in a Final after a penalty box incident involving Rangers striker Derek Johnstone. The Ibrox men won 2–1, with Rougvie and his teammates furiously protesting his innocence. The

two men at the centre of the clash later became teammates at Chelsea, but Rougvie refused to forgive and forget the striker for his part in one of the most disappointing afternoons in football.

The following term he had switched to left-back and made 22 starts in the League Championship-winning team of 1980 to collect his first medal as a Dons player. The Scottish Cup followed in 1982, when Rangers were beaten 4–1 in the Final to pave the way for the European Cup-winners' Cup success in which Rougvie had a major part to play. He missed just two ties in that victorious run to Gothenburg glory, one leg of both the first and second rounds, and answered an SOS from Ferguson for the 2–1 Final win against Real Madrid when he switched from left-back to the right side of the defence to fill the place of the injured Stuart Kennedy.

With another Scottish Cup medal in the bag courtesy of a 1–0 win over Rangers in the 1983 Final, Rougvie was an unmovable member of Ferguson's renowned side and added another Scottish Cup badge to his collection after a 2–1 Final win against Celtic in 1984, as well as a European Super Cup medal when he played in the first leg of the 1983 win against Hamburg.

In December 1983 Rougvie was capped by Scotland manager Jock Stein against Northern Ireland in Belfast. It ended in a 2–0 defeat but completed his set of domestic honours, European success and international recognition by the time he was 27.

In the summer of 1984 Rougvie moved to Chelsea in a £250,000 deal and went on to have spells with Brighton, Shrewsbury and Fulham before returning to his roots with Dunfermline in 1989.

He spent a season with the Pars before, at the age of 34, being appointed co-manager of Montrose with former Pittodrie teammate Chich McLelland. He won promotion to the First Division with the Angus side before being replaced by Jim Leishman in 1992, continuing his career in the Highland League as a player for Steve Pateron's dominant Huntly side of the 1990s. Rougvie succeeded Paterson as manager at Christie Park in 1995 and enjoyed title success before parting company with the club. His last involvement in the senior game was as manager of Cove Rangers immediately after his Huntly tenure, now concentrating instead on his career in Aberdeen's oil industry.

Ian Scanlon

Date of birth: 13 July 1952, Birkenshaw

Aberdeen record:
Appearances: League 92+13, Scottish Cup 10+2, League Cup 18+1, Europe
                  10+2
Goals: League 12, Scottish Cup 6, League Cup 2
Debut: League, 29 April 1978 v Hibs (a) drew 1–1

Also played for: East Stirling, Notts County, St Mirren

Aberdeen had not won the Scottish title for quarter of a century when they travelled to Easter Road on 3 May 1980. The Dons needed a victory against struggling Hibs and for third-placed St Mirren to take a point against second-placed Celtic for the long wait to end, and that afternoon in Edinburgh it all fell into place.

Steve Archibald broke the deadlock in the capital after 26 minutes and two minutes later Andy Watson doubled the advantage. After the interval a double from Ian Scanlon, with a Mark McGhee goal sandwiched in between, put them on easy street.

With a 5-0 win in the bag, a tense wait for the delayed final whistle at Love Street ended when news filtered through that the Saints had held the Parkhead men to a 0-0 win. The Premier Division prize was Aberdeen's and Scanlon was an unlikely hero.

This was unlikely for two particular reasons. The first was that he had actually quit football years earlier, claiming he had become disenchanted with the game. The second was that he had told manager Alex Ferguson he wanted to leave his club 17 months before collecting his Championship medal. Fortunately, on that occasion Ferguson was in a forgiving mood and the wide man remained firmly in his plans.

Scanlon was an unpredictable talent but gave the 1980 title-winning side a valuable outlet on the left wing. His tendency to beat his marker more than once before finally delivering a cross infuriated Ferguson and provoked the famous hair-dryer treatment more than once, but Scanlon kept his place on the team sheet.

In that Championship-winning season he featured in all but seven of the League games, starting 25 and making four appearances from the bench. He scored eight Premier Division goals, including that vital double against Hibs to clinch the flag. In the Scottish Cup that year he scored the only hat-trick of his Dons career, with a treble in the 5-0 win over Arbroath in a third-round replay.

Scanlon was familiar with going home with the match ball. In 1974, while starring for Notts County, he scored three goals in the space of 165 seconds. That still was not enough to win the match, with Sheffield Wednesday claiming a 3-3 draw.

He had arrived at Notts County as a teenager from East Stirling in 1972 and became a Meadow Lane favourite leading the line for the Magpies. At the age of 21 he topped the County scoring chart for the first time and continued to be their main man in attack until his dramatic decision to retire in November 1977, at the age of 25. He claimed to have fallen out of love with the game and planned to use an inheritance to open a pub in the Nottingham area.

His exile proved short and in March 1978 he was back in the game and back at the top, after Aberdeen manager Billy McNeill negotiated a £40,000 deal with Notts County to enable Scanlon to make his comeback with the Dons.

After regaining his sharpness with nine reserve-team outings he made his first-team debut from the bench in the final League game of the 1977-78 season and marked his return to action with the equaliser in a 1-1 draw at Easter Road. That tempted McNeill to include him in the squad for the Scottish Cup Final against Rangers a week later but there was to be no repeat of his super-sub exploits, with the Dons falling to a 2-1 defeat.

Ferguson replaced McNeill that summer and installed Scanlon as his first-choice number 11, but just three months into the campaign he knocked on the manager's door to request a transfer after he and his wife failed to settle in the north east. His target was a return to England or a switch across the Atlantic to America, where his wife's parents were based. Despite interest from the Washington Diplomats the £100,000 price tag scared off the US side and after rejecting the chance to sign for Jack Charlton at Sheffield Wednesday, he gave up on his plans for a Pittodrie exit and focused on his job in the first team.

Despite that off-field unrest Scanlon still appeared in 45 games in the 1978-79 season and was back at his elegant best for the victorious League campaign the following season. He also featured in the 0-0 draw against Dundee United in the League Cup Final and in the 3-0 defeat in the replay.

A League runners'-up medal followed in 1981, when he played in all but one of Aberdeen's games in the Premier Division, before a switch to St Mirren as part of the deal which brought Peter Weir to Pittodrie.

Scanlon finally realised his ambition to venture into the licensed trade when he opened a pub in Glasgow following his departure from the Buddies.

Jocky Scott

Date of birth: 14 January 1948, Aberdeen

Aberdeen record:
Appearances: League 52+11, Scottish Cup 4, League Cup 11+1
Goals: League 17, Scottish Cup 1, League Cup 4
Debut: League Cup, 20 August 1975 v Dumbarton (a) won 1–0
Manager: August 1988 to September 1991

Also played for: Scotland (2 caps), Chelsea, Dundee, Seattle Sounders
Managed: Dundee, Dunfermline, Arbroath, Notts County, Raith Rovers

Jocky Scott was a Cup-double winning co-manager with Aberdeen in his successful stint alongside Alex Smith in the late 1980s and early 1990s, but he also tasted the sweet taste of victory as a Dons player.

Scott's goals helped earn his home-town club a place in the 1976 League Cup Final against Celtic and he was part of the side which defeated Celtic 2-1 to lift the trophy. Drew Jarvie and Davie Robb were the players on target in that Hampden showdown but Scott's own contribution should not be underestimated. He put his name on the scoresheet in the 2-0 quarter-final replay against Stirling Albion and helped himself to a hat-trick in the memorable 5-1 demolition of Rangers in the semi-final.

That Cup run, under Ally MacLeod, was the peak of Scott's time in a red jersey. He was recruited by Jimmy Bonthrone in the summer of 1975 when the Pittodrie manager parted with £15,000 and Ian Purdie to secure the versatile attacker as he prepared for life after Joe Harper.

Scott, who was 27 when he returned home to the north east, had twice been capped by Scotland four years previously but failed to add to those appearances he notched up while playing for Dundee. He had also been capped by Scotland at Schoolboy level while a pupil at Aberdeen Grammar School, traditionally a rugby hotbed, before moving to Chelsea on an apprenticeship in 1963 from Aberdeen Lads' Club Spurs.

Homesickness led him back to Scotland just a year later when his long relationship with Dundee began. With the Dens Park side he established himself as a powerful and potent striker, helping the Tayside men to the League Cup in 1974.

He was a regular in his first full season on the Pittodrie playing staff, following in the footsteps of his father Willie who had turned out for the Dons in the 1930s, but made more sporadic appearances in the next two.

In November 1977, a year after his League Cup Final win and after a brief stint on loan to Seattle in the North American Soccer League, Scott returned to Dens Park in a £15,000 deal and within two years had started his journey in coaching with the club.

He started out as reserve-team coach at Dundee before stepping up to take on first-team duties in 1981 under Donald Mackay, signaling the end of his playing days. He went on to serve under Archie Knox

and had the Dons to thank for his promotion to the Dens Park manager's seat.

When Knox returned to Pittodrie to link up with Alex Ferguson for a second spell in 1986 it was Scott who benefited, becoming a manager in his own right for the first time at the age of 38. Within two years he followed the same route when he was appointed co-manager with Alex Smith in 1988 with the Dons, part of a three-man management team completed by former teammate Drew Jarvie.

The League Cup and Scottish Cup double in the 1989–90 season vindicated the board's decision to go with safety in numbers, but Scott was keen to branch out on his own again and got the chance with Dunfermline in September 1991.

He spent two seasons with the Pars and later went on to serve as a coach under Alex Miller at Hibs, which included a spell as caretaker boss at Easter Road, before a brief stint in charge at Arbroath. Scott returned as manager at Dundee in 1998, earning the club promotion to the SPL, but was replaced by Ivano Bonetti at the start of the club's ill-fated spending spree in 2000.

Notts County then lured him to English football, with a brief return to take charge of Raith Rovers in 2002 where he also served on the coaching staff at Plymouth Argyle and Sunderland. He added Denmark to his CV in 2005 when he spent a season with Viborg.

Scott Severin

Date of birth: 15 February 1979, Stirling

Aberdeen record:
Appearances: League 93+1, Scottish Cup 3, League Cup 5
Goals: League 8
Debut: League, 7 August 2004 v Rangers (h) drew 0–0

Also played for: Scotland (15 caps up to June 2007), Hearts

When the current club captain Scott Severin signed on the dotted line at Pittodrie in the summer of 2004, the club completed a hat-trick by recruiting a defender, midfielder and attacker rolled into one.

Under Jimmy Calderwood the Stirling-born player has patrolled all three of those beats, albeit fleetingly up front, for Aberdeen and proved an accomplished performer in each department. The ideal role is at the centre of the team, but injuries to Dutch sweeper Karim Touzani following his arrival in 2006 forced the Dons boss to use Severin as a more than able deputy in that area.

Strong on the ball and an intelligent passer, Severin is the perfect modern midfielder. His tackling ability and reading of the game make him a well-tuned defender, while a powerful shot have ensured a clutch of spectacular and important goals. A vicious volley to seal a 2–1 win against Hibs in the 90th minute of the October 2006 meeting of the two sides was credited as one of the finest Pittodrie has ever seen.

His qualities have not surprisingly attracted the interest of Scotland's national team bosses and his caps earnt him a place among lofty company in the history of Aberdeen Football Club.

Severin's debut for the national side came as a Hearts player in a 2–1 win over Lithuania at Hampden in 2001, at the end of Craig Brown's tenure as Scotland coach. He added a further 14 appearances at the game's top level under Berti Vogts and Walter Smith up to the start of the 2006–07 season, with seven of those made after his switch from Tynecastle to Aberdeen.

When Alex McLeish was appointed to the national team manager's post in 2007, he included Severin in his first squad and the player looks set to continue to play a part in the Scotland scene.

The versatile player established himself as a mainstay of the Hearts team at the tail end of the 1998–99 season, aged just 19 at the time. The departure of manager Jim Jefferies in 2000 did not hinder his progress in Gorgie and as part of Craig Levein's side he continued to flourish, sampling European football for the first time in the 2000–01 campaign to add to an impressive CV.

Hearts and Severin were back in the UEFA Cup in his final season at the club and by the time he left he had clocked up 175 appearances in just five full seasons.

Frustratingly, European football proved hard to come by with Aberdeen but his move to the north east did coincide with a revival in the club's fortunes, finishing fourth in the SPL in his debut season in 2004–05 compared to 11th the previous term.

Severin has had to overcome niggling injury problems during his time on the Aberdeen staff but has come through those stresses and strains to establish himself as a vital cog in the machine which has emerged as a major player in the top half of the SPL.

His influence both on and off the park was noted when Calderwood appointed him vice-captain to fellow Scotland squad man Russell Anderson. Along with Anderson he emerged as an important influence on the emerging young players around him at Pittodrie, with Calderwood holding the duo up as a shining example of what can be achieved as he aims to propel more of his players into the international set-up. Severin was appointed captain in 2007 following Anderson's move to Sunderland.

Duncan Shearer

Date of birth: 28 August 1962, Fort William

Aberdeen record:

Appearances: League 109+43, Scottish Cup 13+5, League Cup 11+4, Europe 4+4

Goals: League 54, Scottish Cup 8, League Cup 14, Europe 2

Debut: League, 1 August 1992 v Hibs (h) won 3–0

Also played for: Scotland (7 caps), Clach, Chelsea, Huddersfield Town, Swindon Town, Blackburn Rovers, Inverness Caley Thistle

Managed: Buckie Thistle

In 1981 a young and raw striker from Fort William travelled down to Aberdeen and smashed home five goals in a single practice match for the Dons under the watchful eye of manager Alex Ferguson.

The 19-year-old goal machine was Duncan Shearer, and nobody would have predicted that afternoon that it would take him more than a decade to finally take his bow at Pittodrie.

Shearer, then starring for Clach in the Highland League, never won a coveted contract with the north-east side and instead ended up moving from Lochaber to the bright lights of London in 1983 to sign for Chelsea in a £22,000 deal.

Shearer's route to Dons stardom was long and winding, forcing himself to the fringes of the Stamford Bridge first team and making a handful of appearances for the Blues, scoring three goals in two games in the absence of Kerry Dixon and David Speedie before switching to Huddersfield in 1986.

He became a prolific scorer in the English Leagues, continuing his progress with Swindon Town when he moved in a club-record £250,000 deal in 1988. Four years later his penalty box exploits attracted the interest of Kenny Dalglish and a £700,000 move to Blackburn confirmed the pace at which the Highlander's stock was rising.

Shearer spent just four months at Ewood Park before Aberdeen finally moved in and got their man – incredibly at the fourth time of asking. In 1981 a combination of factors saw him slip through the Pittodrie net as a teenager, in 1987 Ian Porterfield received a call from Huddersfield offering the striker at a cut-price £250,000 but rejected the deal while in March 1992, manager Willie Miller lost out to Blackburn when he initially made his move. Miller's persistence paid off in July that year when his £500,000 bid was accepted and Shearer travelled north to finally join the Aberdeen staff.

To say he was worth the wait is an understatement. Shearer finally introduced himself to the Pittodrie crowd on 1 August 1992, when he struck a double in a 3–0 win against Hibs. The account was open, but those two goals were far from the final deposits in that debut season.

Shearer was the runaway scoring king that term, putting 28 goals on the board with a collection that featured a League Cup hat-trick against Falkirk, followed by consecutive trebles in the Premier Division against Partick Thistle and Hearts in incredible games which the Dons won 7–0 and 6–2 respectively. His partnership with Mixu Paatelainen was formidable physically and technically, with the imposing Finnish international adding 20 goals himself as part of a freescoring side. Eoin Jess scored 19 and Scott Booth grabbed 16 – Miller's team was not short of attacking options.

Those goals earned the runners'-up spot in the League and took Aberdeen to both Finals in the knock-out competitions, Shearer's goal in the League Cup not enough to prevent his side slipping to a 2–1 defeat against Rangers after extra-time and the Ibrox men winning the Scottish Cup Final by the same margin.

A haul of 26 goals made Shearer the leading scorer again in the 1993–94 season, but once again honours proved illusive with Rangers pipping the Dons to the title by just three points. It took until November 1995 for Shearer to finally get his hands on silverware with Aberdeen. The striker did his bit to take the trophy back to Pittodrie, giving his side a comfortable 2–0 cushion with his goal to add to the opener from Billy Dodds in the first half of the League Cup Final against Dundee.

The medal was Shearer's major honour from his Aberdeen playing days, but the Dons also helped him realise his Scotland dream. At the age of 31 he made his international debut in a 2–1 win in Austria in 1994 and went on to make six further appearances in dark blue, scoring against Finland and Holland along the way.

In 1997, at the age of 35, the striker returned to his Highland roots when he signed for Steve Paterson at Caley Thistle. He helped the Inverness side gain promotion from the Second Division, earning promotion to assistant manager, and late in 2002 the duo were headhunted by Aberdeen to form a new coaching dream team.

Shearer's second stint at Pittodrie, as assistant manager, ended in May 2004, when Jimmy Calderwood and Jimmy Nicholl were recruited to take charge after a disappointing season in which the club had finished 11th after a huge cost-cutting exercise on the playing front.

Shearer, now living in Inverness, returned to football as manager of Highland League title challengers Buckie Thistle in 2004.

Neil Simpson

Date of birth: 15 November 1961, London

Aberdeen record:

Appearances: League 200+18, Scottish Cup 34, League Cup 33+4, Europe
                 37+5
Goals: League 19, Scottish Cup 5, League Cup 1, Europe 6
Debut: League, 20 December 1980 v Partick Thistle (a) drew 1–1

Also played for: Scotland (5 caps), Newcastle United, Motherwell, Cove Rangers

Neil Simpson is one of the four men who were with Aberdeen every step of the way on the road to glory in Gothenburg in 1983, playing in each of the 11 European Cup-winners' Cup ties and starring throughout. The midfielder was part of the unbreakable spine which ran through Alex Ferguson's side on that run and joined goalkeeper Jim Leighton, defender Willie Miller and striker Mark McGhee on the list of ever presents.

Simpson was among the group of six players who scored in the opening game against Sion as Aberdeen cruised to a 7-0 win, but it was far from his most important strike of the campaign. In the breathtaking, nerve-shredding quarter-final second leg against Bayern Munich at Pittodrie, it was Simpson who cancelled out Klaus Augenthaler's early opener for the Germans, forcing the ball home in the 38th minute from an Erick Black header in his typical never-say-die spirit.

That goal helped the Dons to the famous 3-2 win against Bayern and set-up the semi-final against Watercshei for which Simpson was on form and on target again, rampaging through the Belgian side's defence in the fourth minute to score. It was not the first goal, that honour went to Eric Black two minutes earlier, and the 5-1 home-leg triumph made the return match on the continent academic. Aberdeen were on their way to Gothenburg.

Simpson was a main man for the Dons yet he had only celebrated his 21st birthday six months before he celebrated his finest moment on a football pitch. He was a player who had been tipped for greatness from an early age. Born in London but brought up in Newmachar in Aberdeenshire, he linked up with the Dons as a teenager after learning the game with Middlefield Boys Club in Aberdeen and was part of Andy Roxburgh's Scotland Under-17 and Under-18 sides before he had made his breakthrough at club level.

Simpson was introduced to first-team football by Ferguson on 20 December 1980, as a substitute in a 1-1 draw at Partick Thistle. By the end of the season he was emerging as a key player, starting each of the final 10 League games as Aberdeen lost the title race to Celtic.

Honours soon followed thick and fast as Simpson collected a Scottish Cup-winners' medal after the 4-1 win against Rangers in 1982 and a matching badge the following year after a 1-0 victory against the same side, both Finals going to extra-time.

The European Cup-winners' Cup success in 1983 had propelled the young midfielder to the forefront of European football and he stepped up to the international stage just months later, making his Scotland debut under Jock Stein in a 0-0 draw against Northern Ireland at Hampden.

Simpson, a Scotland Under-21 captain, won a total of five full caps, the first three awarded by Stein before a three-year absence from the national team between the summers of 1984 and 1987, when Simpson was recalled by Andy Roxburgh for an Auld Enemy clash. He patrolled the midfield as Scotland drew 0-0 with England, playing again in the return match the following year at Wembley when the hosts ran out 1-0 winners.

Having added Premier Division Championship-winning medals to his collection in 1984 and 1985, as well as yet another Scottish Cup-winners' badge in 1984 when he played in the 2-1 extra-time victory over Celtic, Simpson also earned a second continental prize when he scored the 47th-minute opener in the 2-0 European Super Cup Final second-leg game at Pittodrie.

In 1990 after 331 appearances and 31 goals, he left his first club behind on the back of 12 years' service in the first team and moved to Newcastle United in a £180,000 transfer. He joined Mark McGhee and Roy Aitken on Tyneside but left a year later to join Motherwell, spending two years at Fir Park before retiring through injury after a brief stint back in Aberdeen with Cove Rangers.

Simpson's expertise was put to good use by the SFA, who appointed him as the north's community development officer, and that post led to a return to Aberdeen as the club's senior community coach before his appointment as assistant director of the Dons youth academy in 2006.

Billy Smith

Date of birth: 1931, Aberdeen

Aberdeen record:
Appearances: League 71, Scottish Cup 6, League Cup 16
Debut: League, 2 January 1952 v East Fife (h) won 2–1

Also played for: Sunnybank, Third Lanark, Deveronvale

You just don't get commitment like you used to in football. In August 1953 Billy Smith broke off from his wedding celebrations to dash from his big day at Garthdee church in his striped morning suit to make the short journey to Pittodrie. Without time to catch his breath, he pulled on the number-three shirt and helped the Dons to a 2–0 win over Airdrie in the group stage of the League Cup. After a quick post-match wash, he made it back to the Palace Restaurant in time to catch the rest of his own wedding reception as it got into full flow.

The following day he took his new bride on a one-day honeymoon – making sure he was back in time for another League Cup tie, against East Fife, three days after he had stood at the alter. Now that's devotion.

Smith was a true unsung hero at Pittodrie, recruited from local junior side Sunnybank as a forward. He made his debut in a 2–1 win against East Fife on home turf on 2 January 1952 and became the man that manager Dave Halliday utilised as a Mr Fixit.

In his first three seasons as a Dons player he played at left-back, right-half, centre-half, inside-right and inside-left. He even stood in for injured goalkeeper Fred Martin twice.

Smith flitted in and out of the team but was always considered a dependable performer when required. His sole Scottish Cup Final appearance of 1953–54 illustrated that point perfectly – called into the side for the Final against Celtic, who won 2–1.

When the utility man finally found a settled position it led to a landmark campaign for Aberdeen. With Smith firmly planted at left-back, the Dons won their first-ever League Championship in the 1954–55 campaign.

He played 25 of the 30 League games that term as well as every League Cup tie and five of the club's six Scottish Cup excursions. In all but one of those games he played at number three – when he switched sides to play right-back, it was with disastrous consequences.

In the Scottish Cup semi-final against Clyde in 1955, as Aberdeen gunned for a League and Cup double, Smith deputised in the number-two shirt after Jimmy Mitchell had fallen ill. He broke his leg shortly after the half-time interval, Clyde equalised in injury time and went on to clinch a place in the Final with victory in the replay.

Smith attempted to come back from that blow just six months later but broke his leg again in a match against an Aberdeenshire junior select and after eight appearances in the 1956–57 season, he was allowed to move on to Third Lanark.

Business commitments took him back north from Glasgow, combining his work in Banff with playing and coaching duties with Deveronvale in the Highland League. He captained the Deveronvale side which produced a Scottish Cup shock by beating Stirling Albion and also led them to Aberdeenshire Cup success.

Smith, who played 93 games for the Dons without scoring, spent nine years with Vale and was awarded a testimonial by the Banffers before emigrating to South Africa in 1967 to continue his work in the poultry industry.

David Smith

Date of birth: 14 November 1943, Aberdeen

Aberdeen record:
Appearances: League 133, Scottish Cup 14, League Cup 19
Goals: League 8, Scottish Cup 1, League Cup 4
Debut: League, 10 January 1962 v St Johnstone (h) drew 1–1

Also played for: Scotland (2 caps), Rangers, Arbroath, Arcadia Shepherds (South
Africa), Los Angeles Aztecs (US), Berwick Rangers, Huntly,
Peterhead
Managed: Berwick Rangers, Huntly, Peterhead

Aberdeen's involvement in the Scottish national side has become a given as season by season and decade by decade, the list of Dons in the dark blue grows. But it has not always been that way. From George Mulhall's appearance against Northern Ireland in October 1959, there was an astonishing international drought at Pittodrie which lasted 79 months.

It was fitting that a home-grown player ended what was by far the most barren spell in the post-war history of the club. On 11 May 1966 it was David Smith who ran out at Hampden to drag his home-town club back out of the international wilderness. Smith's promptings did not prevent Scotland from slipping to a 3–0 defeat against the Dutch masters of Holland, but the long wait for the north-east's legion of Tartan Army members to cheer on one of their own was over.

It proved to be one of the Aberdonian's final acts as a Pittodrie player as just months later he was on his way to join new Scotland colleagues John Greig, Davie Provan, Ronnie McKinnon, Willie Henderson and Willie Johnston at Rangers. His final act was to pull in a club-record fee of £45,000 to boost the Pittodrie coffers and substantially aid the rebuilding exercise Eddie Turnbull was in the process of carrying out.

Smith was just 22 when he became Pittodrie's biggest football export but by that time he was already an established first-team player, with a wealth of experience in the top flight as well as Scotland Under-23 honours.

The former Middlefield Primary and Hilton Academy pupil had caught the eye of the Dons while playing junior football for Aberdeen Lads' Club. He signed for the team at the age of 17 and made his debut on 10 January 1962, in a 1–1 draw against St Johnstone at Pittodrie. He kept his place in the side for the next game, a 1–1 home draw against Airdrie, before returning the number-six shirt to Doug Fraser and biding his time. It took just one game on the sidelines at the start of the 1962–63 First Division season for Smith to get the call from Tommy Pearson and the 18-year-old never looked back, making 35 appearances in his first full term in the first team.

The lack of international recognition in the early 1960s was not an indication of west coast bias, more a reflection on the difficulties the Dons were experiencing at the time. In the season Smith made his fleeting introduction Pearson's charges finished 12th in the 18-team top flight. His full introduction coincided with a mini-revival in fortunes as the Dons clambered to sixth place but throughout his time, finishing in the top half of the table was the main aim rather than a chase for major honours.

Smith's switch to Ibrox in the summer of 1966 brought further recognition, with his second and final cap coming in 1968 in a rematch against Holland which ended 0–0, and his first taste of continental football at club level.

With Rangers he was a losing Finalist in the European Cup-winners' Cup Final of 1967, when Bayern Munich triumphed, but he collected a winners' medal in 1972 after a Man of the Match performance in the Final against Moscow Dynamo in Barcelona.

His performance that season also earned the Scottish Football Writers' Player of the Year Award, his name carved next to the 1971 winner Martin Buchan on the roll of honour. The two Dons of the 1960s remain the only Aberdonians ever to be crowned as the country's Player of the Year.

Smith remained with the Light Blues for eight years, overcoming two leg breaks along the way before becoming player-coach at Arbroath. Playing spells in South Africa and America, alongside George Best in the LA Aztecs team, followed before his return to Scotland as player-manager of Berwick Rangers in 1976. He led Scotland's worst team to the Second Division Championship in 1979, the first honour in the history of the Borders club, before returning to his north-east roots with spells in charge at Huntly and Peterhead in the Highland League in the early 1980s. Smith can now be found behind the bar at the Salutation Inn, the bar and restaurant he and his wife Sheila own in Montrose.

Gary Smith

Date of birth: 25 March 1971, Glasgow

Aberdeen record:
Appearances: League 170+3, Scottish Cup 16+2, League Cup 19, Europe 3
Goals: League 2
Debut: League, 20 November 1991 v Hearts (h) lost 2–0

Also played for: Rennes, Hibs, Cowdenbeath, Dundee

On 15 December 1995 football was rocked to its core when the European Court of Justice in Luxembourg passed the Bosman ruling. The reverberations of the decision that football players should be eligible for free transfers at the end of their contracts could be felt in the corridors of power at every club on the continent.

The waves of fear were as strong at Pittodrie as anywhere else in Europe as the Aberdeen directors weighed up the potential implications of the new regulations. The Dons had been built on a firm financial footing, with the ability to move players on at a massive profit proving to be a long standing and very lucrative tradition. Overnight that financial cornerstone had been removed and since then the club has battled to stem a rising tide of debt.

The player who hammered home the harsh new realities of football was Gary Smith. In November 1995 he was an influential member of the Aberdeen team which ended a five-year wait for silverware when they defeated Dundee 2-0 in the League Cup Final. His contribution prompted the offer of a new deal from manager Roy Aitken, but Smith opted to keep his options open. Under the Bosman ruling he would be free to speak to interested parties from the start of 1996 with a view to moving on that summer.

When he made it clear that that was his plan it sparked a furious reaction from Aitken, who transfer listed the defender and forced him to sit in front of the media and explain himself like a schoolboy who had spoken out of turn in class.

After protracted negotiations, aimed at thrashing out a deal to keep the Glaswegian at Pittodrie, the club admitted defeat and Smith became the first Dons player to exploit the Bosman rule when he joined French club Rennes in August 1996, and a player the Aberdeen management team rated at £1.5 million left for nothing.

The sour ending to the saga tarnished the memories of the outstanding service Smith had given in his four seasons at the club. Signed from Falkirk in a £200,000 deal in the summer of 1991 after helping the Bairns win the First Division Championship, he recovered from a nightmare debut to become a versatile and reliable performer for the Reds.

Smith took his bow at Pittodrie in a midweek Premier Division game against Hearts on 20 November 1991 and was red carded as his new side slumped to a 2-0 defeat.

The 20-year-old showed strength of character to come back even stronger from that early blow and played 16 games in a season in which he had not been expected to even get near to the first team, due to the stiff competition for places in a defence which included Stewart McKimmie, Alex McLeish and Brian Irvine. Injuries to key players led to him filling in at centre-half and right-back and under Willie Miller in the 1992-93 season, he became an automatic selection at the heart of the Pittodrie defence.

Smith was called up to the Scotland squad during that campaign having impressed in the Scotland Under-21 team, but a cap proved illusive for the composed and athletic defender who was promoted to the senior pool by Andy Roxburgh at the age of 21.

The League Cup success of 1995 proved to be his only honour as he suffered the pain of Final defeats against Rangers in both the Scottish Cup and League Cup in 1992-93 season.

Smith spent just a year in France. Before the start of the 1997-98 season he was handed a shock reunion with Roy Aitken as Aberdeen invested £170,000 to bring him back from Rennes. He spent a further three years with the Dons, playing under Aitken, Alex Miller, Paul Hegarty and Ebbe Skovdahl in that rollercoaster period in the club's history before switching to Hibs in 2000.

Six seasons with the Easter Road side were followed by a brief stint as player-coach at Cowdenbeath in 2006, before Smith joined Dundee in the First Division.

Jimmy Smith

Date of birth: 20 January 1947, Glasgow

Aberdeen record:
Appearances: League 103, Scottish Cup 14, League Cup 15, Europe 8
Goals: League 21, Scottish Cup 5, League Cup 8, Europe 3
Debut: League, 4 April 1966 v Morton (h) won 5–3

Also played for: Scotland (4 caps), Benburb, Newcastle United, Celtic

He arrived, thrilled crowds, won international honours and left with a substantial financial legacy trailing in his wake. Jimmy Smith was a flamboyant winger who stood out like a beacon during the transitional early days of Eddie Turnbull's reign at Pittodrie.

Spotted by renowned scout Bobby Calder while playing for Benburb in his home city of Glasgow, Smith's close control combined with the ability to beat defenders and incisive distribution made him stand out as a youngster playing in only his first season in the junior ranks.

Turnbull made his move in the summer of 1965, beating Aston Villa and Wolves to the punch to recruit the promising 18-year-old winger and by the end of the season the new boy had been fast tracked into the first team. 'Jinky' made his debut in a 5–3 home win against Morton on 4 April 1966 and opened his goalscoring account in his fifth start to help the Dons to a 2–1 win over Dundee. It was the first of 37 goals he would score in just three and a quarter seasons at Pittodrie.

In 1966–67 he marked his first full season as a senior player by finishing joint leading scorer for Aberdeen, with 20 strikes in 43 games in all competitions. It was an eventful campaign for Smith, who was called into the Scotland Under-23 team and took part in his first Cup Final as Celtic ran out 2–0 winners in the 1967 Scottish Cup showdown.

That proved to be the final opportunity to compete for a domestic honour with Aberdeen during a short but eventful career with the club, but he did win international recognition. In 1968 he and teammate Bobby Clark lined up together as Scotland faced Holland at the Olympic Stadium in Amsterdam. The game ended 0–0 but Smith did help the national side to victory against Wales in 1974, also picking up caps in a defeat against Northern Ireland in the same year and a 1–1 draw with West Germany in 1974.

Those final three caps came as a Newcastle United player. Smith, after 140 appearances for the Dons, was sold to the English side for £100,000 in the summer of 1969. It was a record for the Magpies and a gamble on a player who was no stranger to suspensions at Pittodrie, mainly after retaliating to meaty treatment dished out by defenders in Scotland. He could also give as good as he got, sent off for a heavy challenge inside the first minute of a Cup tie while playing for Newcastle against Birmingham in 1973.

Manchester City and Celtic, the team Smith had supported as a boy, had both shown an interest in 1969 but were blown out of the water by the six-figure package tabled by Newcastle.

The fanfare surrounding the Scotsman's arrival on Tyneside quadrupled the reserve attendance for his debut, with an 8,000 attendance for his match-winning performance in a second-string encounter against Aston Villa.

Smith was seen as the ideal foil for star striker Malcolm Macdonald but injury wrecked his chances of making a lasting impression, undergoing two knee operations in 1971 alone as years of heavy challenges began to tell.

He returned to fitness and form to reclaim his international place in 1973 and remained in the Newcastle side until a brief loan spell with Celtic in 1976, which ended prematurely when another knee injury began to cause concern and forced his retirement from the senior game at the age of 1979. He remained on Tyneside, working as a taxi driver in Newcastle until heart problems and arthritis forced his retirement.

Joe Smith

Date of birth: 11 November 1953, Glasgow

Aberdeen record:
Appearances: League 142+8, Scottish Cup 12+3, League Cup 34, Europe 3+1
Goals: League 7, Scottish Cup 1, League Cup 3
Debut: League, 16 December 1972 v Rangers (a) drew 0–0

Also played for: Motherwell, Peterhead, Dunfermline

Big brother Jimmy got the Scotland cap as a Dons player but it was Joe who collected a coveted winners' medal with Aberdeen. It took him the best part of a decade, but in 1976 he did it.

Joe Smith was an integral part of Ally MacLeod's side in the 1976–77 season as the Pittodrie side marched into the Final of the League Cup and defeated Celtic 2–1 in front of almost 70,000 at Hampden. Smith played in every game in that run and was on target in the quarter-final against Stirling Albion, rifling home a low shot to make it 2–0 and take the Dons through.

It was the midfielder's finest season in the red of his first club, sitting out just a single League game as MacLeod steered the club to third in the Premier Division. When the manager left Pittodrie at the end of the campaign to take over as Scotland boss he did not forget Smith, a player who built his reputation on the type of skilful running and clever passing his brother was famed for. MacLeod immediately called him up to his squad for the home international series and a South American tour in the summer of 1977. He was on the bench for games against Argentina and Brazil but never made it on to the pitch to win a cap to join the Smith collection started by his big brother.

The Scottish Youth cap would undoubtedly have been in the running to be part of the senior squad for the 1978 World Cup in Argentina, but was cruelly robbed of the chance to continue to impress the national team coach by a knee injury suffered in a League game against Ayr just months into the 1977–78 season.

Initially, medical staff thought the injury, the result of a midfield clash with John Hyslop, would keep their man sidelined for two or three weeks as the ligament damage healed, but weeks turned into seven months and the Aberdeen man watched the World Cup drama unfold from his armchair.

The game against Ayr proved to be his final start for Aberdeen. On his recovery from the knee injury at the start of the 1978–79 season he was sent on loan to Arbroath by new manager Alex Ferguson and made just two appearances from the bench before being reunited with MacLeod, by that time in charge at Motherwell, two days before Christmas in 1978.

The £40,000 deal resulted in a three-year stay at Fir Park before he returned to the north east to play briefly under former Pittodrie teammate Joe Harper

with Peterhead in the Highland League. He returned to the senior ranks with Dunfermline soon after but retired from the senior game in 1983.

Smith had spent 14 years as a professional, joining the Dons as a 15-year-old in 1969 and turning out for Banks o' Dee A in the juvenile Leagues before stepping up to the Dons reserve team a year later.

The Glaswegian, a Celtic supporter as a boy, was handed a baptism of fire on 16 December 1972 when he was named in the team for the first time when Aberdeen travelled to Ibrox to face Rangers. The new boy and his teammates emerged with a point after a 0–0 draw against the Light Blues side who were chasing the Hoops in the First Division title race.

Playing alongside Zoltan Varga, the 6ft-tall 19-year-old midfielder began to make a name for himself in Jimmy Bonthrone's side. By the 1973–74 season he was a regular in the Aberdeen side and began to attract the attention of the international Under-23 and Scottish Football League selectors, turning out for both sides in 1976 – the same year he savoured his finest moment in football with glory at Hampden for his club side.

Theo Snelders

Date of birth: 7 December 1963, Westervoort (Netherlands)

Aberdeen record:
Appearances: League 228+1, Scottish Cup 20, League Cup 29, Europe 14
Debut: League, 13 August 1988 v Dundee (a) drew 1–1

Also played for: Netherlands (1 cap), Twente Enschede, Rangers, MVV
Maastricht

It was always going to take a big man to fill the number-one shirt vacated by Scotland star and Gothenburg hero Jim Leighton, and when that onerous task fell to Alex Smith in 1988 he was forced to look far and wide for a replacement.

Leighton's switch to Manchester United left a huge void at Pittodrie and presented a goalkeeping headache the club had not had to contemplate since he had first broken into the team in 1980.

Signing a new goalkeeper was the first task presented to Smith following his appointment as a successor to Ian Porterfield and he wasted no time in singling out Snelders, watching the Dutchman in action. Theo Snelders had in fact been a target of Alex Ferguson and Manchester United before they switched their attention to luring Leighton from Aberdeen.

Snelders was out of contract with Twente Enschede but, in the pre-Bosman days, still commanded a fee of £300,000. He proved to be worth every single penny and much more.

He had launched his career in Holland's top flight at the age of just 17 and had been voted the best goalkeeper in the country three years prior to his arrival in Scotland. At the age of 24 he made his Dons debut in a 1–1 draw away to Dundee on 13 August 1988 and that season he conceded just 25 goals in 36 Premier Division games to give his new club the best defensive record in the League. However, it was still not enough to prevent Rangers from winning the League and the Ibrox men inflicted a 3–2 defeat on the Dons in the League Cup Final to compound their misery.

That disappointment was tempered by personal joy for one of Scotland's most successful imports, who, after playing in every single one of the 48 games the club took part in, was named as the national players' Player of the Year winner at the end of his first season. He stunned the audience at the awards night in Glasgow by opening his acceptance speech with the line 'fit like', but that would have been no surprise to anyone who had sat in the Pittodrie stands and listened to the 6ft 2in 'keeper roar at his defenders to get 'oot' of their own half.

Snelders was a favourite among his peers and an even bigger favourite among the Aberdeen supporters. The appreciation was mutual. The player, relaxing at his home in the Netherlands, said 'I have very happy memories from Aberdeen. I spent 11 years in Scotland and it was a big part of my life – I have kept all the newspaper cuttings and we took lots of photographs to remind us of the happy times we had. Our two children, Ryan and Kayleigh, were both born in Aberdeen so we will always have a link to the city.

'My wife and I were not married when we moved across. For her it was the first time she had left her parents so it was a big adventure. We sometimes struggled with the accent to begin with but we got the hang of it – I remember when we stayed in a semi-detached house and noticed smoke pouring from the chimney. It was coming from next door but the lady was a true Aberdonian and it was difficult for us to get her to realise. There was a lot of waving of arms and shouting before we got the message across!

'It was a big step into the dark for us. We knew very little about Scotland, let alone Aberdeen. The combination of the city and the club made it for us. I joined at a good time for the club. There were a lot of full Scotland internationals in the side and we were challenging for honours.'

In 1989–90 he completed the process of winning over the Dons' support when he helped his side to a Cup double, first with a 2–1 victory over Rangers in the League Cup and then with his central role in the Scottish Cup win against Celtic. After shutting out the Hoops over 90 minutes and extra-time, Snelders blocked Anton Rogan's penalty in the shoot-out to present Brian Irvine with the opportunity to convert the Cup-winning spot-kick and take the trophy north.

Snelders, who made his debut for the Dutch national team in a friendly in 1989, was continually frustrated in his quest for further trophy success at Pittodrie but amassed 292 games over the course of more than seven years along the way.

He was an imposing figure behind the defence he marshalled so well and an athletic shot-stopper who was never afraid to throw himself into dangerous situations, as he found to his cost when he dived to collect the ball on a wet surface and had his cheekbone shattered by a sliding challenge by Rangers striker Ally McCoist.

Snelders was stretchered off, replaced by Scott Thomson. By the time he recovered from that injury in 1996 a £300,000 bid by Rangers tempted him to Ibrox, where he played 13 games as a back-up 'keeper for the Light Blues.

In 1999 he returned to Holland to wind down his playing career with MVV Maastricht before moving into goalkeeping coaching with Twente Enschede.

Billy Stark

Date of birth: 1 December 1956, Glasgow

Aberdeen record:
Appearances: League 112+12, Scottish Cup 12+4, League Cup 14+3, Europe 11+1
Goals: League 41, Scottish Cup 7, League Cup 11, Europe 1
Debut: League, 20 August 1983 v Dundee (h) won 3–0

Also played for: St Mirren, Celtic, Kilmarnock, Hamilton
Managed: Morton, St Johnstone, Queen's Park Rangers

Billy Stark, the hero of some of Aberdeen's finest moments in Cup football, was the mastermind behind one of the darkest nights in the history of the Dons in knock-out competition.

In his role as manager, it was Stark's plucky amateur Queen's Park Rangers players who dumped the highly-paid Pittodrie side out of the League Cup in 2006 in a penalty shoot-out in Glasgow.

Stark, who was in charge at St Johnstone for three years before taking charge of the Hampden side, has worked wonders with his unpaid team and the result against the Dons confirmed his progress. But then, the manager does know a thing or two about Cup Finals.

In 1985-85 he helped Alex Ferguson's team to a double and scored in both Finals. The League Cup was first on the agenda and Hibs were the opponents as Ferguson aimed for his first triumph in the competition with the Dons. After nine minutes Eric Black opened the scoring and three minutes later Stark settled any lingering nerves, tucking away a John Hewitt cross to make it 2–0. A second from Black after the break wrapped up the tie.

In the Scottish Cup Stark was relegated to the bench for the Final showdown with Hearts but he still had a starring role, heading home a 75th-minute goal to add to John Hewitt's double and make it a season to remember.

Stark was a player who often divided opinion among the supporters in the Pittodrie stands. Many appreciated his cultured promptings going forward and ability to chip in with vital goals, others mistook his languid style for laziness. Scotland managers clearly fell into the latter camp, with Stark surprisingly never earning a cap despite the frequency his colleagues in the Aberdeen team appeared on the international stage. Even at Under-21 level he was denied the chance of playing for his country, despite being involved in the young national squad.

Alex Ferguson did not need to be persuaded about Stark's potential, despite his failure to break into the Under-21 side, and he tried twice to sign him from St Mirren before making it third time lucky in the summer of 1983 with a £75,000 bid.

Stark was joining a club high on the European success of the previous year but was not daunted by the illustrious company he was in, forcing his way into the side for the opening day of the Premier Division campaign as the Dons got off and running on 20 August with a 3–0 win against Dundee at Pittodrie. He signalled his prowess in front of goal with a hat-trick against Raith Rovers in the League Cup just four days later and went on to net 11 times in just 14 starts and six appearances from the bench in his introductory season as he helped his new club to win the Championship and the Scottish Cup, coming on as a substitute in the 2–1 win against Celtic in the Final.

If Stark had played a supporting role in the 1984 Premier Division title win with 11 starts, that claim could not be levelled at him when the Dons defended their crown in 1985. The Glaswegian made the number-four shirt his own and was absent from the starting line up just six times as the League was won with seven points to spare.

The Cup double the following season proved to be his final honours in an Aberdeen shirt and after 169 appearances and 60 goals, he switched to Celtic in a £75,000 deal having jointly led the Dons scoring chart in his final season at the club, despite playing in midfield. He tied on 14 goals with John Hewitt.

Stark won a League-winners' medal in 1988 with the Parkhead side, the third of his career, and capped off a fine season when he appeared in the Scottish Cup Final win against Dundee United – winning three badges in the competition without ever starting in a Final. When he did get a starting place, in the 1990 Final against Aberdeen, he ended up on the losing side as the Dons won on penalties.

After that defeat against Aberdeen Stark linked up with former Hoops teammate Tommy Burns at Kilmarnock, signed for £50,000. In 1991 he moved to Hamilton to combine playing with duties as assistant manager and added a Scottish Football League Challenge Cup-winners' medal to his collection with Accies, before returning to Killie to become right-hand man to Burns and help steer the club back into the Premier League.

The Burns and Stark partnership was recruited by Celtic in 1994 and the duo spent three years in charge. Following their departure from Parkhead the former Dons midfielder became a manager in his own right with Morton in 1997, leading to appointments at St Johnstone and then Queen's Park Rangers. Stark led the Glasgow Amateurs to promotion in 2007.

Gordon Strachan

Date of birth: 9 February 1957, Edinburgh

Aberdeen record:

Appearances: League 183+8, Scottish Cup 29, League Cup 46+3, Europe 34+4

Goals: League 54, Scottish Cup 7, League Cup 20, Europe 8

Debut: League, 5 November 1977 v Dundee United (a) won 1–0

Also played for: Scotland (50 caps), Dundee, Manchester United, Leeds United, Coventry City

Managed: Coventry City, Southampton United, Celtic

All hail football's king of the put down. On the pitch the legend of Gordon Strachan was born when he starred in the European Cup-winners' Cup victory in Gothenburg, off the pitch a new reason for infamy was created in the form of cutting sarcasm the moment he was asked for a quick word by a reporter and responded with 'velocity', before striding off.

As a manager Strachan has perfected a talent for body swerving media questions with his own brand of humour. The journalists so often on the receiving end can't help but come back for more. While in charge of Southampton he was asked in which area he felt Middlesbrough had outplayed his side, responding with 'the big green area out there'.

Confidence was never an area Strachan struggled in as a player and in management that trait continues. Take the time, for example, that he was asked if he was the right man for the job after one of his English appointments, when he hit back with 'No, I think they should have got George Graham because I'm useless.' There's really no answer to that. When asked if he could take the fact an unbeaten run had ground to a halt, Strachan hit back with 'No, I'm just going to crumble like a wreck. I'll go home, become an alcoholic and maybe jump off a bridge.'

One particular one-liner summed up his approach to the media spotlight he has found himself under since branching out into management. When a reporter asked 'You don't take losing lightly do you Gordon?', he was hit with a typically-curt comeback of 'I don't take stupid questions lightly either.'

His love-hate relationship with the media cannot detract from his record in Celtic's top job, leading the club to the Championship in his first season in charge and then into the last 16 of the Champions League in 2006. It was the first time in Celtic's history they had reached that stage and the progress came courtesy of a 1–0 win over a certain Alex Ferguson. Football's a funny old game, as another media-savvy football favourite would testify to.

Strachan's life has been nothing short of extraordinary. Born in Edinburgh, he launched his senior career with Dundee as a teenager and made an immediate impact as he rose to become captain at Dens Park. In 1977 he made the switch to Pittodrie in a deal which took Jim Shirra and £40,000 to Dundee. It was an inspired piece of business by Aberdeen manager Billy McNeill.

The inspirational midfielder was just 20 when he signed, already an Under-21 international, and his best days were certainly in front of him. He had a poor first season by his own high standards and was a target for flak from the Pittodrie fans, but by the time he left the Dons to join Ron Atkinson's Manchester United in 1984 he was laden with honours. The first success came when Alex Ferguson and his Dons side won the Premier Division Championship in 1980, the season in which Strachan's majestic performances won him the Scottish Player of the Year award.

He scored in the 1982 Scottish Cup Final on his way to the first of three winners' medals in that competition in addition to adding another top-flight title in 1983–84 with Aberdeen. Add the European Cup-winners' Cup and European Super Cup into the equation and the considerable sum total of an amazing Pittodrie career is complete. In less than seven years Strachan played 307 games and scored 89 goals after making his debut in a 1–0 win at Dundee United on 5 November 1977.

When he parted company with the club he claimed he was going stale in the Scottish game. He came close to moving to Germany with Cologne but had a late change of heart and signed at Old Trafford in a £600,000 transfer instead.

He was an FA Cup winner with United in his first season before Alex Ferguson followed him to Manchester. The pair's relationship had always been stormy and that intensified in England, to the point Strachan was offloaded to Leeds for £200,000 in 1989.

He became captain at Elland Road, leading them to the Second Division title and earning the English Player of the Year title on their return to the top flight in 1991. The following year the fairytale was complete as Leeds won the First Division ahead of United.

An incredible club career was matched at international level, with Strachan making it into Scotland's hall of fame with his 50-cap tally from his debut in 1980 to his final appearance in 1992. He played in the World Cup Finals in both 1982 and 1986.

He rounded off his playing career with Coventry, the club where he launched his managerial career in 1996. Five years in charge of Coventry were followed by three at Southampton before his appointment to Celtic's top job in 2005 to succeed Martin O'Neill, bringing the title back to Parkhead at the first attempt and defending it in 2007 as part of a League and Cup double.

Dom Sullivan

Date of birth: 1 April 1953, Glasgow

Aberdeen record:
Appearances: League 98+11, Scottish Cup 12, League Cup 21+2, Europe 7+2
Goals: League 11, League Cup 3
Debut: League Cup, 14 August 1976 v Kilmarnock (h) won 2–0

Also played for: Clyde, Celtic, Manchester City, Morton
Managed: Alloa, East Stirling

Within three months of his first appearance as an Aberdeen player, Dom Sullivan had a winners' medal safely tucked away in his pocket. The Glaswegian midfielder could have been forgiven for thinking the streets of Aberdeen were paved with gold, but the League Cup victory in 1976 proved to be his only reward for four years of service under three managers at Pittodrie.

He was a promising Scotland Under-23 international when Ally MacLeod signed him in 1976. Sullivan had spent seven years on the Clyde books, winning a Second Division Championship medal, and was being courted by a string of English clubs alerted by rave reports about the potential of the rising midfield star. He was playing part-time football with the Glasgow outfit but would soon be earning a living from the game he loved.

It was Aberdeen who won the race for his signature with a £25,000 deal and he made the number-seven shirt his own after arriving in the north east, one of five ever presents in the 11-game run to the League Cup Final against Celtic and a key man in the 2–1 win against the Hoops.

Sullivan continued to prove a big hit with MacLeod's successor Billy McNeill and was part of the team which came within two points of pipping Celtic to the League title in 1978, when he was also on the losing side in the Scottish Cup Final against Rangers.

Alex Ferguson became his third boss in as many years when he breezed into Pittodrie in 1978 and he stuck by Sullivan for one term before relegating him to the periphery of the side for the 1979–80 title win, when he made just five appearances.

Before the halfway point in that campaign his desire for a move away from Pittodrie, after a series of rejected transfer requests, was met in October 1979. He had become frustrated by the lack of first-team opportunities but there was no shortage of interest in the player.

Sullivan was reunited with McNeill at boyhood heroes Celtic in a £92,000 transfer, having rejected an approach from Jim McLean at Dundee United. He had spurned the opportunity to sign for the Tannadice club before moving to Aberdeen and refused to reverse his decision later in life.

He was handed a baptism of fire just 24 hours after signing when he starred in Celtic's 1–0 win against Rangers. McNeill raved about the performance of his latest addition and was a huge admirer of his cultured skills in midfield. Celtic went on to win the top flight in his first two full seasons at Parkhead but in 1983 Sullivan was freed and switched to Morton after a month's trial with old mentor McNeill at Manchester City.

He completed his full set of Scottish League-winners' medals with the Cappielow outfit when he helped them to the First Division flag in 1984 to add to his Second Division win with Clyde and Premier Division success with Celtic.

In 1985 Sullivan continued his playing career with Alloa and it was the Wasps who handed him his managerial break the following year, with former Dons teammate Stuart Kennedy recruited to bolster the backroom team. He went on to take the helm at East Stirling before stepping down in 1992 to concentrate on his career in the licensed trade in the central belt.

George Taylor

Date of birth: 9 June 1913, King Edward
Died: 1982, Plymouth

Aberdeen record:
Appearances: League 63, Scottish Cup 8, League Cup 11
Goals: League 6, League Cup 1
Debut: League, 19 March 1938 v Queen of the South (h) lost 1–0

Also played for: Hall Russells, Plymouth Argyle

On 11 May 1946 a wait of more than four decades ended for the hoardes of Aberdeen fans who had trekked south to watch their heroes tackle Rangers in the Southern League Cup Final.

For the Dons fans in the crowd of 135,000 at Hampden it was their first taste of success in a national competition, with the Southern League Cup acting as the precursor to the League Cup. The man who ended a trophy famine stemming from Aberdeen's formation in 1903 was George Taylor, the only north-east player in the starting line up on that momentous day.

The score was poised at 2–2 going into the final minute of an end to end Final. Right-winger Alec Kiddie broke clear and when his cross was only half cleared it was Taylor who stepped forward to crack home the winning goal off the post. It was 3–2 on the day but the magic number was one – the first of many trophies to be inked on the club's honours list.

Taylor started out as a centre-forward with junior side Hall Russell but with Aberdeen he made his name as a left-half. He signed in 1938 and made his debut in a 1–0 loss aginst Queen of the South on 19 March that year.

After the war he remained in the thick of the action at Pittodrie and was Dave Halliday's first-choice number six in the successful 1945–46 season. In addition to the Southern League Cup win the team claimed the third spot in the reformed post-war top flight.

In the following campaign Taylor made it two Cups in the space of two terms when he played in all but one of the seven ties on Aberdeen's run to the Scottish Cup Final against Hibs. For the game against the Easter Road side he switched to left-back and had a key, if unwanted, involvement – watching his back pass slip past goalkeeper George Johnstone in the early stages to give Hibs the lead. His team bounced back to win 2–1 and confirm their rising status in the game, reinforced by another third-place finish in the League.

The chance to add a League Cup-winners' medal passed the King Edward-born player by when he was part of the team that lost 4–0 to Rangers in the inaugural Final in 1947. His final season in the north east saw Taylor sit out just a single game as he continued to thrive in Halliday's team.

He notched up a total of 82 appearances for the Dons and scored six goals before his form tempted Plymouth Argyle to step in and take him south in 1948, and it proved a long and fruitful relationship with the English outfit.

By 1955 he had progressed from playing to become Plymouth's head trainer, looking after six teams at the peak of his powers. He spent more than a decade in that post before becoming chief scout for Argyle in 1966.

Taylor, who moved into the licensed trade following his retirement from football, died in Plymouth in 1982 at the age of 67.

Zoltan Varga

Date of birth: 1 January 1945, Val (Hungary)

Aberdeen record:
Appearances: League 26, Scottish Cup 3, League Cup 2
Goals: League 10
Debut: League, 14 October 1972 v Falkirk (h) drew 2–2

Also played for: Hungary (14 caps), Ferencvaros, Hertha Berlin, Ajax, Borussia
    Dortmund
Managed: Ferencvaros

After Charlie Cooke, the second wild card enters this list of Aberdeen legends at number 89. Zoltan Varga won nothing in his brief dalliance with Scottish football except the undivided attention of a generation of Dons fans.

He spent less than a full season at Pittodrie and competes with Scotland international Alex Jackson for the title of the club's ultimate one-hit wonder. In 1924–25 Jackson wracked up 40 appearances to Varga's 31 before his wing wizardry took him to Huddersfield.

While those who saw Jackson in action are few and far between, the Varga fan club lives on and his bespoke performances at the heart of the Aberdeen team for that one season stay with the paid up members. Can a man who played so few games, with no return in terms of silverware, be categorised as a legend? Perhaps not, but the circumstances of his Scottish sojourn are most certainly the stuff of legend.

Varga, an Olympic gold-medal winner with Hungary's football team in 1964, was a leading light in German football when scandal struck. The Hertha Berlin playmaker was caught up in a bribery row in the Bundesliga and found himself banned for two years.

He had played in two European Finals and the Fairs Cup in both 1965 and 1968, against Juventus and Leeds United, for his first club Ferencvaros after making his debut as a 16-year-old. Yet at the age of 27 and hitting his prime, he found himself out of the club game. Step forward Jimmy Bonthrone, who spent £40,000 of Aberdeen's money to bring the continental master to Scottish shores.

His introduction to the rough and tumble of the game in this country was a harsh one, and the slightly-built Varga required stitches in a head wound after his first training session with his new teammates. It did not put him off, and neither did the fact that his pre-match routine of stretching rather than running or ball striking

drew frowns or that his desire to return after training for extra practice was considered a novelty.

If the Dons fans had questioned their manager's judgement, they had to wait just a matter of weeks for reassurance. Varga, in only his third game for the club, scored one of the most memorable goals Pittodrie has witnessed with a sublime lob against Celtic in a 3–2 defeat in October 1972. He scored both goals that day, two of the 10 strikes on his Scottish record.

His close control, passing ability and eye for goal endeared him to the Dons supporters but the relationship proved short-lived. A knee injury sidelined Varga after that first season and in November 1973 he returned to Europe, citing poor wages at Pittodrie as the reason.

Hertha Berlin repaid the £40,000 the Dons had splashed out and took him back to Germany, but, not for the first time, controversy followed Varga. Just four days after touching down in Berlin there was another transfer – this time Ajax paid £70,000 to take him to Holland and Hertha celebrated a swift £30,000 profit. Not bad for less than one week's work and clearly part of the plan when they moved to end Varga's career with the Dons.

He was recruited as a replacement for Johan Cruyff and lived the life of a superstar with fame and fortune, but failed to sparkle in the Netherlands. Instead, he played out his career back in Germany with Borussia Dortmund. Then a Second Division side, his first training session attracted 2000 to Dortmund's base in the city and the gate for his debut in 1974 leapt by 30,000 to 45,000.

After retiring in the early 1980s he turned to coaching in the amateur ranks in his adopted homeland before returning to take charge of Hungarian champions Ferencvaros in 1996 for a short period.

Michael Watt

Date of birth: 27 November 1970, Aberdeen

Aberdeen record:
Appearances: League 78+2, Scottish Cup 7, League Cup 5, Europe 4
Debut: League, 26 December 1989 v Hibs (h) lost 2–1

Also played for: Blackburn Rovers, Norwich City, Kilmarnock

If anyone can testify to the slings and arrows of outrageous fortune, and misfortune, in life as a professional footballer, it must surely be Michael Watt.

In 1996 the Aberdonian goalkeeper was revelling in his status as one of the country's top-rated shot stoppers and pushing for inclusion in Craig Brown's Scotland squad for Euro '96 in England. It came on the back of his long-awaited promotion to the number-one jersey at Pittodrie and a string of impressive displays on his way to helping the Dons to their first trophy in five seasons.

Watt shut out Dundee in the Final of the 1995 League Cup to become only the fifth 'keeper in the club's history to earn a winners' medal. He was 25 when he held the League Cup aloft and had to be patient before getting his chance.

He had taken over the 'keeper's jersey from Theo Snelders earlier that season and at last held the position he had coveted since joining the club in 1988 upon leaving Robert Gordon's College, where he had gained the qualifications needed to win a university place. Instead of university he chose to study football with the Dons, having caught his home-town club's eye while starring for Cove in the juvenile Leagues.

Watt's talent as an emerging player was never in doubt and he collected 12 caps for the Scotland Under-21 team while serving as understudy to Theo Snelders. After holding down a place in the Dons team in the 1995–96 season, following the Dutchman's move to Rangers, he was propelled into the Scotland B squad and pushing for a place in the senior squad for the Euro '96 adventure.

With Andy Goram and Jim Leighton guaranteed two of the three spots Brown had reserved for a 'keeper, it was down to Watt and rivals Nicky Walker and Bryan Gunn to battle for the remaining place. In the end it was Walker who got the call and ultimately the same man led to the player calling time on his Dons career.

What a difference a year can make in football. Early in 1996 Watt was dreaming of international involvement, even looking forward to continuing his Scotland push ahead of the 1998 World Cup in France as Goram and Leighton moved in to the veteran stage,

but by the end of the year he was seeking a transfer away from Pittodrie.

That request came after he found himself relegated to third choice behind new recruit Walker and young gun Derek Stillie. It was hard to take for a player who made his debut seven years earlier when he deputised for Snelders in a 2–1 defeat at home to Hibs on 26 December 1989.

Watt went on to make 96 appearances for the club, notably when he was thrown in at the deep end for the Premier Division decider at Ibrox in 1991. Rangers needed a victory to prevent the Dons from winning the title and set about trying to intimidate the young opposition 'keeper, with Mark Hateley using his power to knock Watt's confidence at every opportunity. A 2–0 win for the home side ensured the Championship remained in Glasgow.

With his dreams of making it big with Aberdeen fading in the face of competition from Walker and Stillie, Watt came within an ace of a dream move to the Premiership. He had a loan spell at Blackburn Rovers in 1997 to act as support to John Filan, who had stepped up to the Ewood park first team as cover for the injured Tim Flower. Watt broke his jaw in a reserve game – days before Filan broke his arm. Rovers were left with a goalkeeping vacancy in the Premiership but Watt, the man they hoped to have available to fill it, was back in the north east nursing a painful injury which kept him sidelined for almost two months.

When Jim Leighton returned to the Dons it confirmed Watt's time at the club was over and he switched back to England with Norwich City in 1998. The following year, after a handful of top-team appearances for the Canaries, he returned north to sign for Kilmarnock.

After just four games for the Rugby Park club over four months he retired from the game, having just turned 29. More than a decade of fighting for the right to play regular first-team football had taken its toll and Watt, disillusioned with the game, opted to concentrate on a career in the financial services industry in Glasgow. His interest in the game was revived when he began coaching with the Rangers youth teams in 2005.

Peter Weir

Date of birth: 18 January 1958, Johnstone

Aberdeen record:

Appearances: League 160+11, Scottish Cup 19+2, League Cup 28+1, Europe
                  29+3

Goals: League 23, Scottish Cup 7, League Cup 2, Europe 6

Debut: League Cup, 8 August 1981 v Kilmarnock (h) won 3–0

Also played for: Scotland (6 caps), St Mirren, Leicester City, Ayr United

Peter Weir has been tasked with becoming a legend all over again. The Gothenburg Great breezed back into Pittodrie in 2006 to confirm his appointment as the new man in charge of the club's west-coast scouting and coaching network.

His job description, put simply, is to fill the shoes of the late Bobby Calder. It was Calder who unearthed gem after gem for the Pittodrie side decade after decade. His finds included Willie Miller, Alex McLeish, Jim Leighton, Arthur Graham, Archie Glen...the list goes on and the value of the talent runs into millions.

Now Weir, who had earned his stripes scouting opposition teams for Tommy Burns at both Kilmarnock and Celtic as well as during a stint as assistant manager to Billy Stark at Morton before joining the Rangers youth set-up, is back working for the club, which means more to him than any other.

The Glaswegian, recruited by director and former teammate Willie Miller, will have a huge part to play in the future of the Dons but will struggle to match his past achievements with the Pittodrie side. It was Weir's pass which fed Mark McGhee to cross for John Hewitt's famous winner in the European Cup-winners' Cup Final against Real Madrid in 1983.

Up to that point he had missed just the opening tie of the European campaign when Sion had been hammered 7–0. From that point on Weir held the number-11 shirt and a goal in the 2–0 second-round victory against Lech Poznan and the 5–1 semi-final victory against Waterschei helped the Dons on their march to Gothenburg. By that stage he was already a seasoned performer on the European stage, upstaging highly-fancied Ipswich with a stunning double in the 3–1 UEFA Cup victory against the holders in 1981.

Weir believes the legacy of those glory days can help him recruit the next generation of Pittodrie stars. He added, 'Of course we can't say Aberdeen will win a European trophy again but we also can't believe it is impossible. The Gothenburg team was packed full of young players who had come through the ranks at the club and formed a tremendous team and we are striving to return to the days when the club was producing so many quality players.'

Weir's professional association stretches back more than quarter of a century. He had joined the Pittodrie staff in 1981 when Alex Ferguson, who had the player under his wing during his time in charge at St Mirren, tempted the Buddies with a player plus cash offer. Ian Scanlon moved to Love Street along with around £200,000 in cash while the 23-year-old winger travelled north to begin his Aberdeen career.

It was a substantial package, a record at the time, but the club was investing in an international player. Weir had made his Scotland debut in 1980 and had four caps to his credit by the time he left the Paisley side. Despite domestic and European honours he added just two further international appearances as a Dons player, the last in a 2–0 defeat in Northern Ireland at the end of 1983.

The European Cup-winners' Cup was Weir's first trophy success but far from his last. Just 10 days after glory in Gothenburg he added a Scottish Cup medal after helping his team to a 1–0 win against Rangers and another followed in 1983–84 when Celtic were beaten 2–1. That season Weir also starred in both legs of the European Super Cup Final victory against Hamburg, supplying both goals in the crucial 2–0 home win, and played in 27 of the 36 Premier Division games as Aberdeen stormed to the Championship title.

Another League-winners' medal followed in 1985 before Weir collected his third Scottish Cup badge when the Dons defeated Hearts 3–0 in the 1986 season. The winger was a key man in the Final, crossing for John Hewitt to score the second goal of the afternoon, but had an even more important role on the road to Hampden. In the quarter-final replay against Dundee at Pittodrie he scored a sublime goal in the 101st minute of the game, floating the ball over the helpless Bobby Geddes to put Aberdeen through after the game had finished 1–1 at the end of 90 minutes.

Ferguson loved having Weir in his side to give him the width and balance he craved, doing on the left wing what Gordon Strachan and then Joe Miller did on the right. His successor Ian Porterfield was less of a fan and allowed Weir to move on to Leicester City in an £80,000 transfer at the beginning of 1988, after 253 games and 38 goals for the club. Aged 29 at the time, his offer of committing himself to Aberdeen for the rest of his career was rejected by the management team and Leicester took advantage.

After less than a year in England he returned to Scotland with the option of joining either Aberdeen, under Alex Smith, or St Mirren. He opted for the Saints, but later admitted it was his one regret from a tremendous playing career. In 1990 Weir switched to Ayr United before being forced out of the game by an ankle injury at the age of 34.

Derek Whyte

Date of birth: 31 August 1968, Glasgow

Aberdeen record:
Appearances: League 131+2, Scottish Cup 12, League Cup 8, Europe 1
Debut: League, 20 December 1997 v Kilmarnock (a) lost 1–0

Also played for: Scotland (12 caps), Celtic, Middlesbrough, Partick Thistle
Managed: Partick Thistle

On a cold December morning in 1997 there was a moment of realisation for new Aberdeen manager Alex Miller. Less than a month into the job, he trudged off the training field knowing he desperately needed to bolster his defensive options.

Within hours the ink on a cheque for £200,000 was drying and Derek Whyte was packing his bags to leave Middlesbrough behind for a new life with the Dons. Miller, assistant manager to Scotland boss Craig Brown, was convinced he had bagged a bargain, having worked with Whyte during national squad gatherings.

The defender went on to win the final two of his 12 caps while with the Dons, playing in a 1–1 draw against Finland in 1998 and the 1–0 victory against Germany the following year in Bremen when Don Hutchison did the damage for Craig Brown's side.

Whyte's international career began just weeks after his 19th birthday when the promising young Celtic defender was named in the national squad for the European Championship qualifier against Belgium at Hampden in October 1987. Andy Roxburgh sent on the rookie to replace Maurice Malpas as Scotland swept to a 2–0 victory courtesy of goals from Paul McStay and Ally McCoist.

By that stage Whyte was an experienced club campaigner, having made his Hoops debut as a 17-year-old when he was part of the Premier Division-winning squad of 1986 and an established first-team player when the title was won again in 1988. He collected Scottish Cup-winners' medals with the Bhoys in both 1988 and 1989.

When Liam Brady spent £2 million to land Gary Gillespie and Tony Mowbray in 1991, it forced Whyte to fight for his place. The following year he was lured away from Parkhead and joined Middlesbrough, becoming the Teesside club's record signing when he made his £950,000 switch in 1992.

He had made 216 appearances for Celtic and went on to add 196 Boro appearances to his record before returning north to Aberdeen. The Glaswegian was not universally accepted by the Pittodrie supporters but was a solid and dependable servant as well as a captain respected by his teammates. Whyte served as skipper until 2002, when it became clear he would not be renewing his Aberdeen contract and Ebbe Skovdahl handed the armband to Darren Young.

He joined the club during a difficult period, embroiled in a succession of battles against the drop and only avoiding a relegation Play-off in 2000 by virtue of the fact that First Division runners-up Falkirk did not have a ground which met SPL regulations.

The high spots came in the Cup, with the Dons reaching both domestic Cup Finals in the 1999–2000 season. Whyte missed the League Cup showdown with Celtic due to injury but was at the heart of the defence as Rangers ran out 4–0 winners in the Scottish Cup equivalent later that term, a game marred by the facial injury to Jim Leighton which forced the Dons to play with striker Robbie Winter in goal for 88 minutes of the match.

Whyte's final contribution as a Pittodrie employee was to lead his side back into European football courtesy of a fourth-place finish in the SPL in 2002.

By the time the Dons embarked on their UEFA Cup campaign they had lost their captain to Partick Thistle. Whyte's leadership qualities again came to the fore and he captained the Jags before being appointed player co-manger, along with Gerry Britton, in the final month of 2003.

The duo lasted 13 months before being shown the exit door at Firhill and it signalled the end of Whyte's involvement on the frontline of the game. He is now heading a property company in Dubai, utilising his football contacts to source potential investors, and also works as a television football pundit and director of a youth football academy in his new home country.

Robbie Winters

Date of birth: 4 November 1974, East Kilbride

Aberdeen record:
Appearances: League 124+8, Scottish Cup 9+2, League Cup 6+1, Europe 1
Goals: League 41, Scottish Cup 2, League Cup 1, Europe 2
Debut: League, 23 September 1998 v Rangers (h) drew 1–1

Also played for: Scotland (1 cap), Dundee United, Luton Town, Brann Bergen

The date was 26 May 2000 and the venue Hampden Park. Robbie Winters was making Scottish Cup history but he cut a lonely figure as he patrolled the Dons penalty box in unfamiliar goalkeeper's kit.

He had arrived at the national stadium for the Cup Final against Rangers with dreams of becoming an Aberdeen goalscoring hero, but within minutes the script had been torn up. When Jim Leighton crumpled to the turf in the the second minute it was clear the veteran was in trouble. A horrific facial injury forced him out of the game and eccentric Dons manager Ebbe Skovdahl had a problem.

The Dane had opted not to name a back-up goalkeeper among his substitutes and Aberdeen faced playing the remainder of the tie against the Premier League champions with an outfield player between the sticks. Winters was the man to shoulder the burden and despite his valiant efforts the Dons tumbled to a 4–0 defeat.

It was a season of Cup Final heartache for the striker, who had come on from the bench in the League Cup Final earlier that season against Celtic but was unable to prevent a 2–0 defeat. Winters left Pittodrie in 2002 empty handed, save for the precious Scotland cap he collected after joining Pittodrie colleagues Eoin Jess and Derek Whyte in the international side that defeated Germany 1–0 in Bremen in 1999. That appearance for the national side is, to date, his only experience at the top level.

Winters arrived at Pittodrie in September 1998 in the most difficult of circumstances. Manager Alex Miller had paid £500,000 to Dundee United and thrown in fans' favourite Billy Dodds to clinch the deal for a striker who was still only 24.

He had made his debut as a winger under United manager Ivan Golac in 1994 and quickly established himself as a livewire performer with pace to burn. A back injury stalled his progress but in 1997 Winters was named Scotland's Young Player of the Year as his stock continued to rise.

That type of form tempted Miller to gamble on the Dodds deal but Winters had a hard act to follow and the reasonable return of 12 goals in 28 games in his first season did not convince the majority that it had been a good piece of business.

The west-coast player persevered and in his final season with the club he finished at the top of the scoring charts with 14 strikes as the Dons rallied from the relegation-haunted form of previous years to climb to the comparatively heady heights of fourth in the SPL.

Winters played through difficult times during Skovdahl's tenure, with the dubious honour of scoring his single European goal in the embarrassing 2–1 UEFA Cup defeat against Irish outfit Bohemian at Pittodrie in the first leg of the tie which saw the club crash out of the competition at the hands of the underdogs.

Winters switched to Norway with Brann Bergen in 2002, after a short trial with Luton. He has spent four years with the club, carving out a reputation as one of the country's leading marksmen and leading to calls for a return to the Scotland set-up.

Stan Williams

Date of birth: 1 May 1919, South Africa

Aberdeen record:
Appearances: League 72, Scottish Cup 10, League Cup 17
Goals: League 20, Scottish Cup 6, League Cup 8
Debut: League, 26 March 1938 v Hamilton (h) won 1–0

Also played for: Plymouth Argyle, Dundee, Floriana
Managed: Floriana

Of all the imports to have landed on Aberdeen soil, few can claim to match South African star Stan Williams in terms of impact. It was the overseas striker who grabbed a dramatic winner for the Dons in the club's first-ever Scottish Cup victory.

On 19 April 1947 the Pittodrie players were on duty in the Hampden Final against Hibs and it was the Easter Road club who drew first blood inside the first minute. After 36 minutes Williams took a grip on proceedings, crossing for George Hamilton to head home the equaliser. Six minutes later the South African went one better, chasing a Tony Harris through ball and just managing to keep it in play before darting towards the touchline and hammering home what turned out to be the winner from the narrowest of angles.

The red army in the crowd of 82,100 were sent into raptures and Williams was the undoubted star of the show.

The occasion vindicated his decision to travel half way around the globe to pursue his dream of making it big in football. Williams had been taken to Scotland by Dons manager Pat Travers in 1938 and made his debut in a 1–0 win at home to Hamilton that year on 26 March.

The outbreak of war stalled his Pittodrie career, with Williams going on to work in a Glasgow aircraft factory and then in the British forces as a physical instructor in the army, but it was only a temporary break.

When football returned in the 1945–46 season he was in the thick of the action. In the 1946 Southern League Cup, as the club claimed its first national honour with a 3–2 victory over Rangers, he set up Archie Baird for the opening goal in the opening minutes and tucked home the second himself 18 minutes later. Despite a spirited comeback by the Light Blues, it was the Dons who emerged triumphant.

Williams was the goalscoring hero again in the 1947 Scottish Cup Final but his contribution to help get Aberdeen onto the big stage should not be overlooked. In the quarter-final his side tackled Dundee at Dens Park and trailed 1–0 at the break before Williams levelled the tie on the hour mark and volleyed home a spectacular winner after an incredible 39 minutes of extra-time. The SFA had ruled the game would be played to a finish to compensate for a fixture backlog.

The semi-final brought a return to Dens, this time to tackle Arbroath, and once again it was the diminutive but lethal Williams who hit the headlines with a double to clinch a 2–0 win and confirm Aberdeen's place in the Final.

The prolific number nine ended his time in the north east with a record of 34 goals in just 99 games, moving on to Plymouth Argyle in 1949 before returning to Scotland with Dundee in the early 1950s.

He was appointed coach of Floriana in Malta in 1952 and spent two years on the continent before moving back to South Africa to begin life outside of football in the engineering industry of his homeland.

In 2005 the latest generation of the Williams football dynasty made an emotional return to the north east. Keven Williams, a great nephew of Stan brought up on tales of Dons success and inspired by books of press clippings passed down through the family, starred for the Old Benonians youth team at the Aberdeen International Youth Festival.

Billy Williamson

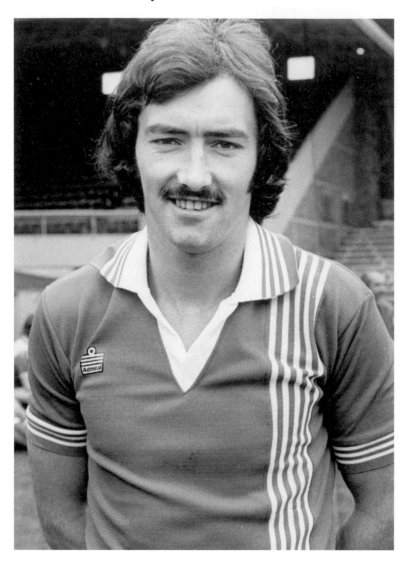

Date of birth: 1952, Dumfries

Aberdeen record:
Appearances: League 93+7, Scottish Cup 10, League Cup 22+6
Goals: League 18, League Cup 5
Debut: League, 10 April 1971 v Cowdenbeath (a) won 2–1

Also played for: Kirkconnel Amateurs, Dundee United, Dundee

Billy Williamson managed to do two things during his Aberdeen career that every aspiring Dons player dreams of doing. Firstly, he performed a one-man demolition act against one half of the Old Firm in front of a jubilant home support and secondly, he walked out at a packed Hampden Park to play his part in a memorable Cup triumph.

On both occasions it was Celtic who were on the receiving end in the two most memorable matches in Williamson's steady spell of service with the club between 1969 and 1977.

At the age of 22 the Dumfries-born player single handedly inflicted Celtic's first defeat at Pittodrie in nine years when he scored his first senior hat-trick in 1975. Amazingly, Williamson was on the transfer list at the time but he did not let the uncertainty put him off his game, opening the scoring from midfield in the 17th minute of the 12 March League game. Few would have predicted the drama about to unfold, with Celtic equalising eight minutes after the break before Aberdeen again took the lead when Williamson completed a double in the 57th minute. Again Celtic came back at the Dons and again they drew level with a 62nd-minute goal. With 12 minutes left on the clock Duncan Davidson was felled by George Connelly and Aberdeen had a penalty; Williamson, unwanted by the club and still relatively inexperienced, accepted captain Willie Young's invitation to make himself a star. He stepped up and sent the spot-kick spinning into the net off the post to make it 3-2 and earn full points.

On 6 November 1977 Williamson enjoyed another defining moment against Celtic when the Dons clinched a 2-1 win in the League Cup Final against the Hoops. This time the versatile borderer claimed the left-back berth, having come into the team in place of Chic McLelland in time for the 5-1 semi-final victory against Rangers.

By the following season Ally MacLeod had departed, replaced by Billy McNeill, and Williamson's days were numbered. He moved to Dundee United in a £14,000 deal late in 1977 and moved across the city to join Dundee the following year for a three-year spell at Dens Park.

The football adventure had started in the final few days of 1969 when a series of trial matches for Eddie Turnbull at Aberdeen won the 17-year-old Kirkconnel Amateurs striker his first professional contract. He was an instant hit with the Dons reserves and a regular scorer, but Turnbull and his backroom staff spotted potential in a different area of the park and in his second season at Pittodrie he was given a taster of first-team action as a right-back in a 2-1 win at Cowdenbeath on 10 April.

Williamson had a frustrating wait for regular first-team action, not truly establishing himself as a regular in the top team until Jimmy Bonthrone put his faith in the versatile squad man in the 1974–75 campaign. He was utilised in defence and attack and missed just three League games, with his appearances including that hat-trick against Celtic.

He went even better the following term, starting 35 of 36 Premier Division games and featuring in the remaining fixture as a substitute as he played in every department for both Bonthrone and new manager MacLeod.

His elevation to a first-team regular vindicated his persistence but the League Cup success of 1977, during a season in which he had drifted back to the periphery of the first team, added him to the elite list of Dons players to have winners' medals under lock and key. Williamson emigrated to Australia after retiring from the game.

Bobby Wishart

Date of birth: 10 March 1933, Edinburgh

Aberdeen record:
Appearances: League 178, Scottish Cup 22, League Cup 36
Goals: League 45, Scottish Cup 7, League Cup 10
Debut: League, 5 December 1953 v Raith Rovers (h) won 2–0

Also played for: Merchiston Thistle, Dundee, Airdrie, Raith Rovers

The usual suspects have dominated League football in Scotland for as long as most people can remember. Rangers, Celtic, Hearts and Hibs won 32 of the first 35 top-flight campaigns to confirm their places at the head of the football food chain.

One man loved breaking that monopoly so much that he did it twice, with two of the only three provincial clubs who upset the establishment between the resumption of football in 1945 and the emergence of Alex Ferguson's dominant Dons in 1980.

Bob Wishart's first Championship medal against the odds was with Aberdeen's legendary title-winning side of 1955. His second came with Dundee in 1962, when he won a place in Dens Park folklore with his contribution to the only League triumph the club has ever savoured.

The Edinburgh-born player was recruited by Aberdeen from juvenile side Merchiston Thistle in 1952. A skilful and creative inside-forward, he made his first start on 5 December the year after he signed as Aberdeen carved out a 2-0 win against Raith Rovers at Pittodrie. By the following season Wishart had taken Joe O'Neil's place at inside-left on a permanent basis, coinciding with Aberdeen's title-winning campaign. He contributed seven League goals in 23 starts but it was the ammunition he supplied for Paddy Buckley and Harry Yorston that made him such a vital piece in Dave Halliday's jigsaw.

His second Dons winners' medal came in the 1955–56 League Cup Final following a 2–1 win against St Mirren in the Hampden Final. Wishart was an ever present in the competition and he came to the fore in the semi-final against old foes Rangers when he scored with a 22-yard rocket after a quick break up field to add to Graham Leggat's opener. The Light Blues pulled a goal back in the second half but could not stop the Dons bandwagon rolling on to the Final. Wishart's performances won recognition at Scotland Under-23 level and for the Scottish Football League select as he embarked on a long and distinguished career in the red of his first senior club.

He missed out on the chance to complete a domestic clean sweep in 1959 when he was part of the Aberdeen side that fell to a 3-1 defeat against St Mirren in the Scottish Cup Final and at the beginning of 1961, with first-team opportunities proving limited at Pittodrie, he was snapped up by Dundee for the bargain price of £3,500 after 236 appearances and 62 goals for the Dons.

At the age of 27 he became a wing-half with Dundee and helped the Tayside outfit pip Rangers to the 1962 First Division prize by just three points. It was an inspired

move by Wishart, with the Aberdeen team he left behind languishing in 12th spot. He went on to play in the European Cup as the Dens Park side progressed to the semi-final of the competition the following term. Wishart wound down his playing days with Airdrie and Raith Rovers before returning to the Edinburgh area, becoming a building society manager. He is now enjoying his retirement in Currie and is able to reflect on the momentous achievements of his life in football. Wishart recalled, 'The League success with Aberdeen was significant because it gave the club a chance to believe in itself. That was a big thing.

'I didn't think we would win the League that year because the team had been put together fairly quickly. When I left to my national service in 1951 it was an ageing team, with players like Tommy Pearson, George Hamilton and Tony Harris. There were good players at the club but the team struggled to get any consistency.

'I came back two years later and the likes of Jack Allister, Fred Martin and Paddy Buckley were breaking through. The team had changed very quickly and we won the League on the back of that.'

Wishart believes Aberdeen were the masters of their own downfall when it came to their failure to add to the initial Championship success. He said 'We slipped up by transferring some of the best reserves to English clubs. That included Ian MacFarlane, Ian McNeill, George Taylor and Bobby Wilson. We left ourselves short.

'When Tommy Pearson came in he instigated a youth policy and, given I had been around the club for a number of years, I didn't fit in with that. I never had any intention of leaving until then. I always got on well with Dick Donald and I'm pretty sure I would have stayed on at the club either in a coaching or even managerial capacity if I had played out my career at Pittodrie.'

Instead of a long-term career with the Dons he embarked on a new playing chapter on Tayside and those days at Dens provide as many happy memories as his Dons adventure. Wishart added, 'What happened with Dundee was quite amazing. I never expected to win another League Championship but I had joined a very good side. Dundee played total football, whereas Aberdeen played good football with a hard-hitting edge.

'I think that Dundee side was as good a team as I had seen in Scotland. Bob Crampsey, a man steeped in the Glasgow game, said that Dundee team played the finest football Scotland had ever produced and that was high praise indeed.'

Stephen Wright

Date of birth: 27 August 1978, Bellshill

Aberdeen record:

Appearances: League 145+7, Scottish Cup 13, League Cup 11+1, Europe 5+1
Goals: League 2
Debut: League, 28 April 1990 v St Mirren (h) won 2–0

Also played for: Scotland (2 caps), Rangers, Wolverhampton Wanderers, Bradford City, Dundee United, Scunthorpe United

In the summer of 1995 Stephen Wright became the most valuable defender in the history of Aberdeen Football Club when Rangers signed a cheque for £1.5 million to add one of Scottish football's most promising players to the Ibrox squad.

Wright made the move in search of the prizes which had eluded him during his time with the Dons. Yet less than four months later he watched his old Aberdeen teammates lift the League Cup while he faced up to the prospect of months on the Ibrox treatment table nursing an injured knee and suffering from a massive dose of bad luck.

The dream move turned into a nightmare for Wright, who damaged his ligaments in a 4–0 European Cup defeat against Juventus at Ibrox just three months into his career with the club. His comeback in 1996 lasted just one game before another knee injury in training led to another frustrating spell on the sidelines and by 1998 he was sent out on loan to Wolves to mark the end of his Rangers days.

It was the Light Blues who made the big investment, but the team in red most certainly got the best days out of a defender who was rated as one of the finest of his generation.

The Bellshill-born player was signed as a schoolboy by Alex Ferguson and joined the Pittodrie groundstaff under Ian Porterfield but got is big break when Alex Smith took charge of the Dons.

Wright was 18 when he appeared as a substitute in a 2–0 home win against St Mirren on 28 April 1990. In the second half of the 1990–91 campaign he stepped in to deputise for Stewart McKimmie at right-back and played 15 consecutive games in the nail-biting conclusion to the season, in which the League was lost on the final day. By that time McKimmie had been switched into the centre of defence to team up with Alex McLeish, with the right-back berth safe in the hands of his teenage deputy.

Wright also went on to prove his versatility and was at home in the centre of the back four as he was on either flank. It was that adaptability which saw him appear in every single one of the 44 games Aberdeen played across four competitions in his final season.

His club form earned almost instant recognition at Scotland Under-21 level, breaking into the team in 1990 and going on to skipper the young Scots. Having already won Youth international caps during his school days in Hamilton, Wright completed a full set when he made his senior debut in a 1–0 defeat against Germany at Ibrox in March 1993. Two months later his second and final cap came when Andy Roxburgh's team beat Estonia 3–0 in Talin courtesy of goals from Kevin Gallacher, John Collins and Pittodrie teammate Scott Booth.

He was still only 21 when he burst onto the big stage with Scotland, but injuries ultimately put paid to Wright's hopes of carving out a long international career. The first knee problems actually came at Aberdeen, with a minor operation in 1991 solving an early recurring injury. The subsequent damage with Rangers proved much more serious and Wright never regained the form which made him a stand-out player for the Dons.

His temporary switch to Wolves was followed by a permanent switch to Bradford in the summer of 1998, and he was part of the squad that won promotion to the Premiership before returning to Scotland to join Alex Smith's Dundee United in 2000. His two-year spell at Tannadice was interrupted by injury and a short stint at Scunthorpe in 2002 brought the curtain down on his playing career. In 2006 Wright was back under Smith's wing once more when he joined former teammates Scott Booth and Gary Smith to be put through their paces alongside fellow pupil Alan Shearer on the SFA top-level coaching course in Glasgow as he prepares for a new chapter in his football story.

Benny Yorston

Date of birth: 14 October 1905, Nigg
Died: 1977, London

Aberdeen record:
Appearances: League 143, Scottish Cup 13
Goals: League 101, Scottish Cup 24
Debut: League, 20 August 1927 v Raith Rovers (a) won 3–2

Also played for: Scotland (1 cap), Mugiemoss, Richmond, Montrose, Sunderland, Middlesbrough

Every striker is judged on black and white statistics and Benny Yorston is the only player in the history of Aberdeen to have a perfect season marked on his Pittodrie report card. In 38 League games in 1929–30 the pocket-sized attacker scored 38 goals.

It does not get much better than that. Or does it? In four Scottish Cup ties in the same season he bagged eight goals to take his total to 46 and that too has never been beaten by any other Dons striker. His breathtaking haul included four hat-tricks and 10 doubles. Standing at 5ft 4in tall, what the Aberdonian star lacked in height he made up for in killer instinct.

He topped the scoring charts in his first four seasons at Pittodrie and was on course to make it five in a row before he dropped out of the side in 1931 to end a torrid time for Scotland's defenders.

Yorston had scored 10 hat-tricks in three full seasons up against the elite of the domestic game. Hamilton, Partick, Queen's Park Rangers twice, Clyde twice, Dundee twice and Raith all felt the force of the fearsome number nine's triple salvos, while he reserved four of his best for Falkirk.

The striker, who had cut his teeth with Sunnybank's juvenile teams and then Mugiemoss and Richmond in the Aberdeen juniors ranks before stepping up to the senior game with Montrose, was signed by Pat Travers in 1927. One of the greatest goalscorers the club has ever had cost £30, just three times his bonus for a single goal at Montrose.

He went on to score 125 goals in just 156 games yet amazingly, Yorston's form in front of goal was not enough to bring silverware to Aberdeen. Even for Scotland he gained scant recognition for his ability, with just one senior cap in a 0–0 draw against Northern Ireland at Windsor Park. Yorston was just 25 at the time, and already a Youth and junior international, but his performance in dark blue was deemed not good enough and the Nigg-born player was cast aside by the international selectors.

At least his home-town supporters appreciated him as a true attacking all rounder, capable of scoring with both feet and his head. Not surprisingly, he came in for heavy treatment from opposition defenders and was known to take to the field with his legs heavily bandaged from top to bottom as the result of the previous week's battles, but Yorston never let it get him down. He would even persuade trainers to treat decoy injuries rather than the one which had really brought him to the turf to ensure his temporary weaknesses were not exposed to the defenders he outfoxed with such regularity.

Yorston's copy book was blotted in 1931 when he and four fellow Dons players were caught up in illegal betting allegations. The group were dumped from the team and a £2,000 move to Sunderland was the striker's escape route in 1932.

Two seasons at Roker Park led to a spell with neighbours Middlesbrough before the outbreak of war effectively ended Yorston's career. He moved into the property business in London, where he remained until his death in 1977.

Harry Yorston

Date of birth: 9 June 1929, Aberdeen
Died: 1992, Aberdeen

Aberdeen record:
Appearances: League 201, Scottish Cup 29, League Cup 47
Goals: League 98, Scottish Cup 21, League Cup 22
Debut: League, 26 December 1947 v Third Lanark (a) lost 3–2

Also played for: Scotland (1 cap), Lossiemouth

Some players take months, some take years and some never succeed, but for Harry Yorston it took all of 300 seconds to show the Aberdeen supporters that he knew how to score goals.

The festive season of 1947 was a time to remember. His new club were on League duty at Third Lanark and Yorston converted the first corner-kick of the match, in the fifth minute, to announce his arrival in style. It was not all smiles, though, with his new side falling to a 3–2 defeat.

Yorston was a bustling striker who did his best to endear himself to the Pittodrie faithful over the course of a decade, banging in 141 goals in 277 games after signing from Aberdeen juvenile side St Clement's in 1946. He had obviously inherited the goalscoring gene from his father's side of the family, with second cousin Benny Yorston already a legend at Aberdeen long before he even set foot inside the ground.

In six starts he had six matching goals in 1948 but it was in the 1949–50 season that the striker really made his mark as he deposed George Hamilton as the club's leading scorer thanks to a 17-goal haul.

Yorston was impossible to shift from Dave Halliday's side and remained in possession of the number-eight shirt right through to his finest year in football. It began on 11 September 1954, when the Dons launched their Championship campaign with a 5–0 win at home to Stirling Albion. Yorston scored the fifth and final goal and went on to net 11 further times in 27 additional League games on the way to the historic title triumph in 1955.

Along the way he collected a coveted Scotland cap when he helped his international colleagues to a 1–0 win against Wales in Cardiff. Paddy Buckley, one of Yorston's teammates at club level, scored the winner. He had previously played for Scotland against Ireland at Dalymount Park in 1951.

With a Championship medal safely secured, the influential inside-forward set about adding a League Cup badge the following season. He scored in the group stages and the quarter-final of the 1955–56 competition and was part of the winning team in the 2–1 Final victory against St Mirren.

Then came the bombshell. On 8 June 1957 Aberdeen fans were left spluttering over their cornflakes when the morning's *Press and Journal* proclaimed in bold type 'Harry Yorston is quitting football for fish.'

It was the type of story that is impossible to comprehend in the current football climate. Yorston, a player at the peak of his powers as a 28-year-old international, who had collected two medals in the space of two seasons, turned his back on the game that had made him a household name and became a porter at Aberdeen's fish market.

Manager Dave Shaw was stunned, the supporters were shocked but Yorston was unmoved. His father had worked in the same job and he knew the rewards were decent, offering a £16.50 weekly wage in comparison to his £16 pay packet as a football player, while the long-term security was assured. The fact he had played in the face of almost constant criticism from his own club's supporters also played a part in his decision.

The job of a porter was highly sought after and a new intake of rookies was welcomed only every two or three years. With an age limit of 30 set by the market, it was a case of now or never for Yorston when his application was accepted sooner than expected.

Despite his clean break from the game at the top level, he was back in the headlines in 1972 and again football was at the root of his fame – when a 25p stake on the pools netted him a £170,000 windfall.

Despite his new-found wealth he returned to work as a driver, a role he combined with a place on Ally MacLeod's backroom team when he returned to Pittodrie to launch a new youth programme in 1976. He also scouted for Manchester United following his playing retirement.

Yorston, who briefly played in the Highland League with Lossiemouth after his split from the Dons, died at the age of 62 in Aberdeen in 1992.

Alec Young

Date of birth: 20 October 1925, Glasgow

Aberdeen record:
Appearances: League 168, Scottish Cup 23, League Cup 30
Goals: League 1
Debut: League Cup, 16 August 1950 v Rangers (a) won 2–1

Also played for: Strathclyde, Kilsyth Rangers, Blantyre Victoria, Ross County
Managed: Ross County

In seven full seasons at Pittodrie Alec Young battled back from three career-threatening knee injuries, a broken ankle and an emergency appendix operation. He kept coming back for more and his persistence was rewarded with the greatest domestic prize of all in 1955 when he helped the Dons to the League title.

His influence on that title-winning team was substantial. Young, Archie Glen and Jackie Hather were the three men who played in each of the 30 League games in that glorious campaign, when Celtic were relegated to the runners'-up spot by Aberdeen's maiden Championship success.

The centre-half was already a proven winner when he signed at Pittodrie in 1950, having collected the Scottish Junior Cup with Blantyre Victoria earlier that year. He went straight into the Dons team in the early stages of the 1950–51 season and, barring injuries, was a defensive rock until he left in 1958. Young racked up 221 appearances in that time, including two unsuccessful Scottish Cup Finals.

Those Cup occasions were the major disappointments of the player's time in the north east as he came desperately close to adding a senior medal to the junior one he had claimed in his native Glasgow, where he had turned out for Strathclyde and Kilsyth Rangers before settling with Blantyre.

In 1953 the Dons took Rangers to a replay before falling to a 1–0 defeat at the hands of the Ibrox men. The following year they were back at Hampden to face Celtic but it was an afternoon to forget for Young, who scored an own-goal in the 2–1 loss to the Hoops.

His League Cup hopes were dashed by injury, and he was sidelined in the 1955–56 season when his teammates lifted the trophy.

Despite captaining Scotland's junior international side he never made the transition to the senior team, despite a string of dominant and impressive performances at the heart of the Aberdeen defence. He became renowned for his split-second timing in the tackle, although his talents had slipped through the net at Parkhead where he had an unsuccessful trial spell with Celtic before linking up with Aberdeen.

Despite spending his youth as a centre-forward, Young's forte was certainly in defence. His goals were collectors' items after he moved into the senior ranks and he scored just one for the Dons, in a 5–0 victory against Airdrie at Pittodrie in 1953.

He was offered the chance to stay on the staff in 1958 but opted instead to join Ross County as player-coach and played on for a further six years before finally calling time. Young changed the mindset at County, ditching a long-ball style for a passing game and importing the fitness regime he had thrived under at Pittodrie as well as the high standards of discipline he had experienced under Dave Shaw.

After leaving County in 1964, on the advice of doctors following a stay in hospital as the result of a perforated ulcer, Young remained in the north to continue running the grocery business he had built up.

Roll of Honour

Edward Adie
Kenneth Adie
Nicol Adie
Catherine Aitchison
Valerie Alexander
Andrew N.P. Anderson
Bill Anderson
Marc Anderson
Harris Anderson
Fergus Anderson
James Anderson
Lewis Archibald
Douglas Auchinachie
James Barron
Keith Benzie
Gordon Birss
Robbie Birss
Sandra Birss
Adam Borthwick
Bradley Boyd
Stanley M. Brechin
 (Canada)
James Bremner
John Brindley
Christopher Bruce
Daniel Bruce
Mark Dylan Budge
Tom Budge
David Buchan
Ian Buchan
Mark Victor Caird
Murray Cameron
Brian Campbell
Mark Campbell
Ryan Campbell
Tyler Campbell
Andy Carswell
Colin Chapman
Aaron Clark
Archie Clark
Audrey Clark
Bryan Clark
Liam Clark
Gary Clark
Charlie Clouston
Michael Clubb
Moray Cocker
Mark Cooper
Elise Cowie
Hannah Dawn Cowie
Richard A Cowie
Robert Glennie Cowie
Evan Cranna
Darren Cruickshank
John Crockett

Graeme Cullen
Grant Cullen
Hugh Cullen
Andrew W.F. Cushnie
Mark A. Cushnie
Mark Dellaquaglia
Alan Donald
Andrew Donald
Ian Donald
Steven C. Dongworth
Craig Douglas
Craig Farquharson
 Duncan
Ian F. Duncan
Ian R. Duncan
Neil John Duncan
Nikki Jane Duncan
Alan Durward
Derek Duthie
Matthew Davidson
 Duthie
Ruth Lesley Duthie
Michael Elder
Bill Ellis
Graeme Ellis
Alan Elrick
Stuart Elsey
Duncan Elsey
Jenny Ewen
Jill Ewen
William Ewen
Jonathan Farrand
Bill Findlay
Alastair J D Flett
Martin Forbes
Keith Fordyce
George Forsyth
Brian Fowler
Ciaran Fowler
Charlie Fowler
Alan A. Fraser
Alan J. Fraser
K.I. Fraser
Les Fraser
Rod Fraser
Steven Fraser
David Gair
Graeme Milne Gammack
Holly Ann Gammack
Calum George Gammack
Jock Gardiner
Marion Gibbs
Ian Glennie
Neil D. Gordon
Christopher S. Graves

Alan Gray
Callum Gray
Craig Gray
Margaret E. Graham
Martin Francis Hale
Barry Hall
Adrian Hay
Kenneth Hay
Kenneth Duguid Hay
Wendy Hay
Greig A Henderson
Bruce Hepburn
Harry Hepburn
Kevin Hepburn
Terry Hossack
Edward Ingram
Maurice Ronald Inkster
David Insch
Stephen Insch
James A Jack
Alfred Jamieson
Betty Jamieson
Callum Jenkins
Peter George Johnston
Joseph Kennedy
Andrew Kilgour
John Kilgour
Sean Kilgour
Graham King
Ralph Kynoch
Brian Laing
Stewart Langdon
Aaron James Leahy
Alastair Learmonth
Dylan J.S. Liebnitz
Hamish Liebnitz
James S. Liebnitz
Christopher Low
Iain McBeath
Alan Scott MacDonald
James Alan MacDonald
Martin A. McElhinney
Dylan A. McGachy
Alison Margaret McGill
George Thomson McGill
Colin Stewart McKay
Miller Brian McKay
Graeme Mackay
Graham Barrie
 MacKenzie
Kenny McKenzie
David McLennan
Colin MacLeod
David McLeod
Ian McLeod

Neil McLeod
Mairi MacNaughton
Stevie McPherson
 (Hopeman)
Craig Mackie
Kenny Mackie
Ryan Mackie
Alan Scot Mair
Brian B. Mair
David Mair
Irene Masson
John Masson
Marie Masson
Dale Mathieson
Greg Mathieson
Peter Mathieson
Roddy Mavor
Cameron Milne
Alan Mitchell
George M Mitchell
Roberto Moretti
Ronald Murray
Alan Napier
Stuart Napier
Alistair Neish
Robert Nicolson
Ross Nicholson
Brian Paterson
Hannah Paterson
Kimberley Paterson
Scott Paterson
Stuart Paterson
Hugh W Patience
William A Patience
Donald Prentice
Raymond Reader
Alexander Reid
Ian D. Reid
Kyle J. Reid
Elizabeth Rennie
Euan Andrew Rennie
Michael Rennie (Sailor
 Man)
Nicholas Stuart Ritchie
William Ritchie
Steven Ian Robb
Yan Robb
Fraser Struan Robertson
Lewis Robertson
Stanley Robertson
Derek A. Rorie
Martin Runcie
Adam Scott
Colin M. Sellar
Ian Shepherd

Jim Shepherd
Ross Shepherd
Gilian Sheran
Billy Alexander Simpson
Daniel Joseph Simpson
Innes Simpson
Shaun Simpson
Ernie Singer
Andrew David Skinner
Duncan Ross Skinner
Chris Smith
Dennis Smith
Richard L. Smith
William Y. Smith
Steven J. Spence
Jim Stewart
Alex Stupart
Ross Stupart
Martin John Strachan
Alison Sutherland
Christopher James
 Sutherland
Craig Thomas Sutherland
Andrew G. Swift
Norman Theobald
Jack Thom
Craig Thomson
Donald J. Thomson
Karen Thomson
Mack Thomson
Richard Thomson
Ian Thomson
Miller Thomson
Scott Thomson
Zander Thornton
Matthew Trotter
Keith George Truscott
Ian B. Tudhope
Mark Turnbull
Veitch Clan
 (Stonehaven)
Alan Walker
Andrew Watt (Elgin)
Rory White
Raymond Willox
Colin R.W. Wilson
Dennis Wilson
Calum G. Wood
Jeremy D. Wood
David Woods
Arthur Wyllie
Bill Yuill